Military Aircraft of the World

JOHN W. R. TAYLOR AND GORDON SWANBOROUGH

LONDON

IAN ALLAN LTD

Contents

First published 1979

ISBN 0 7110 0761 7

Published by Ian Allan Ltd, Shepperton, Surrey, and printed in the United Kingdom by A. Wheaton & Co, Exeter

Front cover, top: An extremely rare colour view of a Polish Air Force Sukhoi Su-17 swing-wing combat aircraft.

Front cover, bottom: Boeing E-3A Sentry Airborne Warning and Control System (AWACS) aircraft, now in service with the USAF's Tactical Air Command and recently the subject of a NATO order for the establishment of a multi-national airborne early-warning squadron.

Title page: Fairchild A-10A Thunderbolt II making a low-level attack on armoured targets during Joint Attack Weapons Systems (JAWS) II trials,

This page: Boeing E-4B.

Introduction

When the first edition of *Military Aircraft of the World* was published, in 1971, the only variable-geometry "swing-wing" combat aircraft in service was the General Dynamics F-111. First operational deployment of this tactical fighter-bomber to Vietnam had proved almost disastrous, with two of the initial batch of six aircraft lost in under a week. The last few months of that war were to produce a very different picture. F-111s achieved near-miraculous results, in an area protected by anti-aircraft defences of unprecedented ferocity, in a kind of war for which they had never been intended. Little wonder that the swing-wing now seems an inevitable feature of the most advanced types of military aircraft like America's Tomcat, Russia's "Backfire", "Flogger" and "Fencer", and Europe's Tornado.

Much else has changed in eight years. The quest for maximum speed, considered the prerequisite for air superiority during half a century from 1915, is now regarded as less urgent. Vietnam and other conflicts have shown that victory is won often by the more manoeuvrable aircraft. First-generation air-to-air missiles seldom hit a tightly turning target whose pilot knew, by signals from his passive ECM (electronic countermeasures equipment), that he was about to be attacked. Guns were put back hastily into fighters like the Phantom and MiG-21. The missile-makers began to concentrate on "dogfight" weapons that could snap into a turn or dive as rapidly as their targets, however short the range. Aircraft designers and air forces began to see new merit in aircraft like the lighter-weight General Dynamics F-16, hundreds of miles an hour slower than many other fighters but needing only half as much sky in which to turn.

To everyone's astonishment, Hawker Siddeley Harriers flown by US Marine pilots outfought US Navy Tomcats—widely regarded as the world's most potent interceptors—in simulated air combat trials. Already convinced that they needed the improved AV-8B Harrier for the 'eighties, the Marines became even more determined to get it. Then the Soviet Navy revealed its Yak-36 counterpart of the Harrier, which proved to be nothing of the sort, lacking some of the features that contributed most to the effectiveness of the all-British type.

That other, older form of VTOL aircraft, the helicopter, has also undergone vast changes in terms of both performance and punch in the 1970s. The US Army set the pace with the Bell HueyCobra gunship; the Soviet Union followed up quickly, and with tremendous skill and imagination. Large formations of Mi-24s, based in East Germany, are now poised to fly squads of tough assault troops speedily behind NATO lines in Europe at the first hint of any trouble, at the same time beating down any opposition with a withering hail of rockets, missiles and large-calibre ammunition.

Every other aspect of modern air power is reflected in this unique book, which has no counterpart as a single-volume, compact guide to all combat and support aircraft now flying throughout the world.

JWRT/GS

Part One

Aeritalia G91

Italy

Single-seat light tactical strike-reconnaissance fighter, in service.

Powered by: Two 2,720lb (1,235kg) st General Electric J85-GE-13A turbojets.
Span: 29ft 6½in (9.01m).
Length: 38ft 3½in (11.67m).
Empty weight: 8,598lb (3,900kg).
Gross weight: 19,180lb (8,700kg).
Max speed: 690mph (1,110km/h) at sea level.
Typical combat radius: 466 miles (750km) at sea level.
Armament: Two 30mm cannon in sides of front fuselage. Four underwing attachments for up to 4,000lb (1,816kg) of bombs, AS.20 missiles, air-to-ground rockets or 0.50in machine-gun pods.

The original G91 was the winner of a design competition for a standardised strike fighter for NATO forces. Three prototypes and 27 pre-production G91s were ordered initially by NATO. The first prototype, with a 4,050lb (1,837kg) st Orpheus B.Or.1, flew on August 9, 1956. After winning the NATO evaluation contest in October 1957, the G91 was ordered into production. The first pre-production model flew on February 20, 1958, and the Italian Air Force formed the first G91 development squadron in August 1958, equipped with the pre-production machines. These were the only pure fighter G91s, subsequent operational aircraft being G91Rs with three Vinten 70mm cameras in a less-pointed nose. Variants, all with 5,000lb (2,268kg) st Orpheus 803, are the G91R/1, R/1A and R/1B, of which 98 were built for the Italian Air Force, and the G91R/3 and R/4 of which 100 were built by Fiat for the German Air Force, with 282 more licence-built in Germany. The R/4s were subsequently acquired by the Portuguese Air Force. Italian G91Rs have four 0.50in guns instead of the cannon fitted to the German versions. Tandem two-seat training versions with a larger wing and longer fuselage are the G91T/1 (more than 80 for Italy) and G91T/3 (66 for Germany). The G91Y was evolved from the G91T for the Italian Air Force, with the same enlarged wing and two J85s replacing the single Orpheus engine. The first of two prototypes flew on December 27, 1966. A pre-production batch of 20 was delivered and these were followed by series production of 45, work on which was completed during 1976; these aircraft currently equip two *Stormi* (Wings) of the Italian Air Force.

Data, photo and silhouette: G91Y.

Aeritalia G222   Italy

Medium-range tactical transport, in production and service.

Powered by: Two 3,400shp General Electric T64-P-4D turboprops.
Span: 94ft 6in (28,80m).
Length: 74ft 5½in (22.70m).
Empty weight: 32,165lb (14,590kg).
Gross weight: 58,422lb (26,500kg).
Max speed: 336mph at 15,000ft (540km/h at 4,575m).
Range: 1,833 miles (2,950km) with 11,025lb (5,000kg) load.
Accommodation: Crew of three and 44 troops, 32 paratroops, or up to 36 stretchers and eight attendants or seated casualties.

Design studies began in 1963, under Italian Air Force contracts, with a view to developing a V/STOL tactical transport. Using a conventional high-wing layout, with two turboprop engines, Fiat proposed to obtain STOL performance by installing four direct-lift engines in each nacelle. This project had the capability of taking off in 230ft (70m) and carrying its design payload a distance of 310 miles (500km), but an alternative was also schemed in which the lift-engines were deleted and the weight saved was taken up by extra fuel, giving a greatly increased range at the expense of take-off performance. Two flying prototypes (and a static test specimen) of this conventional version were eventually ordered by the Italian government, with the stipulation that the work be shared throughout the Italian industry under Fiat direction. First flights of the two prototypes were made on July 18, 1970 and July 22, 1971 respectively, and following evaluation in the early months of 1972 the Italian Air Force confirmed its intention to buy 44 G222s; funds for the first 12 of these were made available in 1974. Production is spread throughout the Italian aerospace industry, with final assembly by Aeritalia (incorporating the former Fiat Aviation Division) now undertaken near Naples. The first G222s were assembled in the Fiat works in Turin, where the first production G222 made its maiden flight on December 23, 1975. The fourth aircraft was the first example exported, to the United Arab Emirates Air Force at the end of 1976, and the first of three ordered by the Argentine Army was delivered in March 1977. A version designated G222 VS was under test for the Italian Air Force in 1978, equipped for the ECM mission, with radomes under the nose and atop the fin. The G222 RM carries equipment for radio and radar calibration.

Data and silhouette: G222
Photo: G222 VS

Aermacchi MB326, Embraer AT-26 Xavante and Atlas Impala
Italy

Basic trainer and light attack aircraft, in production and service.

Powered by: One 4,000lb (1,814kg) st Rolls-Royce Viper 632-43 turbojet.
Span: 35ft 7in (10.85m).
Length: 35ft 0¼in (10.67m).
Gross weight: 13,000lb (5,897kg).
Max speed: 553mph (890km/h) at 5,000ft (1,525m).
Typical combat radius: 81 miles (130km) with max weapon load.
Armament: Two 30mm DEFA cannon in lower front fuselage: six underwing pylons for up to 4,000lb (1,814kg) of external stores.

**Data: MB326K. Photo: Impala 2.
Silhouette: Xavante.**

The first of two prototypes of this widely-used tandem two-seat basic trainer flew on December 10, 1957 powered by a 1,750lb (794kg) st Rolls-Royce Viper 8 turbojet. Production models had the 2,500lb (1,134kg) st Viper 11 and the first of 100 for the Italian Air Force flew on October 5, 1960. Delivery of this batch was completed in 1966 but 30 more were ordered subsequently, including, in 1974, 12 MB326E (six of them conversions) with new equipment and strengthened wing with six weapon attachments. Eight MB326B and seven MB326F, delivered to the Tunisian and Ghana Air Forces respectively, are similar. In the spring of 1967, Aermacchi flew the prototype MB326G, an armed version with a 3,410lb (1,547kg) st Viper 540 engine. Production versions are known as the MB326GB and orders include 17 for Zaïre, 8 for the Argentine Navy, 23 for the Zambian Air Force and 167 similar MB326GCs for the Brazilian Air Force (the majority made by Embraer in Brazil as the AT-26 Xavante). In 1976, Brazil supplied three Xavantes to Togo. MB326H is the version for the Royal Australian Air Force and Navy, with Viper 11 engine; 12 were supplied by Aermacchi, with the balance of orders totalling 87 for the RAAF and 10 for the RAN built by CAC in Australia. In South Africa, Atlas Aircraft built about 150 MB326M Impalas, similar to the MB326G with armed capability, and subsequently put into production the Impala 2, similar to the single-seat MB326K. The latter is a single-seat attack/trainer version with Viper 632 engine, first flown on August 22, 1970; its two-seat counterpart is the MB326L. Orders for these later variants included three Ks and one L for the United Arab Emirates Air Force (Dubai), six Ks for Ghana, eight Ks and four Ls for Tunisia, and seven Ks for South Africa pending delivery of Impala 2s.

Antonov An-12
(NATO code-name: Cub)

USSR

Medium/long-range transport, in service.

Powered by: Four 4,000ehp Ivchenko AI-20K turboprops.
Span: 124ft 8in (38.0m).
Length: 108ft 3in (33.0m).
Gross weight: 134,480lb (61,000kg).
Max cruising speed: 373mph (600km/h).
Range: 2,110 miles (3,400km) at 342mph (550km/h) with 22,050lb (10,000kg) payload.
Accommodation: Crew of five and troops, vehicles or freight.
Armament: Two 23mm cannon in tail turret.

Developed from the An-10 commercial airliner, this turboprop transport has been standard equipment in the Soviet Air Force for paratroop-dropping, air supply and heavy transport duties for many years. Its undercarriage has four-wheel bogie main units, retracting into fairings on each side of the cabin, and is fitted with low-pressure tyres, enabling the An-12 to operate from unprepared airfields. Take-off and landing runs are under 2,500ft (750m). A loading ramp for vehicles and freight forms the undersurface of the up-swept rear fuselage and can be opened in flight for air-dropping of troops and supplies. Size of the main cabin is 44ft 3½in (13.50m) long, by 9ft 10in (3.0m) wide and 7ft 10½in (2.40m) high.

Current Soviet Air Force An-12s have an enlarged under-nose radome. A special ECM "jamming" version is known to NATO as *Cub-C*; examples have been operated by the Egyptian Air Force as well as the Soviet Air Force.

Foreign air forces which have been supplied with troop and cargo transport An-12s (*Cub-A*) include those of Algeria, Bangladesh, Egypt, India, Iraq, Poland, Syria and Yugoslavia. A civil version, known as the An-12V, without the tail gun turret, is operated on pure freight services by Aeroflot and has been supplied to several other nations in the Soviet bloc. At least one Aeroflot An-12 has been operated on skis during service in the Arctic and is one of the largest aeroplanes ever equipped in this way.

Data and silhouette: Cub-A.
Photo: Cub-C.

Antonov An-22
(NATO code-name: Cock)

USSR

Long-range heavy strategic transport, in service.

Powered by: Four 15,000shp Kuznetsov NK-12MA turbo-props.
Span: 211ft 4in (64.40m).
Length: 189ft 7in (57.80m).
Max payload: 176,350lb (80,000kg).
Gross weight: 551,160lb (250,000kg).
Max speed: 460mph (740km/h).
Range: 6,800 miles (10,950km) with max fuel and 99,200lb (45,000kg) payload; 3,100 miles (5,000km) with max payload.
Accommodation: Crew of five or six: 28–29 passengers plus freight.

First flown on February 27, 1965, the Antonov An-22 was the World's largest transport aircraft until the appearance of the Lockheed C-5A and Boeing 747. A natural progression from the An-10/12 series, the An-22 was in service with Aeroflot and the Soviet Air Force by mid-1967, at which time two prototypes in civil markings were operating an experimental freight service and three others in military markings took part in the display at Domodedovo. The latter disgorged, after landing, batteries of *Frog-3* and *Ganef* missiles on tracked launchers. The An-22 has a normal payload of 176,350lb (80,000kg) but in a series of record flights in October 1967, a max load of 221,443lb (100,445kg) was lifted. In two other series of record flights in 1972 and 1974, An-22s carried payloads of up to 110,230lb (50,000kg) over distances of up to 3,108 miles (5,000km) at speeds up to 378mph (608km/h). A feature of the An-22 design is that four gantries are installed on overhead rails running the entire length of the cabin to facilitate freight handling through the rear door and ramp. Early examples carried the scanner for a navigational radar in a radome under the starboard wheel housing, but later service versions have it relocated under the nose. By 1969, An-22s were in service with several Soviet Air Force units, and in 1970 one was lost in the Atlantic during relief flights after the Peruvian earthquake. Production was terminated in 1974, after about 50 had been built.

Antonov An-26 (and An-24 and An-32)   USSR
(NATO code-names: Curl, Coke and Cline)

Tactical personnel and supply transport, in production and service.

Powered by: Two 2,820ehp Ivchenko AI-24T turboprops plus, in the starboard nacelle, one 1,985lb (900kg) st RU19-300 turbojet for standby use.
Span: 95ft 9½in (29.20m).
Length: 78ft 1in (23.80m).
Empty weight: 33,113lb (15,020kg).
Gross weight: 52,911lb (24,000kg).
Cruising speed: 264-270mph (425-435km/h).
Range: 560 miles (900km) with 9,920lb (4,500kg) payload.
Accommodation: Flight crew of five (two pilots, radio operator, flight engineer and navigator) and up to 40 paratroops or 24 stretchers.

The An-26 (NATO code-name *Curl*) is a variant of the An-24 (NATO code-name *Coke*) short-range general purpose transport, more specifically adapted to military needs, although civil versions have been seen in service. The An-24 itself was first flown in 1960 and was produced in large quantities, initially for use by Aeroflot and then for export to other airlines and for military use. The An-26, which made its appearance in 1969, differs primarily in having a redesigned rear fuselage with a "beaver-tail" incorporating ramps and loading doors so that vehicles can be accommodated. The rear door forming the ramp for loading can also be swung down and forward beneath the fuselage to allow direct loading from trucks into the cabin, which has an electrically or manually operated conveyor fitted flush in the floor. Among the air forces known to have put An-24s or An-26s into service—mostly in small numbers—as troop and personnel carriers, in addition to the Soviet Air Force itself, are those of Bangladesh, the Congo Republic (Brazzaville), Czechoslovakia, Egypt, East Germany, Hungary, Iraq, North Korea, Mongolia, Peru, Poland, Romania, the Somali Republic, North Vietnam and South Yemen. During 1977, a development of the An-26 was offered to the Indian Air Force to meet its requirements for a tactical transport, this being designated An-32 (NATO *Cline*) and having uprated AI-20 engines to improve its performance in hot and high airfield conditions. The An-32 is probably in service with the Soviet Air Force.

Data: An-26. Photo and silhouette: An-24.

9

Avro Shackleton

Great Britain

Long-range maritime reconnaissance and AEW aircraft, in service.

Powered by: Four 2,455hp Rolls-Royce Griffon 57A piston-engines.
Crew: 10.
Span: 119ft 10in (36.52m).
Length: 92ft 6in (28.19m).
Gross weight: 98,000lb (44,452kg).
Max speed: 260mph (418km/h). Patrol endurance, up to 10hrs.
Armament: None.

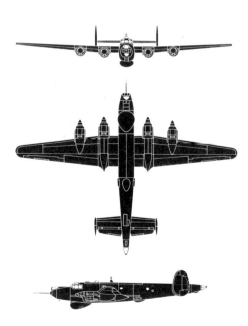

Data, photo and silhouette: Shackleton AEW.Mk 2.

Only survivors of the 188 Shackletons built for the RAF are AEW.Mk 2s, converted from MR.Mk 2Cs and assigned to No 8 Squadron for long-range airborne early warning duties from RAF Lossiemouth. For this purpose, they have had all armament removed and a range of new equipment added, including AN/APS-20 (F) I search radar (transferred from retired Gannet AEW.Mk 3s) in a chin radome, *Orange Harvest* wideband passive ECM, APX7 IFF and Doppler navigator. Since these Shackletons entered service, they have been further updated by the addition of AMTI (Airborne Moving Target Indicator) units. The first of 12 AEW Mk 2 conversions flew on September 30, 1971, and they will remain in service until the AEW.Mk 3 version of the Nimrod is introduced in the 'eighties. The Shackleton MR.Mk 1 (77 built) first entered service with No 120 Squadron of RAF Coastal Command late in 1951. The Mk 1 aircraft could be distinguished from later versions by their shorter, more rounded nose with fixed undernose radome, and blunt rear fuselage. The MR.Mk 2 (prototype WB833) was developed in 1952 with a longer, more streamlined nose, pointed tail-cone and retractable ventral radar. With equipment brought up to Mk 3 standard, the Mk 2C continued in RAF service until 1972. The Shackleton MR.Mk 3 had wingtip tanks, nose-wheel undercarriage in place of the former tail-wheel type and other refinements. Sixty-nine Mk 2 and 42 Mk 3 aircraft were built. To increase the capabilities of the RAF's Mk 3 Shackletons, they underwent extensive modification to Phase 3 standard, including structural strengthening, increase in fuel capacity and the addition of two Rolls-Royce Bristol Viper auxiliary turbojets, mounted in the rear of the outboard engine nacelles, to improve take-off performance. A squadron of eight Mk 3 Shackletons, without the Viper boost engines, serves with the South African Air Force.

BAC Lightning

Great Britain

Single-seat supersonic fighter, in service.

Powered by: Two 16,360lb (7,420kg) st Rolls-Royce Avon 301 turbojets with afterburning.
Span: 34ft 10in (10.61m).
Length: 55ft 3in (16.84m).
Gross weight: approx. 50,000lb (22,680kg).
Max speed: Mach 2 (1,320mph; 2,124km/h).
Armament: Two Red Top or Firestreak air-to-air missiles, or two packs of 24 air-to-air rockets plus, optionally, two 30mm guns in ventral pack.

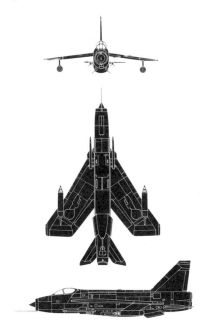

The Lightning F.Mk 1, evolved from the P. 1A research aircraft, first flew on April 4, 1957. This version (20 built) and the F.Mk 1A (28 built), with provision for flight refuelling, equipped three RAF squadrons. The F.Mk 2, first flown on July 11, 1961, introduced many improvements and could carry Red Top as well as Firestreak.Thirty were modified to F.Mk 2A, with some features of the F. Mk 6, for service in RAF Germany with Nos 19 and 92 Squadrons. First flown on June 16, 1962, the F. Mk 3 had Series 300 Avons, a larger square-tip tail fin and much improved equipment, although the two 30mm Aden guns fitted in earlier marks were deleted. From it was evolved the fully-developed F. Mk 6 (prototype flown on April 17, 1964), in which the outer portion of the wing leading-edge has slightly less sweep and incorporates conical camber, and the capacity of the ventral fuel tank was more than doubled. This version can carry two overwing fuel tanks for long-range ferrying. Since 1974, the RAF's Lightnings have been progressively replaced by Phantoms in the interceptor role, and in 1978 only two squadrons of Mk 6 aircraft remained operational in the UK. These and the Lightning Training Squadron also use a few T. Mk 5s (prototype first flown March 29, 1962; 22 built) which are side-by-side dual-control fully-operational counterparts of the F.Mk 3. Saudi Arabia purchased 35 Lightning F.Mk 53 multi-role interceptor/ground-attack fighters, six T.Mk 55 trainers, and five ex-RAF Mk 2 and two Mk 4 as F.Mk 52 and T.Mk 54 respectively. These remain first-line equipment in 1978, but the 12 F.Mk 53 and two T.Mk 55 Lightnings bought by Kuwait were withdrawn from service in 1977.

Data and photo: Lightning F.Mk 6.
Silhouette: Lightning F.Mk 53.

BAC VC10 Great Britain

Long-range troop and freight transport, and flight refuelling tanker, in service.

Powered by: Four 21,800lb (9,888kg) st Rolls-Royce Conway R.Co.43 Mk 550 turbojets.
Span: 146ft 2in (44.55m).
Length (without refuelling probe): 133ft 8in (40.74m).
Gross weight: 323,000lb (146,510kg).
Max cruising speed: 581mph (935km/h).
Typical range: 3,900 miles (6,275km) with 57,400lb (26,030kg) payload at 425mph (683km/h) at 30,000ft (9,145m).
Accommodation: 150 passengers in rearward-facing seats, or freight.

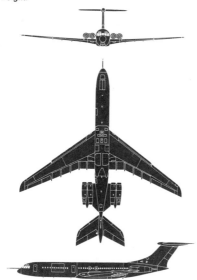

Although similar in overall dimensions to the original BOAC version, the RAF's VC10 C.Mk 1 (Model 1106) has the more powerful Conway 43 engines and fin fuel tank of the Super VC10. Other changes include the installation of a large cargo door at the front of the cabin on the port side, an optional nose-probe for flight refuelling and an Artouste auxiliary power unit in the tail-cone for engine starting and electric power on the ground. The primary duty of the RAF's VC10s is to carry troops or personnel at high speed to any part of the world. The first C.Mk 1 made its first flight on November 26, 1965. Deliveries began on July 7, 1966, and were completed in 1968; 14 originally went into service with No 10 Squadron, but this number was reduced to 11 as part of the 1976 defence cuts. The aircraft are named individually after holders of the Victoria Cross.

To fulfil the increased flight refuelling requirement anticipated with the phase-in of the Tornado, the RAF purchased in 1978 five VC10 and four Super VC10 airliners operated previously by Gulf Air and East African Airways respectively, for conversion into tankers by BAe at Bristol. The VC10 tankers will supplement the Victor K.Mk 2s at RAF Marham. One other VC10 operates in military colours, this being an ex-British Caledonian Airways standard VC10 used at the RAE Bedford for a variety of research tasks. Another standard VC10, sold by British Airways to the Sheik of Abu Dhabi, operates as a VIP transport in the colours of the Federation of Arab Emirates.

Data and silhouette: VC10 C.Mk 1.
Photo: V.1101 VC10.

BAe HS748, Andover and Coastguarder

Great Britain

Short/medium-range tactical transport, in production and service.

Powered by: Two 2,280ehp Rolls-Royce Dart 534-2 turboprops.
Span: 98ft 6in (30.02m).
Length: 67ft 0in (20.42m).
Gross weight: 51,000lb (23,133kg) in overload condition.
Cruising speed: 281mph (452km/h).
Range: 1,105 miles (1,778km) with max payload.
Accommodation: Flight crew of two and up to 58 troops or 48 paratroops and despatchers.

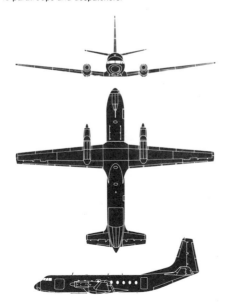

Data: HS748 Srs 2A.
Photo and silhouette: Andover VC.Mk 1.

The Avro company (subsequently part of Hawker Siddeley, now British Aerospace) began design of this twin-Dart transport in January 1959, initially for commercial use, and the prototype flew on June 24, 1960. More than 300 examples have been built to date and a number have been delivered to air forces around the world for use as VIP, staff or troop and supply transports, in some cases fitted with a large air-openable freight-loading door in the port side of the rear fuselage. Military operators include the Argentine Air Force (1), RAAF (10), RAN (2), Belgian Air Force (3), Brazilian Air Force (12), Brunei (1), Colombian Air Force (3), Ecuadorean Air Force (4), Nepal (1), South Korea (2), Thailand (2) and Zambian Air Force (1). The Indian Air Force has acquired a total of 62, of which the first four were lower-powered Srs 1s; these aircraft are assembled by HAL at Kanpur from British components. The RAF uses four HS748s as Andover C.Mk 2s and two others assigned to the Queen's Flight are designated Andover CC.Mk 2. The Andover C.Mk 1 was a special version for the RAF with a redesigned rear fuselage incorporating a stright-in loading ramp. The first example flew on December 21, 1963, being a converted HS748, and the first of 31 Andover C.Mk 1s for the RAF flew on July 9, 1965. The Andover C.Mk 1 was retired as an RAF tactical transport in 1975, but six were subsequently modified to Andover E.Mk 3s for radio and radar calibration duties and 10 others were sold to the RNZAF, of which one was modified to have a VVIP interior, one a VIP interior and the remainder are used as troop and supply transports. On February 18, 1977, Hawker Siddeley flew the prototype of an HS748 specially equipped for maritime surveillance, with MAREC radar in a radome under the centre fuselage, this version being known as the Coastguarder.

BAe HS Harrier

Great Britain

Single-seat V/STOL strike and reconnaissance aircraft, in production and service.

Powered by: One 21,5000lb (9,752kg) st Rolls-Royce Pegasus 103 vectored-thrust turbofan.
Span: 25ft 3in (7.70m).
Length: 45ft 6in (13.87m).
Gross weight: VTOL approx. 17,000lb (7,710kg); STOL approx. 23,000lb (10,433kg); max over 25,000lb (11,339kg).
Max speed: over 737mph (1,186km/h).
Typical radius of action: 500 miles (805km).
Armament: Three under-fuselage and four underwing attachments for 5,000lb (2,268kg) of stores. Typical load includes a 1,000lb bomb and two 30mm gun pods under fuselage; two pods of nineteen 68mm SNEB rockets and two 1,000lb bombs under wings.

Data: Harrier GR.Mk 3.
Photo and silhouette: Harrier GR.Mk 3A.

The Harrier is the operational development of the P.1127 Kestrel, first aircraft to utilise the Pegasus vectored-thrust turbofan. The four rotating exhaust nozzles on this engine make possible either vertical take-off and landing or, where a forward run is possible, short take-off with a heavier weapon load. The first of six pre-production Harriers made its first hovering flight on August 31, 1966, and all six were flying by mid-1967. The first of 114 single-seat Harriers for the RAF flew on December 28, 1967, with the designation GR.Mk 1 and powered by the Pegasus 101 engine. Engines of this type were later modified to the more powerful Pegasus 102 standard, the aircraft being then designated GR.Mk 1As: a further change of engine to 21,500lb (9,752kg) Pegasus 103 changed the designation to GR.Mk 3, and aircraft with laser target-marking equipment in the nose are GR.Mk 3A.

The RAF also acquired 17 tandem two-seat Harrier T.Mk 2s with revised front fuselage and tail unit; the first two flew on April 24 and July 14, 1969, respectively. The same engine changes as described above changed the designations to T.Mk 2A and T.Mk 4 respectively.

Deliveries to the RAF began in April 1969, and No 1 Squadron, the only Harrier unit in No 38 Group of Strike Command, began working up on the type in the latter half of that year. Two Harrier squadrons are assigned to RAF Germany (Nos 3 and 4). The US Marine Corps received on January 6, 1971 the first of 102 Harriers ordered as AV-8As; eight two-seat TAV-8As have also been ordered. The first ten had Pegasus 10 (F402-RR-400) engines; the remainder have the 21,500lb st Pegasus 11 (F402-RR-401). The Spanish Navy has ordered, through the US, eleven AV-8As and two TAV-8As, known in Spain as Matadors. A single Harrier Mk 52 has been built as a two-seat demonstrator.

BAe HS Nimrod

Great Britain

Four-engined long-range anti-submarine aircraft, in service.

Powered by: Four 12,140lb (5,506kg) st Rolls-Royce Spey Mk 250 turbofans.
Span: 114ft 10in (35.0m).
Length: 126ft 9in (38.63m).
Gross weight (typical): 192,000lb (87,090kg).
Max speed: 575mph (926km/h).
Typical ferry range: 5,755 miles (9,265km).
Armament: Mines, bombs, depth charges and torpedoes in weapon-bay.

Data, photo and silhouette: Nimrod MR.Mk 1.

The Nimrod has an airframe basically similar to that of the Comet 4C airliner, with an unpressurised pannier containing a weapon-bay added under the fuselage. The centre fuselage is fitted out as a navigational and tactical centre for the operators of the wide range of submarine detection devices. There is a searchlight in the front of the fuel pod on the starboard wing leading-edge and an electronic countermeasures pod on the fin-tip. The 12-man crew includes two pilots and an engineer on the flight deck, and two navigators and seven sensor operators in the forward cabin. Up to 45 passengers can be carried when the Nimrod is operated in its secondary trooping role. The first of two prototype Nimrods, converted from Comet transports, flew on May 23, 1967. A total of 46 MR.Mk 1 production models was ordered to replace the RAF's Shackletons and the first of these (XV226) flew on June 28, 1968. Deliveries to No 201 Squadron of Strike Command, at Kinloss, began on October 2, 1969. Nimrods now equip four Strike Command squadrons, (Nos 42, 120, 201 and 206) and the OCU (No 236). Three additional aircraft, designated Nimrod R.Mk 1, serve in an electronic reconnaissance role with No 51 Squadron at RAF Wyton. During 1978, work was proceeding on an updated avionics fit for the Nimrod which, when fully operational, will result in a change of designation to Nimrod MR.Mk 2. It was also announced that 11 Nimrods will in due course be converted to operate in the AEW role, replacing Shackletons in No 8 Squadron, and a Comet airframe converted to serve as a prototype of this configuration flew on June 28, 1977. One of the final batch of production MR. 1s is being used as an MR. 2 development aircraft; two others have been allocated to AEW.Mk 3 development.

BAe HS Sea Harrier

Great Britain

Single-seat carrier-based fighter/strike/reconnaissance aircraft, in production.

Powered by: One 21,500lb (9,760kg) st Rolls-Royce Pegasus 104 vectored-thrust turbofan.
Span: 25ft 3¼in (7.70m).
Length: 47ft 7in. (14.50m).
Gross weight: Over 25,000lb (11,340kg) for STO.
Max speed: Over 737mph (1,186km/h) at low altitude.
Radius of action: 100 miles (161km) plus loiter time on combat air patrol.
Armament: Provision for two gun pods under fuselage, each carrying one 30mm Aden cannon, and four wing pylons plus one fuselage pylon to carry AAMs, ASMs, bombs, rockets, etc.

Development of a version of the Harrier (see page 14) more specifically intended for carrier-based operations in the naval strike fighter role began in the early 'seventies, although the Harrier in unmodified form has proved fully capable of operating from carrier decks and is so used by the US Marines and Spanish Navy. As eventually ordered by the Royal Navy in May 1975 for operation from the new *Invincible* class of through-deck carriers, the Sea Harrier FRS.Mk 1 differs from the basic RAF Harrier in having a new front fuselage with a raised cockpit and changed avionics; a modified engine (Pegasus 104 instead of 103) in which two major magnesium components have been eliminated; a new cockpit conditioning system and single auto-pilot; increased roll power from roll control valves; increased tailplane incidence travel; revised liquid oxygen system; a hold-back system on the main undercarriage leg; an emergency brake system; updated Martin-Baker ejection seats; magnesium components eliminated from airframe structure; strengthened centre fuselage structure and provision for air-to-air and air-to-ground guided weapons to be carried under the wings, to RN requirements. The RN order for Sea Harriers is for 34 aircraft, of which the first three are development airframes to be used in a flight test programme which started in 1978. Initial Sea Harrier deployment is expected to be on board HMS *Hermes* from 1980 onwards, pending the commissioning of *Invincible*; they will be operated by Nos 800, 801 and 802 Squadrons, FAA.

BAe (BAC 167) Strikemaster (and Jet Provost)

Great Britain

Two-seat counter-insurgency strike aircraft and trainer, in service.

Powered by: One 3,410lb (1,546kg) st Rolls-Royce Viper 535 turbojet.
Span: 36ft 10in (11.23m).
Length: 33ft 8½in (10.27m).
Gross weight: 11,500lb (5,215kg).
Max range: 1,382 miles (2,224km).
Max speed: 472mph (760km/h) at 20,000ft (6,100m).
Armament: Two 7.62mm FN machine-guns in fuselage. Four wing strong points for maximum underwing load of 3,000lb (1,360kg).

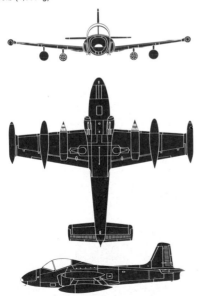

Data, photo and silhouette: Strikemaster.

The BAC 167 Strikemaster was developed from the basic armed Jet Provost to meet the needs of small air forces for a relatively cheap armed counter-insurgency aircraft and trainer. It differs from the RAF's Jet Provost T.Mk 5 trainer primarily in having an uprated engine, permanently-attached tip-tanks and increased armament capability. Common to both the Strikemaster and the Jet Provost 5 is a pressurised cockpit. The first Strikemaster flew on October 26, 1967, and 140 have been built for the Saudi Arabian Air Force (25 Mk 80 and 21 Mk 80A), the South Yemen People's Republic (4 Mk 81, later sold to Singapore), the Sultan of Oman's Air Force (12 Mk 82 and 12 Mk 82A, of which five sold later to Singapore), the Kuwait Air Force (12 Mk 83), the Singapore Air Defence Command (16 Mk 84), the Kenya Air Force (6 Mk 87), the Royal New Zealand Air Force (16 Mk 88) and the Ecuadorean Air Force (16 Mk 89). A total of 110 Jet Provost T.Mk 5s were built for the RAF, with 2,500lb (1,134kg) st Viper 202, pressure cabin and optional wing-tip tanks. They replaced the Jet Provost T.Mk 4, which was unpressurised. The T.Mk 3 which had a 1,750lb (794kg) st Viper 102 engine remains in service alongside the T.Mk 5; both of these variants have undergone a refit programme, completed in 1976, since when they have been redesignated T.Mk 3A and T.Mk 5A. Export models of the Jet Provost, with provision for two 0.303in machine-guns in the air intake walls and limited underwing stores capability, were the T.Mk 51 (Viper 102) for Ceylon, the Sudan and Kuwait and T.Mk 52 (Viper 202) for Venezuela, Sudan, Iraq and the South Yemen. Five examples of an armed version of the Jet Provost T.Mk 5 were sold to the Sudan to supplement its Mk 51s and 52s, and were designated Jet Provost 55 (BAC 145), remaining in service in 1978.

Beriev M-12 (Be-12) (NATO code-name: Mail)

USSR

Maritime reconnaissance amphibian, in service.

Powered by: Two 4,000shp Ivchenko AI-20D turboprops.
Span: 97ft 6in (29.70m).
Length: 107ft 11$\frac{1}{4}$in (32.9m).
Gross weight: 65,035lb (29,500kg).
Max speed: 379mph (610km/h).
Range: 2,485 miles (4,000km).
Armament: Attack weapons on four underwing pylons and in bomb-bay in rear of hull.

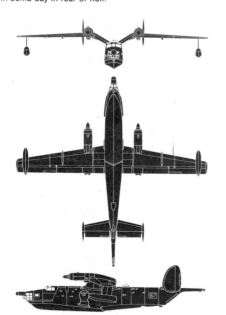

Data are estimated.

Existence of this turboprop-engined amphibian became known in 1961, when a single example appeared during the Soviet Aviation Day fly-past over Moscow. This fleeting appearance revealed the type to be a close relative of the piston-engined Be-6 which was then standard equipment in flying-boat squadrons of the *Morskaya Aviatsiya* (Soviet Navy Aviation). The prototype is believed to have flown for the first time during 1960.

Little more was heard of the new type until October 1964 when a series of altitude records was established by the Be-12, named Tchaika (Seagull) and designated M-12 by the Soviet forces. These records showed that the Be-12 was capable of lifting a payload of 22,266lb (10,100kg) and of reaching nearly 40,000ft (12,185m) with no payload.

Several examples of the M-12 participated in the display at Domodedovo in July 1967, showing that it had entered service, presumably as a replacement for the Be-6. Although resembling the latter type in all general respects other than the engines and undercarriage, in detail it shows many design refinements. A speed record of 351 mph (565km/h) around a 500km circuit was set up by an M-12 in April 1968, in the flying-boat, rather than amphibian, category; and M-12s now hold all 38 records for turboprop flying-boats and amphibians.

About 100 M-12s are thought to have been built, and they are operational with units of the Soviet Northern and Black Sea fleets. For a period, some were based in Egypt for patrol duties over the Mediterranean.

Boeing B-52 Stratofortress   USA

Strategic heavy jet bomber, in service.

Powered by: Eight 17,000lb (7,718kg) st Pratt & Whitney TF33-P-3 turbofans.
Span: 185ft 0in (56.42m).
Length: 160ft 0in (48.77m).
Gross weight: over 488,000lb (221,350kg).
Max speed: About 650mph (1,040km/h) at 50,000ft (15,240m).
Range: 12,500 miles (20,120km).
Armament: One 20mm multi-barrel cannon in remote-control rear turret. Primary armament comprises eight SRAM internally and six under each wing, as alternative to conventional HE bombs internally.
Accommodation: Crew of six.

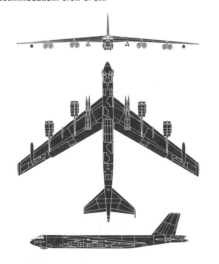

Data: B-52H.
Photo and silhouette: B-52G.

Development of the B-52 began in mid-1945, and production totalled 744 between 1954 and 1962. First operational version was the B-52B, in service from June 1955 onwards. Continual refinement and introduction of new equipment and more powerful engines resulted in the B-52C, B-52D, B-52E and B-52F. Most-produced variant was the Wichita-built B-52G, distinguished by a "wet" wing with integral fuel tanks for greater capacity and hence range, and provision for a Hound Dog missile (since retired) under each wing. A remotely-controlled rear turret was introduced on this version, production of which totalled 193. Final variant was the B-52H, with turbofan engines, instead of the former P & W J57 turbojets, and improved defensive armament. The B-52H first flew on March 6, 1961, and 102 were built at Wichita, the last being delivered to SAC in October 1962. Stratofortresses were operational against targets in Vietnam from bases in Thailand, especially in the closing stages of the campaign, carrying large numbers of non-nuclear bombs under their wings and internally. In a major modification programme started in 1972, 96 B-52s of the G and H models were adapted to carry 20 Short Range Attack Missiles (SRAM) each, for continued service with SAC. Another programme, begun in 1973, introduced AN/ASQ-151 Electro-optical Viewing System (EVS) which provides forward-looking LLTV and IR capability and is indicated by two small steerable chin turrets under the nose. About 270 B-52s were modified to have EVS by the end of 1976. In 1978, SAC still used 80 structurally modified B-52Ds and about 165 Gs and 90 Hs, which are now expected to remain in the active inventory for the rest of this century, as cruise missile carriers.

Boeing E-3A Sentry

USA

Seventeen-seat airborne warning and control system aircraft, in production and service.

Powered by: Four 21,000lb (9,525kg) st Pratt & Whitney TF33-P-100/100A turbofans.
Span: 145ft 9in (44.42m).
Length: 152ft 11in (46.61m).
Gross weight: About 330,000lb (149,685kg).
Search range: 7 hr endurance at 29,000ft (8,840m) at a distance of 1,150 miles (1,850km) from base.
Armament: None.

Following evaluation of proposals by McDonnell Douglas and Boeing, the USAF selected the latter company as prime contractor for its new Airborne Warning and Control System (AWACS) aircraft on July 8, 1970. The Boeing proposal was based on the airframe of the commercial Model 707-320B, with the addition of an extensive range of equipment for the airborne early-warning command-and-control role, including a downward-looking radar in a large rotating dorsal radome. Two prototypes were ordered, and the first of these flew on February 9, 1972. Designated EC-137D, they were used for competitive evaluation of Hughes and Westinghouse radars, the latter being selected later in 1972. Two more 707 airframes were ordered subsequently for conversion to E-3A prototypes, this being the production designation, and these aircraft flew (without AWACS electronics) in February and July 1975. One of the EC-137Ds also became an E-3A prototype while the other was modified up to full production standard. The USAF was expected to acquire 34 E-3As (including the three prototypes) eventually, although the programme suffered successive stretch-outs and by 1978 only 19 had been firmly ordered. Fourteen were scheduled for delivery by the end of that year. The E-3A was originally intended to be powered by eight General Electric TF34 engines but this was later changed, on grounds of economy, to the same four-engined arrangement as the commercial model, with P & W engines.

Boeing KC-97 Stratofreighter

USA

Transport and flight refuelling tanker, in service.

Powered by: Four 3,500hp Pratt & Whitney R-4360-59 piston-engines.
Span: 141ft 3in (43.1m).
Length: 110ft 4in (33.64m).
Empty weight: 82,500lb (37,450kg).
Gross weight: 175,000lb (79,450kg).
Max speed: 375mph (603km/h) at 25,000ft (7,620m).
Max range: 4,300 miles (6,880km) at 297mph (478km/h).
Accommodation: Crew of 5; up to 96 troops or 69 litters.

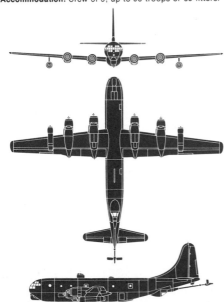

The first of three prototypes of the Boeing XC-97 flew on November 15, 1944, the design having originated as a transport version of the B-29 Superfortress. It had the same wing, power plant and tail unit, with a new fuselage of double-bubble section. Production began in 1945 and Boeing built a series of different transport versions for the USAF designated YC-97, YC-97A, YC-97B, C-97A, VC-97A, C-97C and VC-97D. After trials with three modified C-97As, fitted with the Boeing-developed Flying-Boom refuelling gear, the KC-97E tanker went into production in 1951. It was followed by the KC-97F and KC-97G models. Production ended in July 1956 with 888 C-97s built, 811 of these being tankers. The 592 KC-97Gs delivered to the USAF were replaced in due course by KC-135As. Many were converted (by Hayes) to KC-97L with the addition of two 5,200lb (2,360kg) st J47-GE-23 jet pods, one beneath each wing, and these equipped five Wings and Groups of the Air National Guard in 1978, to provide tanker services for Tactical Air Command. In another programme, 135 were converted (by AiResearch) to plain C-97Gs in cargo configuration, and another 26 went to SAC for mission support duties in passenger configuration as C-97Ks. Fairchild Stratos converted 28 to HC-97G for search and rescue. The Israeli Air Force had about a dozen KC-97s and ex-civil Stratocruisers in service as two-point flight refuelling tankers, troop and freight transports and on ECM duties, but these have been retired as newer types became available.

Data: KC-97G. Photo and silhouette: KC-97L.

Boeing KC-135 Stratotanker and C-135 Stratolifter

USA

Refuelling tanker and strategic transport, in service.

Powered by: Four 13,750lb (6,237kg) st Pratt & Whitney J57-P-59W turbojets.
Span: 130ft 10in (39.88m).
Length: 136ft 3in (41.53m).
Empty weight: 98,466lb (44,663kg).
Gross weight: 297,000lb (134,715kg).
Max speed: 585mph (941km/h) at 30,000ft (9,144m).
Range: 1,150 miles (1,850km) with full load of transfer fuel.
Accommodation: Crew of six and up to 80 passengers.

Data, photo and silhouette: KC-135A.

The KC-135A jet tanker-transport first flew on August 31, 1956 and deliveries of 732 began in June 1957. The 600 operational with eight Air National Guard Wings and Groups, and two Reserve Squadrons, are standard flight refuelling tankers for Strategic Air Command bombers, each with a total fuel capacity of 31,200 US gallons (118,100 litres), and can also be used as cargo or personnel transports.

For use by MATS as interim jet transports, the C-135A and turbofan C-135B were ordered in 1961, with tanker gear deleted and space for 87,100lb (39,510kg) of cargo or 126 troops; eleven C-135Bs became VC-135Bs when fitted with VIP interiors. Only 11 C-135s remained in USAF service in 1978. France purchased 12 C-135F tankers similar to the KC-135A, to refuel Mirage IVs. Other aircraft in the KC-135A series were modified during production for special duties, bringing the total quantity built (all as Boeing Model 717 or 739) to 820. These special variants were 14 KC-135B (later EC-135C) SAC Airborne Command Posts; 4 RC-135A for photo-reconnaissance and mapping; and ten RC-135B for electronic reconnaissance. Other designations were applied to various aircraft which changed their role after initial delivery; these included ten WC-135Bs for weather reconnaissance, RC-135C, D, E, M, S, U and V electronic reconnaissance versions and EC-135G, H, J, K, L and P command posts. Eight EC-135Ns serve as advanced range instrumentation aircraft for space mission support. The KC-135Q variant was specially adapted to refuel Lockheed SR-71s; the KC-135R and KC-135T were for special reconnaissance. Military versions of the Boeing 707 are described separately on page 23.

Boeing Model 707 and VC-137   USA

VIP transport and flight refuelling tanker, in service.

Powered by: Four 19,000lb (8,626kg) st Pratt & Whitney JT3D-7 turbofans.
Span: 145ft 9in (44.42m).
Length: approx 158ft 0in (48.16m).
Gross weight: 333,600lb (151,315kg)
Max speed: 620mph (998km/h).
Range: Over 7,000 miles (11,263km).

Data for 707-320C.
Photo: Iranian 707-3J9C tanker/transport.

Since 1974, the Iranian Imperial Air Force has put into service a fleet of 12-15 Boeing 707-320Cs specially adapted to serve as flight-refuelling tankers as well as cargo or personnel transports. These aircraft, identified by Boeing as Model 707-3J9Cs, are basically commercial 707-320Cs with side-loading cargo doors and can be readily adapted to have full passenger or executive interior layouts. In addition, each carries a Beech Model 1080 hose-and-drogue refuelling pod under each wingtip, and has a Boeing "flying boom" under the rear fuselage, with an operator's station below the cabin floor. Fuel capacity has been increased by 5,000 US gallons (18,925 litres) to a total of more than 28,000 US gallons (109,008 litres). The Canadian Armed Forces acquired five 707-320Cs in 1970, which are operated as CC-137s, and two have Beech underwing pods (but no "flying boom" equipment). The *Luftwaffe* operates four standard 707-320Cs as personnel and freight carriers; the Portuguese Air Force had two, but transferred them to TAP after the loss of Angola. One 707-320B is operated as a presidential and VIP transport by the Argentine Air Force, and another serves the same role in Egypt. The most famous military 707, however, is Air Force One, the personal transport of the president of the USA. Basically a 707-320B, this has a VIP interior and is designated VC-137C. Air Force One is operated from Andrews AFB by the 89th Military Airlift Wing, which also has on strength three smaller 707-120s, bought by USAF for VIP duties as VC-137As and modified to VC-137Bs when turbofans replaced the original piston engines.

Breguet Br.1050 Alizé

France

Three-seat carrier-borne anti-submarine aircraft, in service.

Powered by: One 2,100eshp Rolls-Royce Dart R.Da.21 turboprop.
Span: 51ft 2in (15.6m).
Length: 45ft 6in (13.86m).
Empty weight: 12,565lb (5,700kg).
Gross weight: 18,100lb (8,200kg).
Max speed: 292mph (470km/h) at 10,000ft (3,050m).
Endurance: 5hr 10min at 144mph (230km/h) at 1,500ft (460m).
Armament: Internal weapon bay for three 353lb (160kg) depth charges or one torpedo. Racks under inner wings for two 160kg or 175kg depth charges. Racks under outer wings for six 5in rockets or two AS.12 air-to-surface missiles. Sonobuoys in front of wheel housings.

Development of the Alizé began in 1948 when Breguet designed the two-seat Br.960 Vultur mixed power plant (turboprop and jet) strike aircraft to meet a French Navy requirement. When the Navy abandoned this concept in 1954, Breguet was given a contract to adapt the Vultur design into a three-seat single-engined anti-submarine aircraft, and this became the Br.1050 Alizé. The first stage was to modify the second prototype Vultur into an aerodynamic prototype of the new design. A more powerful (1,650shp) Mamba turboprop was installed; the Nene turbojet was removed to make way for a large retractable "dustbin" radome in the rear fuselage and dummy undercarriage/sonobuoy nacelles were fitted to the wings. This aircraft flew for the first time on March 26, 1955. Meanwhile, two genuine prototypes and three pre-production Alizés had been ordered, with Dart turboprop in place of the Mamba. The first of these flew on October 6, 1956, and the first of 75 production Alizés for the French Navy, with detail changes, was delivered on March 26, 1959. The remaining 40 aircraft equip two French Navy squadrons, Flotilles 4F and 6F, for service on board the carriers *Foch* and *Clémenceau* and for training. About 20 Alizés are to be updated to equip one Flotille on board the two carriers throughout the '80s, with improved radio and navaids, and Thomson-CSF Iguane radar. Twelve Alizés were supplied to the Indian Navy and two more were acquired later, ex-Aéronavale; about five continue to equip No 310 Squadron at INS *Garuda*, one detached flight from the squadron normally serving on board the carrier INS *Vikrant*, from which Alizés were in operational use during the 1971 Indo-Pakistan War.

Breguet Br.1150 Atlantic

France

Long-range maritime reconnaissance aircraft, in service.

Powered by: Two 6,105eshp SNECMA/Rolls-Royce Tyne R.Ty.20 Mk 21 turboprops.
Span: 119ft 1in (36.30m).
Length: 104ft 2in (31.75m).
Gross weight: 95,900lb (43,500kg).
Max speed: 409mph (658km/h).
Max range: 5,590 miles (9,000km) at 195mph (320km/h).
Crew: 12.
Armament: Internal weapon bay accommodates all standard NATO bombs, 385lb (175kg) depth charges and homing torpedoes. Underwing pylons for air-to-surface rockets, air-to-surface missiles, etc.

Two prototypes of the Atlantic were ordered in December 1959, following a NATO design competition for a Neptune replacement which had attracted a total of 25 entries from manufacturers in several countries. The governments of France, Federal Germany, Belgium, the Netherlands and USA assumed joint responsibility for the programme, and design and manufacture of the aircraft was undertaken by a consortium of companies in several countries, under the overall leadership of Breguet. The first of the prototypes flew on October 21, 1961. Two pre-production aircraft (the first of which flew on February 25, 1963) introduced a 3ft (1m) longer front fuselage, giving more room in the operations control centre. Breguet then delivered 40 production machines for the French Navy, to equip three squadrons, and 20 for the German Navy, five of the latter now being used for ECM duties with special equipment. The first delivery of an operational Atlantic was made to Aéronavale on December 10, 1965. In 1968, further orders were placed by the Netherlands for nine aircraft, and by Italy for 18; and during 1974, Aéronavale sold three of its Atlantics to Pakistan. In the same year, work was started on converting an existing aircraft into a prototype Atlantic Mk II, planned to have AM.39 Exocet air-to-surface missiles and a new standard of electronics primarily for an air-to-surface-vessel attack role. By 1977 this had evolved into the more refined Atlantic ANG, of which Dassault-Breguet expected to fly a prototype in late 1980. Aéronavale has a requirement for 42 aircraft to replace its existing Atlantics in the mid-eighties, and the French Defence Ministry authorised resumption of Atlantic production in 1978, to meet this need.

Canadair CL-41
(including CT-114 Tutor)

Canada

Two-seat basic trainer and light attack aircraft, in service.

Powered by: One 2,950lb (1,340kg) st General Electric J85-J4 turbojet.
Span: 36ft 6in (11.13m).
Length: 32ft 0in (9.75m).
Empty weight: 5,296lb (2,400kg).
Gross weight: 11,288lb (5,131kg).
Max speed: 480mph (774km/h) at 28,500ft (8,700m).
Max range: 1,340 miles (2,156km) with six underwing tanks.
Armament: Up to 4,000lb (1,815kg) of missiles, bombs, rockets and gun pods on six attachments under wings and centre-section.

The first of two prototypes of the Canadair CL-41 two-seat basic trainer flew on January 13, 1960, powered by a 2,400lb (1,090kg) st Pratt & Whitney JT12A-5 turbojet. It was developed to meet the anticipated needs of the RCAF for a basic jet trainer and, after evaluation of the prototypes, the RCAF ordered 190 CL-41A production models, powered by the locally-built 2,633lb (1,194kg) st General Electric J85-Can-40, under the designation CT-114 Tutor. The first of these was delivered on October 29, 1963, and all were in service by 1966. They continue in service in 1978 as the standard basic trainer of the Canadian Armed Forces. In June 1964, Canadair flew a Tutor converted to CL-41G configuration as a light counter-insurgency aircraft and armament trainer. This prototype had four underwing points for bombs, rockets or Minigun pods, but production CL-41Gs had two additional strong points under the centre-section. Twenty CL-41Gs were supplied to the Royal Malaysian Air Force in 1967/68 and currently equip two squadrons—No 6 for light strike duties and No 9 for training, both based at Kuantan. The RMAF name for the CL-41G is *Tebuan* (Wasp).

Data and photo: CL-41G.
Silhouette: CT-114 Tutor.

Canadair CP-107 (CL-28) Argus   Canada

Maritime reconnaissance aircraft, in service.

Powered by: Four 3,700hp Wright R-3350-EA-1 Turbo-Compound piston-engines.
Span: 142ft 3½in (43.38m).
Length: 128ft 9½in (39.25m).
Empty weight: 81,000lb (36,740kg).
Gross weight: 148,000lb (67,130kg).
Max speed: 315mph (507km/h) at 20,000ft (6,100m).
Max range: 5,900 miles (9,495km) at 223mph (359km/h).
Crew: 15.
Armament: Approx. 8,000lb (3,630kg) of weapons internally, plus 3,800lb (1,725kg) under each wing if required.

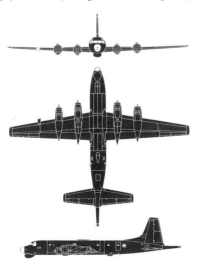

Development of the Argus began in 1953 when the RCAF drew up a specification for a new long-range overwater reconnaissance aeroplane to replace the Avro Lancasters then in service. To meet this requirement, Canadair projected an aeroplane based on the Bristol Britannia, and having secured an RCAF contract to go ahead, obtained a licence for Britannia development on March 16, 1954. In the CL-28 design, a completely new fuselage was introduced, and Wright R-3350 Turbo-Compound engines were adopted to obtain the necessary long duration at sea level. The basic Britannia wing design was retained, together with the tail unit, undercarriage and some other components. Equipment for the search role includes a large nose radome, MAD in the tail and a 70-million candle-power searchlight on one wing. The CL-28 first flew on March 28, 1957 and the first squadrons, Nos 404 and 405, were equipped at Greenwood, Nova Scotia, on May 17, 1958. After production of 13 Mk 1s, including the prototype, Canadair built 20 Mk 2s with new equipment identifiable by a smaller chin radome, production being completed in July 1960. Two further squadrons, Nos 407 and 415, have been equipped, and all four squadrons, with six aircraft each, are scheduled to continue flying the Argus until the introduction of the Lockheed CP-140 Aurora in 1980-81. Canadian Armed Forces designation of the Argus is CP-107.

Photo and silhouette: Argus Mk 2.

27

Cessna A-37 Dragonfly (and T-37) USA

Light attack aircraft and basic jet trainer, in service.

Powered by: Two 2,850lb (1,293kg) st General Electric J85-GE-17A turbojets.
Span: 35ft 10½in (10.93m).
Length: 29ft 3½in (8.93m).
Gross weight: 14,000lb (6,350kg).
Max speed: 507mph (816km/h) at 16,000ft (4,875m).
Ferry range: 1,010 miles (1,628km).
Armament: One 7.62mm multi-barrel Minigun; eight underwing strong points for more than 5,000lb (2,270kg) of ordnance.

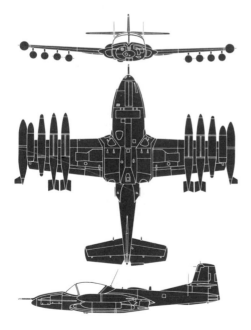

Data and silhouette: A-37B.
Photo: T-37C of the Royal Jordanian Air Force.

Cessna's first design for a jet aeroplane won a competition in 1954 for a primary jet trainer for the USAF. The first of two XT-37 prototypes flew on October 12, 1954, and the first of an evaluation batch of 11 T-37s flew a year later. A total of 416 T-37As were built, with two Continental J69-T-9 turbojets, before being superseded in production by the T-37B with 1,025lb (465kg) st J69-T-25 engines and revised equipment. All T-37As were converted to 'B' standard, and production of the T-37B continued into 1976, side-by-side with the export T-37C. The latter has provision for underwing armament, including machine-gun pods, rockets and bombs. Through MAP and by direct purchase, T-37Bs have been delivered to Thailand, Cambodia, Chile and Pakistan, while Germany purchased 47 for use in its training programmes based in the USA. Recipients of T-37Cs included Portugal, Peru, Brazil, Chile, Colombia, Greece, Pakistan, S. Korea, Thailand and Turkey. A total of 1,268 T-37s of all types had been built by the time production ended.

The A-37 was evolved from the T-37 for service in Vietnam, following evaluation by the USAF of two YAT-37D prototypes (first flown on October 22, 1963). In August 1966 the USAF ordered Cessna to complete 39 T-37Bs then in production as A-37As and the first of these was delivered in May 1967. These aircraft had eight underwing hardpoints, J85-GE-17A engines each de-rated to 2,400lb (1,090kg) st, and other changes and were operational in Vietnam by 1969. Deliveries began in May 1968 of the A-37B, with fully-rated engines, in-flight refuelling provision, 6g airframe stressing, provision for increased fuel capacity and other operational improvements. By late 1977, when production ended, a total of 538 A-37Bs had been built, recipients in addition to the USAF being Peru, Chile, Guatemala and Honduras. Many A-37Bs were transferred by USAF to the Vietnamese Air Force and nearly 100 were left in Vietnam when the war ended. Others serve with the USANG in two Tactical Fighter Groups, and the Air Force Reserve in four squadrons.

Convair F-106 Delta Dart

USA

Interceptor fighter, in service.

Powered by: One 24,500lb (11,123kg) st Pratt & Whitney J75-P-17 afterburning turbojet.
Span: 38ft 3½in (11.67m).
Length: 70ft 8¾in (21.56m).
Empty weight: 23,646lb (10,726kg).
Gross weight: About 35,000lb (15,875kg).
Max speed: Mach 2.3 (1,525mph; 2,450km/h) at 36,000ft (11,000m).
Range: 1,150 miles (1,850km).
Accommodation: Pilot only (pilot and observer in F-106B).
Armament: One Douglas AIR-2A Genie or AIR-2B Super Genie rocket and four Hughes AIM-4F or AIM-4G Super Falcon air-to-air missiles in internal weapons bay, supplemented by one 20mm M-61 cannon in modified aircraft.

Development of the F-102 to accommodate the more powerful J75 engine began in 1955. The designation was initially F-102B but this was later changed to F-106. While the wing remained substantially unchanged, the fuselage was extensively redesigned with the air intakes moved farther aft and the cockpit moved relatively farther forward. The shape of the fin and rudder was changed, the undercarriage was improved and provision was made for later weapons in the bomb-bay. A Hughes MA-1 guidance and control system was introduced to permit the F-106 to operate with the SAGE defence system. The first F-106A flew on December 26, 1956. Production of 277 was completed by the end of 1960, deliveries to Air Defense Command having begun in mid-1959. On April 9, 1958, the first of 63 F-106Bs flew; this variant is a combat trainer with two seats in tandem and full operational capability. The F-106A and F-106B still equip the majority of Aerospace Defense Command units, some 231 Delta Darts being shared by six active and five ANG squadrons. New drop tanks suitable for supersonic operation and capable of being refuelled in flight were added to the F-106s some years ago. Another modification programme, started in 1973, has made most F-106As capable of carrying an M-61 multi-barrel 20mm cannon, together with a Snap-Shoot gunsight. This enhanced the dog-fighting capability of the F-106, which will remain in ADC service throughout the 'seventies.

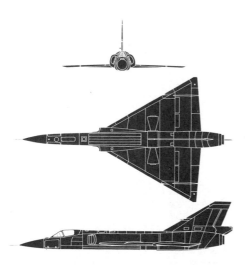

Photo and silhouette: F-106A.

Dassault Mirage IV-A   France

Two-seat supersonic strategic bomber, in service.

Powered by: Two 15,400lb (6,985kg) st SNECMA Atar 09K afterburning turbojets.
Span: 38ft 10½in (11.85m).
Length: 77ft 1in (23.50m).
Empty weight: 31,965lb (14,500kg).
Max gross weight: 73,800lb (33,475kg).
Max speed: Mach 2.2 (1,460mph; 2,350km/h) at 36,000ft (11,000m).
Tactical radius: 770 miles (1,240km).
Armament: One nuclear weapon recessed into bottom of fuselage, or sixteen 1,000lb bombs or four Martel air-to-surface missiles under fuselage and wings.

To meet French Air Force requirements for a supersonic bomber to deliver France's atomic bomb, Dassault scaled up the Mirage III fighter design and the result was the prototype Mirage IV, which flew for the first time on June 17, 1959. Powered by two 13,225lb (6,000kg) st Atar 09 turbojets with afterburning, this aircraft exceeded Mach 2 during its 33rd test flight. It was followed by three pre-production Mirage IVs, of which the first flew on October 12, 1961. The first two had 14,110lb (6,400kg) st Atar 09Cs and introduced a circular under-fuselage radome and dummy missiles, some containing test equipment. The third pre-production machine, first flown on January 23, 1963, was to operational standard, with Atar 09Ks, flight-refuelling nose-probe and armament. A total of 62 production Mirage IV-As were ordered for the French Air Force. The first of these flew on December 7, 1963, and all had been delivered to the French Air Force by 1967. During the time that they represented the primary French nuclear strike force (*Force de Frappe*), the aircraft were kept in protective shelters, and could take off straight out of the shelters with their engines running at full power. The nuclear bomb was designed for free-fall delivery, carried semi-recessed in the underside of the fuselage. As land-based and submarine-launched nuclear missiles have taken over the primary strike role, the Mirage IV-A force has been re-assigned to a low-level tactical strike role, carrying HE bombs or a tactical nuclear weapon with a 70KT yield. A dozen of the original fleet had been lost by 1978, when the remainder equipped nine squadrons in three wings, with no replacement expected before 1985. Four Mirage IV-As have been assigned to the strategic surveillance role, carrying reconnaissance equipment in a large pod.

Dassault-Breguet Etendard IV and Super Etendard

France

Single-seat carrier-based fighter-bomber and reconnaissance aircraft, in production and service.

Powered by: One 11,025lb (5,000kg) st SNECMA Atar 8K-50 turbojet.
Span: 31ft 6in (9.60m).
Length: 46ft 11½in (14.31m).
Gross weight: 20,280-25,350lb (9,200-11,500kg).
Max speed: approx. Mach 1 (660mph; 1,062km/h) at 36,000ft (11,000m).
Radius of action, with AM39 missile: 403 miles (650km)
Armament: Two 30mm DEFA cannon. Four underwing attachments for 882lb (400kg) bombs, Magic air-to-air missiles or rocket pods. Alternatively, one Exocet AM39 air-to-surface missile under starboard wing and external fuel tank under port wing.

Data, photo and silhouette: Super Etendard.

The Etendard began life as a low-level land-based strike fighter to meet French Air Force and NATO requirements, prototypes of the Etendard II, IV and VI variants being built and flown. None of these models progressed beyond the prototype stage, but the French Navy decided to adapt the Etendard IV for service from its two attack carriers, the *Clémenceau* and *Foch*, and the prototype of the navalised Etendard IV-M flew on May 21, 1958. It was followed by five pre-production and 69 production IV-Ms, used to equip two seagoing squadrons (*Flot* 11F and 17F) and one shore-based training unit. Compared with the land-based version, these have a long-stroke undercarriage, deck hook, catapult fittings, folding wingtips, modified nose containing AIDA all-weather fire-control radar, and a high-lift system combining leading-edge and trailing-edge flaps, plus two under-fuselage air-brakes. Some of the IV-Ms were delivered with nose refuelling probes and "buddy" refuelling packs. Also in service is the Etendard IV-P, of which 21 were delivered (plus one prototype) as dual-purpose reconnaissance/tankers, with nose and ventral camera positions, no cannon, self-contained navigation system and flight refuelling nose-probe. These equip one squadron (*Flot.* 16F) of the Aéronavale. During 1973, the French Navy ordered development of the Super Etendard to replace the IV-M and F-8E(FN) Crusader, the principal new features being Agave X-band radar in a larger nose radome, uprated Atar 8K-50 non-afterburning turbojet instead of the 9,700lb (4,400kg) st Atar 8B of the Etendard IV, and improved wing leading-edge and trailing-edge flaps. The first of three prototype/trials aircraft converted from standard Etendard IVs flew on October 28, 1974. The first of a planned production series of 71 Super Etendards flew on November 24, 1977, and deliveries to the Aéronavale began on June 28, 1978.

Dassault-Breguet Mirage III

France

Single-seat long-range fighter-bomber, in production and service.

Powered by: One 13,670lb (6,200kg) st SNECMA Atar 09C afterburning turbojet and, optionally, one 3,307lb (1,500kg) SEP 844 rocket-engine.
Span: 27ft 0in (8.22m).
Length: 49ft 3½in (15.03m).
Empty weight: 15,540lb (7,050kg).
Max gross weight: 29,760lb (13,500kg).
Max speed: Mach 2.2 (1,460mph; 2,350km/h) at 40,000ft (12,000m).
Tactical radius: 745 miles (1,200km) in ground attack configuration.
Armament: Two 30mm cannon in fuselage and one AS.30 air-to-surface missile or Matra R.530 air-to-air missile under fuselage, and two rocket pods or 1,000lb bombs under wings. Two Sidewinders can also be carried.

The Mirage III was designed as an all-weather fighter capable of operating from short unprepared airstrips and has proved to be one of the most successful jet fighters of the 1960-1980 period, with about 1,820 sold to some 20 nations (including 470 Mirage 5 variants—see next page).

Data, photo and silhouette: Mirage III-E.

The prototype flew on November 17, 1956, with a 9,900lb (4,500kg) st Atar 101G turbojet. It was followed by the Mach 2 Mirage III-A with 13,225lb (6,000kg) st Atar 9B turbojet, of which ten were built, and the generally-similar Mirage III-C (first flown October 9, 1960) of which 95 were built for all-weather interception and day ground attack duties with the French Air Force, with optional 3,307lb (1,500kg) thrust rocket-engine in the rear fuselage, and one for the Swiss Air Force. Others were delivered to Israel (III-CJ) and to South Africa (III-CZ). The Mirage III-C was followed by the III-E, first flown on April 5, 1961. This is a long-range fighter-bomber version with Atar 09C engine, fuselage lengthened by 1ft (30cm) and new nav/attack equipment. French orders for over 300 have been supplemented by export orders from the Argentine (III-EA), Brazil (III-EBR), Pakistan (III-EP), South Africa (III-EZ), Spain (III-EE), Lebanon (III-EL) and Venezuela (III-EV). Alongside the Mirage III-C, Dassault developed and produced the III-B, a tandem two-seat trainer which is 2ft (60cm) longer and retains the same strike capability as the III-C. This version first flew on October 20, 1959, and has been produced for the French Air Force, Israel (III-BJ), Lebanon (III-BL), Switzerland (III-BS), South Africa (III-BZ and III-DZ), Australia (III-D), Pakistan (III-DP), Brazil (III-DBR), Spain (III-DE) and the Argentine (III-DA). The III-BE is a two-seat version of the III-E for the French Air Force. A reconnaissance version of the III-E is designated Mirage III-R and was first flown in prototype form in November 1961. It carries five cameras in the nose and has been built for the French Air Force (III-R and III-RD, the latter with improved equipment), Pakistan (III-RP), Switzerland (III-RS), South Africa (III-RZ and III-RDZ) and Abu Dhabi (III-RAD). A version of the III-C was built in Switzerland as the III-S, with Hughes radar and Falcon missiles; a version of the III-E built in Australia was designated III-O, a two-seat version being the III-D. Some late-production Mirage IIIs have the Atar 9K-50 engine, including the III-D2Z and III-R2Z for South Africa.

Dassault-Breguet Mirage 5 and 50   France

Single-seat fighter-bomber, in production and service.

Powered by: One 13,670lb (6,200kg) st SNECMA Atar 09C afterburning turbojet.
Span: 27ft 0in (8.22m).
Length: 51ft 0¼in (15.55m).
Empty weight: 14,550lb (6,600kg).
Gross weight: 29,760lb (13,500kg).
Max speed: Mach 2.2 (1,460mph; 2,350km/h) at 40,000ft (12,000m).
Combat radius: 400–805 miles (650–1,300km) with 2,000lb (907kg) bomb-load.
Armament: Two 30mm cannon in fuselage. Typical external weapon load comprises two 1,000lb bombs, ten 500lb bombs and two 250lb bombs, plus two external fuel tanks. Other weapons can include one AS.30 or R.530 missile, rocket pods and Sidewinder missiles.

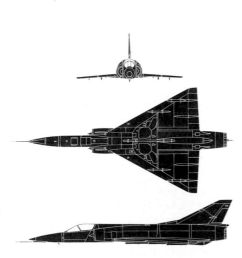

By simplifying the electronics and other systems of the basic Mirage III-E airframe, Dassault produced a day fighter-bomber with increased internal fuel capacity, considerably greater weapon-carrying capability and reduced maintenance requirements, known as the Mirage 5. The prototype flew on May 19, 1967. Subsequently, 50 Mirage 5-J were ordered by Israel, but delivery of these was blocked by the French government and in 1972 they were taken into service with the French Air Force as Mirage 5-Fs. Belgium ordered a total of 106 in three versions: the 5-BA for ground attack (27), the 5-BR reconnaissance model (63) and the 5-BD two-seater (16). The first of three Belgian Mirage 5s completed by Dassault flew on March 6, 1970; the remainder were then assembled in Belgium by SABCA. Other customers include Peru (5-P and 5-PD two-seaters); Libya (5-D, 5-DE, 5-DR and two-seat 5-DD); Colombia (5-COA, plus camera-equipped 5-COR and two-seat 5-COD); the United Arab Emirates Air Force-Abu Dhabi (5-AD and 5-RAD, plus two-seat 5-DAD); Venezuela (5-V and two-seat 5-DV); Gabon (5-G and two-seat 5-DG); Zaïre (5-M and two-seat 5-DM); Pakistan (5-PA) and Saudi Arabia (5-SDE and two-seat 5-SDO). The Mirage 5s supplied to Saudi Arabia were transferred immediately to the Egyptian Air Force, on whose behalf they were bought. Dassault developed a derivative of the Mirage III/5 family known as the Milan (Kite), with retractable 'moustache' fore-planes which improve the low-speed handling. After trials on a Mirage III-R, a prototype Milan S-01 with Atar 09K-50 flew on May 29, 1970, but was not put into production. However, Sudan has ordered 24 Mirage 50s which are basically Mirage 5s with the Atar 09K-50 engine.

Data, photo and silhouette: Mirage 5.

Dassault-Breguet Mirage F1   France

Single-seat all-weather multi-purpose fighter, in production and service.

Powered by: One 15,798lb (7,166kg) st SNECMA Atar 09K-50 afterburning turbojet.
Span: 27ft 6¾in (8.40m).
Length: 49ft 2½in (15.00m).
Empty weight: 16,314lb (7,400kg).
Gross weight: 32,850lb (14,900kg).
Max speed: Mach 2.2 (1,460mph; 2,350km/h) at 40,000ft (12,000m). Mach 1.2 at low altitude.
Endurance: 3 hr 45 min.
Armament: Two 30mm DEFA cannon in forward fuselage. One underfuselage strong point, and two under each wing, for max external load (in F1-E) of 8,820lb (4,000kg). Provision for Sidewinder missile attached at each wingtip.

Data, photo and silhouette: Mirage F1-C.

This multi-purpose fighter is a development of the Mirage III-E, with a basically similar fuselage and the same weapon systems. Its primary role is all-weather interception at all altitudes, but versions are also available with ground attack capability. The sweptback wing, contrasting with the delta wing of other Mirage types, is fitted with a drooping saw-tooth leading-edge and large double-slotted flaps, enabling the Mirage F1 to take off and land in under 700 yards (640m) and to use unprepared runways. The prototype flew for the first time on December 23, 1966, but was destroyed on May 18, 1967. Three replacements were ordered by the French Air Force, and the first of these, the F1-02, flew on March 20, 1969, followed by F1-03 on September 18, 1969 and F1-04 on June 17, 1970. For its first 62 flights, F1-02 was powered by an Atar 09K-31, but the definitive 09K-50 was then fitted, and powered the subsequent pre-production aircraft. The French Air Force ordered 105 Mirage F1-Cs and plans procurement of further batches. The first production F1-C flew on February 15, 1973 and deliveries began in March to the 30e *Escadre* at Reims, followed in due course by the 5e and 12e *Escadres*. Export orders from Spain, Greece, Kuwait, Iraq, Ecuador, South Africa, Libya and Morocco, plus licensed production in South Africa, brought total sales to 554 by early 1978, including some two-seat F1-Bs, the first example of which flew on May 26, 1976. The F1-A (also included in the sales total) has simplified electronics. The F1-E designation was first used for a single prototype, first flown on December 22, 1974, with 18,740lb (8,458kg) st M53 engine, but is now used for an Atar-engined advanced attack version, of which the F1-D is the two-seat equivalent.

Dassault-Breguet Mirage 2000 (and Super Mirage 4000)

France

Single-seat air superiority and long-range interdiction fighter, under development.

Powered by: One 18,740lb (8,500kg) st SNECMA M53-2 or 19,840lb (9,000kg) st M53-5 turbofan with afterburning.
Span (estimated): 29ft 6in (9.00m).
Length (estimated): 50ft 3½in (15.33m).
Gross weight: About 20,000lb (9,000kg) as interceptor.
Max speed: Approximately Mach 2.3 (1,520mph; 2,440km/h) at 40,000ft (12,200m) and above.
Radius of action (air superiority role): 435 miles (700km).
Armament: Built-in armament of two 30mm DEFA cannon. Two Matra Super 530 and two Matra 550 Magic air-to-air missiles in air superiority role (plus provision for two drop tanks). Four underwing pylons and five fuselage hardpoints for up to 11,000lb (5,000kg) of ordnance in interdiction role.

Data, photo and silhouette: Mirage 2000.

First flown on March 10, 1978, with a second prototype scheduled to fly before the end of the year, the Mirage 2000 is being developed as the principal new tactical fighter for the *Armée de l'Air*, with which it is expected to become operational in 1983. The Mirage 2000 follows the delta-wing configuration of the highly successful Mirage III/5 series, but is designed for a high overall performance and increased combat capability. The initial version is intended for interceptor and air superiority roles, in which it will carry two 30mm DEFA cannon and two Matra Super 530 and two Matra 550 Magic missiles. A large Thomson-CSF/EMD X-band radar will be carried, and with a thrust-to-weight ratio of nearly 1:1, the Mirage 2000 is expected to be able to reach Mach 2.0 at a height of more than 49,000ft (15,000m) within four minutes of brake release. Carrying two drop tanks in addition to the four air-to-air missiles, it will have about twice the endurance of the Mirage F1 on combat air patrols, and in the secondary role of long-range low-altitude interdiction and reconnaissance it will be able to carry up to 11,000lb (5,000kg) of bombs on four wing and five fuselage hardpoints. The French government has funded four prototypes of the Mirage 2000, of which one will be a two-seater; in addition, a company-funded prototype is being built, primarily as a demonstrator for a simplified and lightened export model. The initial *Armée de l'Air* requirement is for 130 of the air superiority version, in single-seat and two-seat variants, perhaps to be increased to 200 eventually, in addition to about 200 long-range interdiction and reconnaissance versions. A related twin-engined multi-role fighter (with M53-5s) is under development as a Dassault-Breguet private venture and is named Super Mirage 4000.

Dassault-Breguet/ Dornier Alpha Jet

France/Germany

Light strike aircraft and basic/weapons trainer, in production and service.

Powered by: Two 2,975lb (1,350kg) st SNECMA-Turboméca GRTS Larzac 04 turbofans.
Span: 29ft 11in (9.11m).
Length: 40ft 3in (12.29m).
Empty weight: 7,660lb (3,475kg).
Gross weight: trainer, 10,010lb (4,540kg); close support, 13,227lb (6,000kg); max permissible, 15,432lb (7,000kg).
Max speed: 616mph (991km/h) at sea level, Mach 0.85 at altitude.
Radius of action: close support, 390 miles (630km).
Armament: Provision for gun pod under fuselage (one 30mm or two 0.50in), and four wing pylons carrying max combined load of 3,760lb (1,710kg).

The project to develop a new basic trainer to meet the joint requirements of France and Germany was initiated in July 1969. After evaluation of competitive designs submitted by teams comprising Dassault/Dornier and Nord (Aérospatiale)/ Messerschmitt (MMB), the former was selected for development. Basis of this design was a Dornier project, with tandem seating and two SNECMA-Turboméca Larzac 02 engines. After development began in 1971 against expected purchases of 200 each for the *Armée de l'Air* and the *Luftwaffe*, the latter changed its requirement to that of a light close air-support and battlefield reconnaissance aircraft and the Alpha Jet was developed around more powerful Larzac 04 engines to have extra wing pylons and higher operating weights, as quoted above. The first of two "basic" prototypes flew in France on October 26, 1973, followed by the second in Germany on January 9, 1974. Prototype No 3, also flown in France, was first airborne on May 6, 1974 and represented the *Luftwaffe* configuration, while No 4, flown in Germany on October 11, 1974 was a French trainer. The first truly representative production French trainer flew on May 19, 1978; the first Alpha Jet A for the *Luftwaffe* had flown in Germany on April 12, 1978; and the first Alpha Jet B for Belgium flew in France on June 20, 1978. The *Armée de l'Air* received its first Alpha Jet E in November 1978, one month after the *Luftwaffe* accepted its initial operational aircraft. The Belgian Air Force has placed an initial order for 16 Alpha Jets with 17 more on option. Others have been ordered by Ivory Coast (6), Togo (5) and Morocco (25).

De Havilland Venom

Great Britain

Single-seat fighter-bomber, in service.

Powered by: One 4,850lb (2,200kg) st de Havilland Ghost 103 turbojet.
Span: 41ft 8in (12.70m).
Length: 31ft 10in (9.70m).
Gross weight: 15,400lb (6,985kg).
Max speed: 640mph (1,030km/h).
Range: over 1,000 miles (1,610km) with external fuel.
Armament: Four 20mm cannon in nose and up to 2,000lb (907kg) of bombs or rockets under wings.

The D.H.112 Venom prototype first flew on September 2, 1949, as a direct modification of the Vampire with thinner, slightly sweptback wings, tip-tanks and Ghost turbojet. Production deliveries of the Venom FB. Mk 1 to the RAF began in 1951 and the type was used to equip squadrons of the 2nd TAF in Germany and others in the Middle and Far East. Re-equipment of these squadrons with the Venom FB. Mk 4, with powered ailerons, redesigned tail unit and other changes, began in the mid-fifties; and the two-seat, radar-equipped Venom NF. Mk 2 and 3 night fighters were also supplied to several squadrons. All Venoms had been phased out of operational service with the RAF by 1962; but the FB. 50 version of the Mk 1 remains operational in Switzerland, where 150 were built under licence, followed by 100 Venoms similar to the FB. Mk 4. Additional avionic equipment has been fitted in a recontoured nose to enhance the ground attack capability of the Swiss Venoms, about 150 of which remain in service with nine squadrons. Progressive replacement by F-5Es was to begin in 1978.

Data: Venom FB. Mk 4.
Photo and silhouette: Swiss Venom FB.4 and FB.50 respectively, with recontoured nose.

De Havilland (Canada) DHC-4 Caribou

Canada

Light tactical transport, in service.

Powered by: Two 1,450hp Pratt & Whitney R-2000-7M2 piston-engines.
Span: 95ft 7½in (29.15m).
Length: 72ft 7in (22.13m).
Empty weight: 18,260lb (8,283kg).
Normal gross weight: 28,500lb (12,928kg).
Max speed: 216mph (347km/h) at 6,500ft (1,980m).
Range: 242 miles (390km) with max payload.
Accommodation: Crew of 3 plus 32 combat troops or 26 paratroops or 22 litters and 8 other persons.

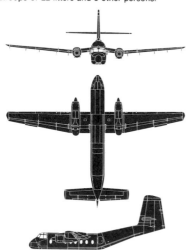

De Havilland Canada began design of this STOL tactical transport in 1955. The project gained US Army support in 1957 with a contract for five prototypes designated YAC-1; the Canadian Government ordered two, of which one was for RCAF evaluation as the CC-108.

The first Caribou flew on July 30, 1958 and the first YAC-1 in March 1959. Deliveries to the US Army began in October 1959 and the first of a continuing series of production orders was placed in 1960. The US Army AC-1s (later redesignated CV-2As) were delivered with a gross weight of 26,000lb (11,790kg); later aircraft (CV-2Bs) were to DHC-4A standard with a weight of 28,500lb.

A total of 159 Caribou were acquired by the US Army; 134 still in service in January 1967 were taken over by the USAF and redesignated C-7A. They are operated currently by two Tactical Airlift Groups of the AF Reserve and ANG. Four Caribou Mk 1A (DHC-4) ordered by the RCAF in August 1960 were allocated to UN forces in the Congo and five Mk 1B (DHC-4A) were purchased later, all with the CC-108 designation. Two CV-2As were transferred to the Indian Air Force in 1963 for evaluation, and 20 Caribou were subsequently purchased by India. Other air forces which bought Caribou, and continued to fly them in 1978, were those of Australia (26), Kuwait (2), Kenya (4), Zambia (5), Malaysia (16), Tanzania (10), Spain (12), Oman (2), Zaïre (2) and Abu Dhabi (3).

Photo: Caribou of Zambia Air Force.

De Havilland (Canada) DHC-5 Buffalo

Canada

Assault transport, in production and service.

Powered by: Two 3,133shp General Electric CT64-820-4 turboprops.
Span: 96ft 0in (29.26m).
Length: 79ft 0in (24.08m).
Empty weight: 25,050lb (11,362kg).
Gross weight: 49,200lb (22,316kg).
Max speed: 288mph (463km/h) at 10,000ft (3,050m).
Range: 690 miles (1,112km) with max payload.
Accommodation: Crew of 3; up to 41 troops or 35 paratroops or 24 litters and 6 other people.

Data apply to DHC-5D.
Photo: DHC.5D of Zaïre Air Force.

As the Caribou II, this design originated in a US Army requirement which was put out to industry in May 1962. De Havilland Aircraft of Canada, one of 25 companies invited to submit designs, had already sold three earlier types to the US Army in quantity—the Beaver, Otter and Caribou. The DHC-5, which was selected as winner of the design competition, was based on the Caribou wing and had the same general configuration, with a new, more capacious fuselage, a T-tail and T64 turboprop engines. The US Army ordered four DHC-5s for evaluation and development, originally with the designation YAC-2, this being changed later to YCV-7A and then to C-8A when the USAF took over US Army transports in January 1967. The first of these aircraft flew on April 9, 1964 and was delivered a year later. Late in 1964, the Canadian Armed Forces ordered 15 Buffaloes, of which most are now assigned to search and rescue duties. These are designated CC-115 and have a 20in (50cm) increase in overall length due to the nose radome, and more powerful engines. Twenty-four similar aircraft were ordered for the Brazilian Air Force and 16 by Peru, deliveries taking place in 1971/72. The DHC-5D version, with uprated engines and higher operating weights, entered production in 1974 and first flew on August 1, 1975. Orders to date include four for Zaïre, two for Togo, six for Zambia, two for Ecuador, four each for Kenya, Sudan, Tanzania and the United Arab Emirates and two for Mauritania.

Embraer EMB-111 and EMB-110 Bandeirante

Brazil

Twin-turboprop patrol aircraft (EMB-111) and light transport (EMB-110), in production and service.

Powered by: Two 750shp Pratt & Whitney (Canada) PT6A-34 turboprops.
Span: 52ft 4½in (15.96m).
Length: 48ft 8in (14.83m).
Gross weight: 15,430lb (7,000kg).
Cruising speed: 251mph (404km/h) at 10,000ft (3,050m).
Range: 1,693 miles (2,725km).
Armament: Provision for six air-to-surface rockets or three bombs or depth charges under wings.
Accommodation: Crew of five or six.

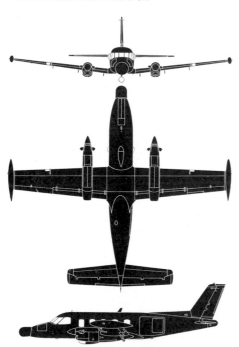

The EMB-111 is a shore-based maritime patrol aircraft developed initially to meet a requirement of the Brazilian Air Force, which placed an order for 12 at the end of 1975. The design is a variant of the EMB-110 Bandeirante transport, from which it differs externally in having AIL AN/APS-128 search radar in a large nose radome, a podded searchlight in a nacelle on the starboard wing, wingtip tanks, and provision for rockets under the wings. The internal equipment is also extensively revised to suit the coastal surveillance role. The first EMB-111M for the FAB made its first flight in August 1977, and deliveries have been interspersed with six similar EMB-111Ns for Chile. The design of the EMB-110 itself was evolved initially by the aircraft department (PAR) of the official Aeronautical Technical Centre (CTA). Designated YC-95, the prototype first flew on October 26, 1968, and was followed by the slightly modified second prototype on October 19, 1969. These prototypes carried 7–10 passengers and had 550shp PT6A-20 engines; basic production aircraft have 12 passenger seats and 680shp PT6A-27 or 750shp PT6A-34 engines. The Brazilian Air Force has ordered 89 Bandeirantes, of which 60 are the basic EMB-110 model (C-95); 20 are EMB-110K1 freighters (C-95A) with enlarged fuselage door, six are EMB-110B air survey versions (R-95) and three are EMB-110A navaid checking and calibration aircraft (EC-95). The Chilean Navy has acquired three EMB-110C(N)s and the Uruguayan Air Force has five EMB-110Cs.

Data, photo and silhouette: EMB-111.

English Electric Canberra (and Martin B-57)

Great Britain (USA)

Three-seat tactical light bomber, reconnaissance aircraft, trainer and target, in service.

Powered by: Two 7,400lb (3,357kg) st Rolls-Royce Avon 109 turbojets.
Span: 63ft 11½in (19.51m).
Length: 65ft 6in (19.96m).
Gross weight: 55,000lb (24,950kg).
Max speed: 580mph (933km/h) at 30,000ft (9,145m).
Range: 3,790 miles (6,100km).
Armament: As bomber carries 6,000lb (2,720kg) of weapons internally. Later aircraft modified to carry up to 1,000lb (455kg) of bombs, rocket pods or guided weapons under each wing.

Data: Canberra B.Mk 6.
Photo: Canberra B(I).Mk 12 (SAAF).
Silhouette: EB-57E.

Up to 100 Canberras remain in RAF service or in reserve, and others are in service with several foreign air forces. Principal RAF service versions are the PR. Mk 7 photographic reconnaissance aircraft and PR. Mk9 with greater wing area and uprated engines, used by one UK-based squadron. Original B.Mk 2 and B.Mk 6 bombers are used for special duties and as trainers, and the T.Mk 4 trainer continues in service at the Canberra OCU. The E.Mk 15 is a modification of the B.Mk 6 for calibration duties and other modified variants are the T.Mk 17 ECM trainer, the T.Mk 19 radar target and the TT.Mk 18 target tug. The T. Mk 22 was the final British variant designated, for use as a special RN radar target. Among the users of exported Canberra versions, some of which are refurbished ex-RAF aircraft, are Rhodesia, using B.Mk 2s; Ethiopia, which acquired four similar B.Mk 52s; Peru with B.Mk 72s and Venezuela with B.Mk 82s. Peru also has B(I).Mk 56s and B(I).Mk 78s (the final digit in these mark numbers corresponds with equivalent RAF variants); Venezuela has B(I) Mk 88 intruders. Also similar to the B(I).Mk 8 intruders are the B(I).Mk 12s of the RNZAF and SAAF, and the B(I).Mk 58s of the Indian Air Force, while Argentina has B.Mk 62s and India has B.Mk 66s. Several of these air forces also operate reconnaissance and training variants— e.g., PR.Mk 57s and T.Mk 67s in India, PR.Mk 82s and T.Mk 84s in Venezuela, T.Mk 74 in Peru, T.Mk 13 in the RNZAF and T.Mk 64 in Argentina. Under licence from the UK government, the Glenn L Martin company put a version of the Canberra into production for the USAF. All but the initial B-57A/RB-57A variants featured a new cockpit arrangement with tandem seating, and versions up to B-57G were designated. These included tactical bombers, trainers and high altitude reconnaissance aircraft (the RB-57D and RB-57F) with extended span and (F only) underwing jet pods. Last of the USAF Canberras in service, with a few still operational in 1978, were the EB-57B and EB-57E electronic counter-measures variants.

Fairchild A-10A Thunderbolt II   USA

Single-seat close support aircraft, in production and service.

Powered by: Two 9,065lb (4,112kg) st General Electric TF34-GE-100 turbofans.
Span: 57ft 6in (17.53m).
Length: 53ft 4in (16.26m).
Empty weight: 20,796lb (9,433kg).
Gross weight: 47,400lb (21,500kg).
Max combat speed: 449mph (723km/h), clean, at sea level.
Combat radius (close air support): 288 miles (463km), with 2 hours in combat area.
Armament: One 30mm GAU-8/A multi-barrel gun and up to 16,000lb (7,257kg) external ordnance on 11 pylons.

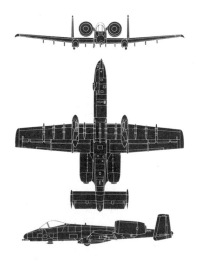

Following evaluation of preliminary designs for an attack aircraft in the USAF's A-X programme, those submitted by Fairchild and Northrop were chosen for prototype construction and a fly-off competition. The two prototypes of the Fairchild design, designated YA-10, first flew on May 10 and July 21, 1972, respectively and after an intensive series of trials at Edwards AFB, the A-10 was declared winner on January 18, 1973. Competitive development of a new 30mm multi-barrel gun was also undertaken, and the General Electric GAU-8/A was chosen for the A-10 in August 1973, the first in-flight firing trials from the No 1 prototype taking place on February 26, 1974. A batch of six R & D A-10As was funded in the 1974 Defense Budget and the first of these flew on February 15, 1975. The total projected USAF requirement is put at 739, and funding for the initial production batch of 22 was included in the FY75 budget, followed by 73 in the FY76 appropriation, 100 in FY77 and 144 in FY78. The first production A-10A flew on October 21, 1975 and deliveries began in the spring of 1976, to the 333rd TF Training Squadron at Davis-Monthan AFB. A year later, the first A-10As began to reach the first operational wing to form on the type, at Myrtle Beach AFB, South Carolina, with initial operational capability achieved in January 1978. Deployment of A-10 wings to bases in the UK began at the end of 1978; eight-aircraft detachments from these bases are rotated to forward operation locations (FOLs) in Germany. Standard equipment includes a Pave Penny laser target designation pod, for use with laser homing weapons.

FMA I.A.58 Pucara

Argentina

Counter-insurgency attack aircraft, in production and service.

Powered by: Two 1,022shp Turboméca Astazou XVIG turboprops
Span: 47ft 6$\frac{2}{4}$in (14.50m).
Length: 46ft 9in (14.25m).
Empty weight: 8,900lb (4,037kg).
Gross weight: 14,990lb (6,800kg).
Max speed: 310mph (500km/h).
Range: 1,890 miles (3,042km).
Accommodation: Two seats in tandem.
Armament: Two 20mm Hispano cannon and four 7.62mm FN machine-guns in fuselage. Three strong points under fuselage and wings for up to 3,300lb (1,500kg) of stores.

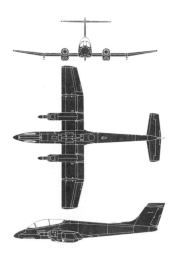

The Pucara is the latest product of the Argentinian Military Aircraft Factory (the Fábrica Militar de Aviones) at Cordoba. It is a counter-insurgency and light tactical aircraft designed to meet the requirements of the Argentine Air Force, which is reported to have plans to acquire about 70 production examples. Flight testing of the design (originally named the Delfin) began with a full-scale unpowered prototype, with dummy engines and fixed undercarriage, which was first flown on December 26, 1967. This was followed by a powered prototype with 904shp Garrett-AiResearch TPE 331-U-303 engines, first flown on August 20, 1969, and a second prototype with 1,022shp Turboméca Astazou XVIG engines, first flown on September 6, 1970. Work on an initial production batch began in 1972 and the first of these flew on November 8, 1974, by which time the Argentine Air Force had placed a firm order for 30. Deliveries began in the first half of 1976. Projected developments include a navalised version with folding wings, arrester gear and catapult spools, for operation from aircraft carriers, and an advanced trainer, designated I.A.60, with basically the same airframe but Astafan engines in fuselage-side nacelles.

Fokker-VFW F.27M Troopship   Netherlands

Short/medium-range military transport aircraft, in production and service.

Powered by: Two 2,210shp Rolls-Royce Dart R.Da.7 Mk 532-7 turboprops.
Span: 95ft 2in (29.00m).
Length: 77ft 3½in (23.56m).
Empty weight: 23,430lb (10,628kg).
Gross weight: 45,000lb (20,410kg).
Normal cruising speed: 302mph (486km/h) at 20,000ft (6,100m).
Range: 1,285 miles (2,000km) with max payload.
Accommodation: Crew of two or three and up to 45 troops, or freight.

Data and silhouette: Mk 400M Troopship.
Photo: F.27 Maritime.

Although it is best-known as a 40/56-seat airliner, the F.27 Friendship—built by Fokker-VFW in Holland and Fairchild in America—is also in service as a military transport. The Royal Netherlands Air Force has three more-or-less standard Friendship airliners and the Philippine Air Force has one for VIP duties and nine for cargo-carrying and trooping. In addition, the RNAF has six F.27M Troopships with accommodation for 45 paratroops, 13,800lb (6,260kg) of freight or 24 litter patients and 7 attendants in an air ambulance role. The Troopship has a large cargo door at the front on the port side and an enlarged rear cabin door, for parachuting, on each side. Three former RNAF examples have been transferred to the RNN as navigation trainers. Four F.27Ms, of which two remain, were supplied to the Sudanese Air Force in 1965 and the Argentine Air Force acquired 12 F.27s (including eight Troopships), primarily for use by LADE, an Air Force organisation which provides regular air transport services in underdeveloped areas of Argentina. The Uruguayan Air Force acquired two F.27s, together with two Fairchild FH-227Bs; the Imperial Iranian Air Force has 14 Troopships and six F.27 Mk 600s, four of the Mk 400Ms being equipped to serve as target tugs. The Iranian Army has two F.27s and the Navy has four. Late in 1971, Nigeria ordered six F.27s from Fokker, of which four were Troopships, and has since acquired more. One F.27 and one Troopship are in service in the Republic of the Ivory Coast, and in 1973 the Ghana Air Force ordered six, including two Srs 600 with a large cargo door. The Indonesian Air Force has eight Mk400Ms, and six F.27s bought by Air Algerie are also available for use by the Algerian Air Force. On March 25, 1976, Fokker-VFW flew the prototype of the F.27 Maritime, a version equipped for maritime patrol duties, with Litton AN/APS-503F radar in the fuselage. Two examples have been bought by the Peruvian Navy and three by the Spanish Air Force.

GAF Mission Master and Search Master   Australia

STOL utility transport, in production and service.

Powered by: Two 400shp Allison 250-B17B turboprops.
Span: 54ft 0in (16.46m).
Length: 41ft 2¼in (12.56m).
Empty weight: 4,666lb (2,116kg).
Gross weight: 8,500lb (3,855kg).
Normal cruising speed: 193mph (311km/h).
Range: 840 miles (1,352km).
Accommodation: Two pilots and up to 14 persons in cabin.

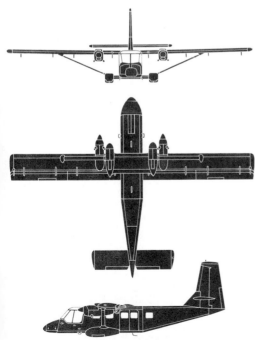

Design of a small utility transport with both military and civil applications began at the Government Aircraft Factories at Fishermen's Bend in 1965, this being the first full-scale design project of the GAF. Previously the Factories had built a number of European aircraft under licence, including the Canberra and Mirage, and had developed and produced the Jindivik target and the Ikara anti-submarine weapon. The transport design was designated Project N and evolved as a conventional high-wing aircraft with single fin and rudder, retractable undercarriage, and emphasis upon simple construction and ease of operation. Two prototypes were built, making their first flights respectively on July 23 and December 5, 1971, and these subsequently became known as Nomad 22s. During 1972, an initial production batch of 20 was ordered by the Australian government, of which 11 were earmarked for service with the Australian Army Aviation Corps and six were to be supplied to the Indonesian Navy in the maritime patrol role, under the terms of Australian aid for Indonesia. By the beginning of 1978, production of 95 aircraft had been authorised in four versions. The basic civilian model is the N22B, and a lengthened 19-passenger civilian version is available as the N24A. The Mission Master is the standard military counterpart of the N22B for the Australian Army (11), Papua New Guinea (3) and the Philippines (12). A derivative is the coastal surveillance Search Master, with optional Litton radar and advanced navigation system, of which the Indonesian Naval Air Arm has six.

Data and silhouette: Mission Master.
Photo: Search Master (Indonesia)

General Dynamics F-16

USA

Single-seat advanced combat fighter and two-seat operational trainer, in production.

Powered by: One Pratt & Whitney F100-PW-100 turbofan, rated at approx. 25,000lb (11,340kg) st with afterburning.
Span: 31ft 0in (9.45m).
Length: 47ft 7¾in (14.52m).
Empty weight: approx. 14,000lb (6,350kg).
Max gross weight: 33,000lb (14,968kg).
Max speed: Above Mach 2.
Radius of action: More than 575 miles (925km).
Armament: One internally-mounted M61A-1 20mm multi-barrel gun with 500 rounds of ammunition. One advanced Sidewinder air-to-air missile on each wingtip. Underwing attachments for other stores; max external load, 15,200lb (6,895kg).

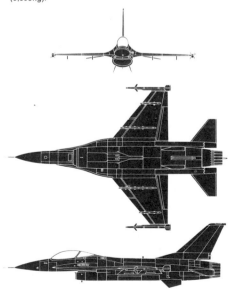

Two prototypes of this aircraft were ordered in April 1972, under the USAF's Lightweight Fighter (LWF) programme, simultaneously with two prototypes of the Northrop YF-17. All four aircraft were intended originally as technology demonstrators, to examine the military capability of small, relatively low-cost fighters embodying the latest design concepts and materials, and to show how they might complement larger, conventional types such as the F-14 and F-15. Not being tied to any defined military requirement, the manufacturers were free to utilise whatever they considered to be the optimum configuration and power plant. Thus, Northrop settled on a twin-fin, twin-engined design, while General Dynamics chose a single-fin layout, with a fixed-geometry underbelly engine air intake and a single afterburning turbofan of the same basic type as that used in the USAF's F-15 Eagle. The first YF-16 flew on January 20, 1974, followed by the second on May 9. By then, the USAF had decided to re-orientate the programme as a competitive flight evaluation for a new Air Combat Fighter. In January 1975, the YF-16 was named as winner of the ACF evaluation, with a first order for six single-seat F-16As and two two-seat F-16Bs for "full-scale development"; the tandem-seat F-16B has the same overall dimensions but reduced internal fuel to accommodate the second seat. The first of these F-16As flew on December 8, 1976 and the first F-16B (fourth of the FSD batch) flew on August 9, 1977. Total USAF requirement is 1,388, including 204 F-16Bs. In 1975, the F-16 was chosen as an F-104 replacement by four European NATO nations and plans were announced for acquisition of 116 by Belgium, 58 by Denmark, 102 by the Netherlands and 72 by Norway, including a combined total of 58 F-16Bs.

Data, photo and silhouette: F-16A.

46

General Dynamics F-111　　　USA

Two-seat tactical fighter, in service.

Powered by: Two 25,100lb (11,385kg) st Pratt & Whitney TF30-P-100 afterburning turbofans.
Span: 63ft 0in (19.20m) spread; 31ft 11½in (9.74m) swept.
Length: 73ft 6in (22.40m).
Empty weight: 47,481lb (21,537kg).
Max gross weight: 100,000lb (45,359kg).
Max speed: Mach 2.5 (1,650mph; 2,655km/h) at 36,000ft (11,000m).
Max range: 2,925 miles (4,707km) on internal fuel.
Armament: One M61 multi-barrel 20mm cannon and two bombs in weapon bay; external stores on six underwing pylons.

Initial contracts for 18 F-111A (USAF) and five F-111B (USN), for development flying, were followed by production of several variants of this tactical fighter for the USAF. The Navy's F-111B was abandoned after production of seven aircraft, including the five development models. The F-111A first flew on December 21, 1964, and the variable-sweep wing was operated on the second flight, on January 6, 1965. The first F-111A (a trials aircraft) delivered for service went to a training unit, the 4,480th TF Wing, in July 1967. The first operational unit was the 474th TFW, which received its first aircraft (the 31st F-111A) in October. Production of the F-111A totalled 141 (excluding the trials aircraft), followed by 94 F-111Es which have revised intake geometry. The first of these swing-wing aircraft deployed to Europe were F-111Es assigned to the 20th TFW at Upper Heyford in September 1970, where they were still operating in 1978. These were followed by 96 F-111Ds, with uprated avionics, and 106 F-111Fs with TF30-P-100 turbofans to equip two more TAF Wings, the 27th and 366th respectively. Many of the F-111Fs moved to the UK in 1977, with the 48th TFW. Two F-111Ks, intended for but not delivered to the RAF, went to USAF as YF-111As; one development aircraft was flown as RF-111A, and the RAAF acquired 24 F-111C strike aircraft. Two F-111As were converted to EF-111A tactical jamming aircraft by Grumman, with pallet-mounted ALQ-99 jamming system in the weapons bay and a large fin-tip radome, and with all ordnance provision deleted. A partial aerodynamic prototype EF-111A flew on December 15, 1975 and in fully representative form in March 1977, followed by the second prototype with full avionics. The USAF hopes to acquire 40 similar EF-111A conversions eventually.

Data and photo: F-111F.
Silhouette: F-111E.

General Dynamics FB-111A   USA

Two-seat strategic bomber, in service.

Powered by: Two 20,350lb (9,230kg) st Pratt & Whitney TF30-P-7 afterburning turbofans.
Span: 70ft 0in (21.34m) spread; 33ft 11in (10.34m) swept.
Length: 73ft 6in (22.40m).
Gross weight (estimated): 100,000lb (45,360kg).
Max speed: Mach 2.5 (1,650mph; 2,655km/h) at 36,000ft (11,000m).
Range: 4,100 miles (6,600km) with external fuel.
Armament: External points for four 2,200lb (1,000kg) Boeing AGM-69A SRAM short-range attack missiles, with two more in weapons bay. Provision for up to 31,500lb (14,285kg) of conventional weapons. Typical load comprises two 750lb bombs in internal weapon-bay and 36 in twin clusters of three on six underwing attachments with wings at 26° sweep. (Only 20 such bombs can be carried at full wing-sweep.)

The FB-111A was derived from the original swing-wing F-111 (previous page) to provide Strategic Air Command of the USAF with an advanced super-sonic bomber to supplement its B-52 force. Pro-curement of as many as 253 FB-111As was plan-ned originally, but development hold-ups, cost escalation and changes in the US strategic posture led to successive reductions to a total production run of 76, completed in 1971, to equip only two wings. The FB-111A airframe is a hybrid, using the larger wing, with six pylons, developed originally for the Navy's F-111B, with the fuselage and intakes of the F-111E. It also has a new avionics fit, higher gross weight, beefed-up struc-ture and landing gear, and uprated engines. The FB-111A prototype was a conversion of the last F-111A development airframe (No 18), first flown on July 30, 1967. Two other modified F-111As were used in the development programme before the first flight of the first production FB-111A on July 13, 1968 (fitted temporarily with TF30-P-3 engines). The first SAC unit to equip with the new bomber was the 340th Bomb Group at Carswell AFB, on October 8, 1969; this unit provides combat crew training for the two two-squadron wings which are equipped with the FB-111A—the 509th Bomb Wing at Pease AFB, NH, and the 380th Strategic Aero-space Wing at Plattsburgh, NY. Following cancel-lation of the B-1, development of an improved version of the FB-111 was suggested, and a pro-posal is being studied to convert two aircraft to this new FB-111H configuration with lengthened fuselage, General Electric F101 engines, increased bomb-load and other changes.

Grumman A-6 Intruder

USA

Two-seat carrier-based strike and reconnaissance aircraft, in production and service.

Powered by: Two 9,300lb (4,218kg) st Pratt & Whitney J52-P-8A or 8B turbojets.
Span: 53ft 0in (16.15m).
Length: 54ft 7in (16.64m).
Empty weight: 25,630lb (11,625kg).
Max gross weight: 60,400lb (27,397kg).
Max speed: 643mph (1,035km/h) at sea level.
Armament: Up to 17,280lb (7,838kg) of assorted stores on four underwing attachments and in a semi-recessed fuselage bay.

US Navy and Marine Corps experience in Korea led to a new requirement for a long-range, all-weather low-altitude attack aircraft, able to carry a heavy load of conventional or nuclear weapons. A design competition was held in May 1957 and Grumman was named the winner at the end of that year. Features of the Grumman design, originally called A2F-1, included tilting tailpipes on the engines, to help shorten take-off distances, but production aircraft have a fixed downward tilt on the jet pipes. The US Navy ordered eight Intruders for trials and the first flew on April 19, 1960. Production of the A-6A followed, and this became the standard all-weather attack aircraft for Navy and Marine squadrons. Production totalled 482, of which 19 became A-6B carrying AGM-78A Standard ARM anti-radar missiles, and 12 became A-6C with FLIR (forward-looking infra-red) in a dorsal pod. A prototype KA-6D "buddy" flight-refuelling tanker flew on May 23, 1966, and 62 A-6As were converted to this standard. Second major Intruder production variant was the A-6E, first flown on February 27, 1970, with Norden multi-mode navigation and attack radar. By FY 1979, 123 new A-6Es had been ordered by the USN, from a planned total of 159; another 159 A-6As are being modified up to A-6E standard. Most new and converted A-6Es are in due course to have target recognition attack multisensor (TRAM) equipment, first flown on October 22, 1974, and Harpoon missile capability.

Data, photo and silhouette: A-6E.

Grumman E-2 Hawkeye

USA

Five-seat carrier-borne airborne early warning and fighter control aircraft, in production and service.

Powered by: Two 4,910shp Allison T56-A-422/425 turbo props.
Span: 80ft 7in (24.56m).
Length: 57ft 7in (17.55m).
Empty weight: 38,009lb (17,256kg).
Gross weight: 51,900lb (23,540kg).
Max speed: 348mph (560km/h).
Ferry range: 1,605 miles (2,583km) with full internal fuel.
Armament: None.

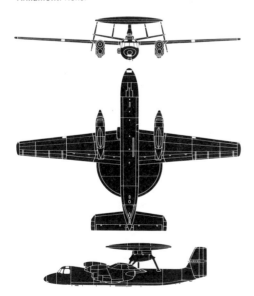

Data, photo and silhouette: E-2C.

Like the E-1 Tracer which it replaced, the E-2 carries a large saucer-shaped radome above the fuselage, and a mass of electronic devices to process the information provided by the radar. The complete installation is called Airborne Tactical Data System—ATDS—and the information provided by it is transmitted to a Naval Tactical Data System. Taking information from a team of E-2s disposed around a Naval task force, the NTDS can assess and act upon the threat of attack from any direction.

An aerodynamic prototype of the E-2 flew on October 21, 1960, followed by the first with full electronic equipment on April 19, 1961. Deliveries began on January 19, 1964, and the first Hawkeye unit, VAW-11, became operational in 1966, followed by VAW-12, both squadrons providing detached flights on board operational aircraft carriers. Production of the E-2A ended in 1967 with a total of 59 built. A few became TE-2As with the ATDS removed and training equipment added. Between 1969 and 1971, the entire remaining E-2A force was modified to E-2B standard by installation of an updated general-purpose computer of increased capacity. The E-2C has a completely revised electronic system and improved engines. A prototype flew on January 20, 1971 and a second followed later in the year. The first production E-2C flew on September 23, 1972 and procurement of 86 is expected to be complete by 1980, to allow each operational USN carrier to keep one of its four E-2Cs airborne continuously for an extended operational period. From 1976, E-2Cs have been delivered with improved AN/APS-125 radar. A small number of TE-2C training versions is in service. Four E-2Cs have been ordered by Israel and Japan plans to acquire nine, with deliveries starting in 1982.

Grumman EA-6B Prowler

USA

Four-seat carrier-based electronic counter-measures aircraft, in production and service.

Powered by: Two 9,300lb (4,218kg) st Pratt & Whitney J52-P-8A, -8B or -408 turbojets.
Span: 53ft 0in (16.15m).
Length: 59ft 5in (18.11m).
Empty weight: 34,581lb (15,686kg).
Max gross weight: 65,000lb (29,483kg).
Max speed: 656mph (1,055km/h).
Range: 1,180 miles (1,897km) with max load and reserves.
Armament: Normally unarmed; external weapons attachment points retained as on A-6A.
Accommodation: Pilot, navigator and two radar operators.

A version of the Intruder (see page 49) intended specifically for electronic countermeasures duties was developed soon after the basic A-6A had entered service in 1963. Designated EA-6A, this was selected for operation by the US Marine Corps and differed in having an extensive array of special electronic detection and jamming devices, carried internally, in pods on the fuselage and underwing strongpoints and in a new radome atop the fin. A prototype, converted from an A-6A, flew in 1963 and 27 production EA-6As were built (including six converted A-6As). The single remaining operational detachment will serve on USS *Midway* until the ship is retired in the mid-eighties.

To enhance the ECM capability of the aircraft, the EA-6B was developed, with a new front fuselage section incorporating two additional seats for radar/ECM operators. The avionic equipment was also revised and updated. First flight of a prototype was made on May 25, 1968 and production began to provide the US Navy with a new standard ECM (tactical jamming) aircraft to replace the EKA-3B. A total of 77 EA-6Bs had been ordered by 1978, with further procurement planned for 1981-82, to meet Marine Corps as well as Navy requirements. After entering service, this variant was named Prowler to avoid confusion with the Intruder attack versions of the A-6.

Three EA-6Bs are included in each of 12 carrier air wings, and 15 are to be available to the Marine Corps.

51

Grumman F-14 Tomcat

USA

Two-seat carrier-borne air superiority and general purpose fighter, in production and service.

Powered by: Two 20,600lb (9,344kg) st Pratt & Whitney TF30-P-412A afterburning turbofans.
Span: 64ft 1½in (19.54m) spread; 38ft 2in (10.12m) swept.
Length: 61ft 10½in (18.86m).
Empty weight: 38,930lb (17,659kg).
Max gross weight: 74,348lb (33,724kg).
Max speed: Mach 2.34 (1,564mph/2,517km/h) at 40,000ft (12,190m).
Armament: One General Electric M61-A1 multi-barrel gun in port side of front fuselage. Four missile bays semirecessed under fuselage for Sparrow air-to-air missiles, or four Phoenix missiles on pallets. Two underwing pick-ups for a combination of a fuel tank and two Sidewinder air-to-air missiles on each pylon; or a Sparrow or Phoenix plus one Sidewinder on each pylon.

The US Navy issued a Request for Proposals for a new carrier-based air superiority fighter to five US aerospace companies on June 21, 1968. From the initial proposals, the Navy selected Grumman and McDonnell Douglas for final competition, as a result of which the Grumman G.303 was selected on January 15, 1969. Since that date, the company has received a series of contracts, the first two of which were each for six development aircraft; the subsequent contracts brought firm orders to 343 by 1978, with planned total procurement of 521 Tomcats to equip 18 USN squadrons by FY 1983. The prototype F-14A first flew on December 21, 1970, but was lost on its second flight. Testing resumed on May 24, 1971, and seven more of the test aircraft flew during that year. Two prototypes of an F-14B version were flown, with more powerful YF401 engines; but problems with this engine led to planned procurement of 179 F-14Bs being dropped by the Navy. Initial F-14A deliveries were made to VF124 for training, and the first operational units were VF1 and VF2, which were serving on board the USS *Enterprise* by September 1974, followed by VF14 and VF32 on board the USS *John F. Kennedy* in 1975. Fourteen squadrons were to be equipped with Tomcats by the end of 1978. During 1974, the Iranian Imperial Air Force ordered 80 F-14As in two batches; the first of these flew on December 5, 1975 and deliveries began in January 1976.

It was announced in 1978 that F-14s fitted with reconnaissance pods will serve as interim reconnaissance aircraft until a definitive replacement for the RA-5C and RF-8G is available.

Data, photo and silhouette: F-14A.

Grumman OV-1 Mohawk

USA

Two-seat observation aircraft, in service.

Powered by: Two 1,150eshp Lycoming T53-L-701 turbo-props.
Span: 48ft 0in (14.63m).
Length: 41ft 0in (12.50m).
Empty weight: 12,054lb (5,467kg).
Gross weight: 18,109lb (8,214kg).
Max speed: 308mph (496km/h) at 5,000ft (1,520m).
Range: 1,010 miles (1,625km) with external tanks.
Armament: Six wing strong-points allow for pylon-mounted bombs, rockets, etc., if required.

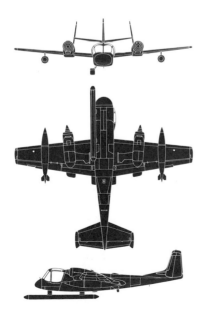

Designed originally to meet joint US Army and Marine Corps requirements, the Mohawk is now exclusively an Army aircraft, and was the first turboprop-engined type to go into service with the US Army. The primary mission for which it was designed (as the Grumman G-134) was tactical observation and battlefield surveillance in direct support of Army operations, flying from unprepared fields and having a STOL performance. Initial contracts were for nine test aircraft designated YAO-1AF (later YOV-1A); the first of these flew on April 14, 1959. Production models were the OV-1A, primarily for photographic reconnaissance; the OV-1B with SLAR (side-looking airborne radar) in a long container under the fuselage, and the OV-1C with infra-red mapping gear. Deliveries to the Army began in 1961 and production of the three models totalled 64, 101 and 133 respectively. During 1968, four Mohawks were completed to OV-1D standard, with side-loading doors to accept pallets with SLAR or infra-red or other sensors; this version also added a third photographic system, comprising a vertical, panoramic camera. Production of 37 OV-1Ds followed successful evaluation of the prototypes, and a programme to convert 108 OV-1Bs and OV-1Cs to OV-1D standard began in 1974.

Some OV-1C and OV-1D were permanently modified for electronic reconnaissance as RV-1C and RV-1D respectively. In addition, the Army studied a proposal to convert OV-1Bs to EV-1 electronic surveillance aircraft, with AN/ALQ-133 radar target locator system in pods on the centreline and under each wingtip.

Data, photo and silhouette: OV-1D.

Grumman S-2 Tracker USA

Four-seat carrier-based anti-submarine attack aircraft, in service.

Powered by: Two 1,525hp Wright R-1820-82WA piston-engines.
Span: 72ft 7in (22.13m).
Length: 43ft 6in (13.26m).
Empty weight: 18,750lb (8,505kg).
Gross weight: 29,150lb (13,222kg).
Max speed: 265mph (426km/h) at sea level.
Ferry range: 1,300 miles (2,095km).
Armament: 60 echo-sounding depth charges in fuselage; one Mk 101 or Mk 57 nuclear depth bomb or similar store in bomb bay; 32 sonobuoys in nacelles; four float lights; six underwing pylons for 5-inch rockets, torpedoes, etc.

First flown on December 4, 1952, the S2F-1 (as the Grumman G-89 was originally designated) went into production for the US Navy for combined

Data, photo and silhouette: S-2E.

"hunter-killer" operations in the anti-submarine role. Of 755 S-2As built, over 100 were for export to Argentina, Brazil, Italy, Japan, South Korea, the Netherlands, Taiwan, Thailand and Uruguay, and are still serving with most of these nations.

The S2F-1T (later TS-2A) was used as a trainer. The 60 S-2Cs (S2F-2s) had enlarged bomb-bays to accommodate two homing torpedoes and have mostly been converted to US-2C utility aircraft. The S-2D (originally S2F-3) had an 18in (45cm) front fuselage extension, a 35in (89cm) greater span, a wider cockpit and improved equipment. Production totalled 119, and deliveries began in May 1961. In October 1962, the S-2E succeeded the S-2D with more advanced ASW equipment, and 245 were built. Similar equipment added to early S-2As changed their designation to S-2B and, with further modifications, to S-2F. In 1972, Martin Marietta produced a prototype YS-2G and kits for 49 more S-2Gs, to be converted by the USN, this version having updated equipment for interim use until the S-3A entered service. The Tracker was phased out of first-line USN service in 1976. Conversion programmes produced the US-2A, US-2B, US-2C and US-2D versions for target towing and utility transport duty; the TS-2A and TS-2B trainers and RS-2C photo-survey version.

Production of the S-2E ended in 1968 with a batch of 14 for the RAN. All but four of these were destroyed in a hangar fire in December 1976 and 16 ex-USN S-2Gs were acquired by the RAN in 1977 to bring the inventory back to strength. The Royal Canadian Navy obtained 100 Trackers built by D.H. Canada, of which 17 later went to the Netherlands; the first 43, starting in January 1957, were CS2F-1s and the final 57, starting in October 1958, were CS2F-2s, with improved equipment. Redesignated CP-121, 16 remained in service in 1978.

Based on the S-2D, Grumman developed the TF-1 Trader as a nine-seat transport for COD duty; the 87 built were later redesignated C-1A and four TF-1Qs became EC-1As.

HAL Ajeet and (HSA) Gnat

India

Light interceptor and close support fighter, in production and service.

Powered by: One 4,500lb (2,043kg) st Rolls-Royce Orpheus 701–01 turbojet.
Span: 22ft 1in (6.73m).
Length: 29ft 8in (9.04m).
Gross weight: 9,195lb (4,170kg).
Max speed: 716mph (1,152km/h) at sea level.
Combat radius: 127 miles (204km) with two 500lb bombs and underwing tanks.

The Ajeet (Invincible) is a locally developed, improved version of the Gnat lightweight fighter, evolved by Hindustan Aeronautics during 1972–1974 to meet the specific requirements of the Indian Air Force. Prior to the appearance of the Ajeet, the first prototype of which flew on March 5, 1975, the IAF had received 213 Gnat 1s built under licence by HAL at Bangalore to the original design of W.E.W. Petter and with the assistance of the UK parent company, Folland Aircraft Ltd (later Hawker Siddeley Aviation). In early 1978 the IAF had eight squadrons equipped with Gnats, which have given satisfactory service in two conflicts with Pakistan, and the Ajeet (originally Gnat Mk 2) was developed to improve on the Gnat's characteristics and overcome certain inherent shortcomings. The major differences comprise the use of a "wet" wing and doubling the number of wing hardpoints to four, to allow a greater variety of weapons to be carried. There are also some equipment changes, similar to those applied to some Gnat 1s which, when modified, became Gnat 1As. The last two Indian Gnat 1s (Nos 214 and 215) served as Ajeet prototypes, and the first production Ajeet of more than 100 on order flew on September 30, 1976. An Ajeet trainer, with fuselage lengthened by 4ft 7in (1.40m) and a raised rear cockpit for an instructor, is under development.

The Gnat, in its original form, first flew in the UK on July 18, 1955, and over 40 single-seaters were built for evaluation and for export to India, Finland and Yugoslavia. From it was evolved the Gnat trainer, some 15 per cent larger all round and with a second cockpit in tandem. The first of an evaluation batch of 14 for the RAF flew on 31 August 1959, and 91 Gnat T. Mk 1s were then built for RAF Training Command. Their replacement by HS Hawks began in 1977.

Data, photo and silhouette: Ajeet.

HAL HF-24 Marut

India

Single-seat fighter, in service.

Powered by: Two 4,850lb (2,200kg) st Rolls-Royce Orpheus 703 turbojets.
Span: 29ft 6¼in (9.00m).
Length: 52ft 0¾in (15.87m).
Gross weight: 24,048lb (10,908kg).
Max speed: Mach 1.02 (673mph; 1,083km/h) at 40,000ft (12,200m).
Normal range: 750 miles (1,200km).
Armament: Four 30mm cannon in nose and retractable pack of 48 air-to-air rockets in fuselage aft of nose-wheel bay; four 1,000lb bombs or rockets under wings.

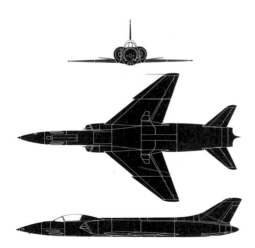

First supersonic fighter designed in any Asian country outside of the Soviet Union, the HF-24 Marut (Wind Spirit) was developed initially under the leadership of Professor Kurt Tank, whose earlier products included the wartime Focke-Wulf Fw 190 fighter. Design studies were started in 1956, to meet an Indian Air Force requirement, and early research work included flight testing of a full-scale wooden glider version of the HF-24. The prototype HF-24 Mk 1 fighter flew for the first time on June 17, 1961. It was followed by a second prototype and then by the first of a production batch of about 125 Mk 1s in March 1963. The initial flight of Mk 1s was accepted formally by the Indian Air Force on May 10, 1964, and three squadrons, Nos 10, 31 and 220, have been equipped with the type. In addition to the single-seat Mk 1s, HAL built 20 tandem two-seat Mk 1T trainers, the first prototype of which flew on April 30, 1970.

In an attempt to improve the performance of the Marut, HAL projected a Mk II version with Adour engines, but this was not built. In another programme, HAL developed a reheat system for the Orpheus engines, flying a prototype installation in a Marut 1A in September 1966. Two more trials aircraft with afterburners were designated Marut 1R, but one of these crashed on January 10, 1970, and further development was subsequently cancelled.

One HF-24 was sent to Egypt as a flying test-bed for the Helwan E-300 afterburning turbojet and, as the Mk 1BX, flew with this engine on March 29, 1967; but the E-300 was eventually abandoned.

Data, photo and silhouette: Marut Mk 1.

Handley Page Victor K.Mk 2   Great Britain

Five-seat flight refuelling tanker, in service.

Powered by: Four 20,600lb (9,344kg) st Rolls-Royce Conway R.Co 17 Mk 201 turbojets.
Span: 117ft 0in (35.69m).
Length: 114ft 11in (35.0m).
Gross weight: 223,000lb (101,242kg)
Max speed: Over 600mph (966km/h) at 40,000ft (12,000m).
Max range: 4,600 miles (7,400km).
Armament: None.

The first production Victor B.Mk 1 bomber with Sapphire turbojets flew on February 1, 1956, and deliveries to the RAF began in 1958, production of 50 aircraft being sufficient to equip four squadrons. Late production aircraft were designated B.Mk 1A, signifying equipment changes and the addition of ECM radar in the rear fuselage, and 24 were eventually converted to this standard. Subsequently, six were modified to B(K). 1A two-point flight refuelling tankers and 24 others to K.1 or K.1A three-point tankers. The B.Mk 2 (first flown on February 20, 1959) had Rolls-Royce Conway turbojets and the wing span increased from 110ft (33.5m) to 120ft (36.6m). Deliveries to No 139 Squadron began late in 1961 and this was the first Victor unit to become operational with the Blue Steel missile in February 1964, 21 of the 34 production B.2s being converted for this role. Another nine were modified for strategic reconnaissance duties as Victor SR.2, for service with No 543 Squadron until 1974. They were then replaced by Vulcans and, together with B.Mk 2s, were allotted for conversion to K.Mk 2 tanker configuration by Hawker Siddeley. The first K.Mk 2, with slightly reduced wing span and other modifications, plus three-point refuelling as in the K.Mk 1/1A, flew on March 1, 1972 and the first delivery to the RAF was made on May 8, 1974, for service with No 232 OCU. A total of 24 K.Mk 2s was delivered by mid-1977, to equip Nos 55 and 57 Squadrons as the RAF's sole tanker force, until the addition of a squadron of VC10s.

Hawker Hunter

Great Britain

Single-seat fighter and two-seat trainer, in service.

Powered by: One 10,000lb (4,540kg) st Rolls-Royce Avon 207 turbojet.
Span: 33ft 8in (10.26m).
Length: 45ft 10½in (13.98m).
Gross weight: 24,000lb (10,885kg).
Max speed: Mach 0.92 (710mph; 1,140km/h) at sea level.
Range: 1,840 miles (2,965km) with external tanks.
Armament: Four 30mm cannon in nose; underwing attachments for two 1,000lb bombs, or two packs each containing up to 37 × 2in rockets, or 12 × 3in rockets on inner pylons, plus up to 24 × 3in rockets outboard.

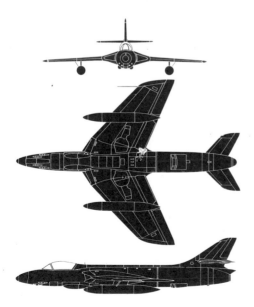

Data: Hunter FGA.Mk 9.
Photo: Hunter F.Mk 58.
Silhouette: Hunter F.Mk 6.

As the Hawker P.1067, the prototype Hunter (WB188) first flew on July 20, 1951. The Avon-powered F.Mk 1 made its first flight on May 16, 1953, and aircraft of this mark equipped the first RAF squadron, No 43, in mid-1954. This version is no longer in service; nor are the Sapphire-powered F.Mk 2 and 5. The Mk 1 was superseded in production by the F.Mk 4, with Avon 115, more internal fuel and provision for underwing weapons or fuel tanks, and this mark saw service in Denmark (F.Mk 51) and Peru (F.Mk 52). It was followed by the F.Mk 6 (prototype first flown January 22, 1954), with Avon 203, and export versions are still flying in India (FGA.Mk 56), Switzerland (F.Mk 58), Lebanon (F.Mk 6 and 70) and Oman (F.Mk 73 and FGA.Mk 6). Final version in RAF service was the FGA.Mk 9, a ground attack development of the Mk 6 with tail parachute and increased weapon load, still serving in various training roles in 1978. Versions of the Mk 9 also serve with the Rhodesian, Chilean (FGA.Mk 71) and Iraqi (FGA.Mk 59) Air Forces. Singapore has over 30 FGA.74s, some modified as FGA. 74Bs with additional wing and fuselage weapon pylons, and four FR.74s; the Sheikhdom of Abu Dhabi acquired ten FGA Mk 76s and FR.Mk 76As, and two two-seat T Mk 76As. Four Mk 78 were supplied to Qatar and in 1974 Kenya acquired about six Hunters, including single and two-seaters. Other side-by-side two-seat trainer versions of the Hunter include the RAF's T.Mk 7 and Royal Navy's T.Mk 8, and variants delivered to Peru (T.Mk 62), India (T.Mk 66), Switzerland (T.Mk 68), Iraq (T.Mk 69), Chile, Kuwait (T.Mk 67), and Singapore (T.Mk 75). Late in 1970 Switzerland ordered 30 refurbished Hunters, for final assembly by the Federal Aircraft Factory, and a second batch of 30 was ordered subsequently, bringing the total inventory in the Swiss Air Force to 140.

Hawker Siddeley Buccaneer　　　Great Britain

Two-seat carrier-borne and land-based low-level strike aircraft, in service.

Powered by: Two 11,100lb (5,035kg) st Rolls-Royce RB.168 Spey Mk 101 turbofans.
Span: 44ft 0in (13.41m).
Length: 63ft 5in (19.33m).
Max gross weight: 62,000lb (28,123kg).
Max speed: Mach 0.85 (646mph; 1,038km/h) at 200ft (60m).
Typical strike range: 2,300 miles (3,700km).
Armament: Internal weapons-bay, with rotating door, for nuclear or conventional (four 1,000lb) bombs, or camera pack; four underwing attachments for Bullpup or Martel missiles, 1,000lb bombs (three on each pylon) or rocket packs. Max. weapon load 16,000lb (7,257kg).

Data, photo and silhouette: Buccaneer S.Mk 2B.

Work on what was then known as the Blackburn B.103 began in the early 'fifties to meet the requirements of the Naval specification NA.39 for a carrier-launched aircraft capable of flying at transonic speed close to the ground or sea to strike at enemy objectives. A pre-production batch of 20 B.103s was ordered in July 1955 and the first of these flew on April 30, 1958. The name Buccaneer S.Mk 1 was adopted in August 1960.

A production order for 50 aircraft was placed in October 1959, and the first 40 of these were delivered as S.Mk 1s to equip Nos 801, 809 and 800 Squadrons, starting in July 1962. The final 10 aircraft were completed as S.Mk 2s, with Speys replacing the 7,100lb (3,220kg) st Gyron Junior 101s in the first version. The prototype S.Mk 2 flew on May 17, 1963, followed by the first production model on June 6, 1964. Orders for 74 more S.Mk 2s were placed by the Royal Navy, and the type entered service with No 801 Squadron in October 1965. Nos 809, 800 and 803 were also equipped. Those remaining in Navy service until the end of 1978 were designated S.Mk 2C (without Martel capability) or S.Mk 2D.

In 1968, the RAF ordered 26 Buccaneer S.Mk 2Bs, with revised equipment, a bomb-door fuel tank and provision for carrying Martel missiles, followed by a second contract for 17 in 1972, plus three for use as weapons trials aircraft at the RAE, West Freugh, and two as test-beds for Panavia Tornado equipment. About 60 ex-Navy aircraft have been converted to S.Mk 2A (without Martel capability) or S.Mk 2B for the RAF. The first RAF Buccaneer squadron, No 12, became operational in July 1970 and was joined subsequently in Strike Command by No 208. The first of two squadrons to fly the Buccaneer in Germany, No 15, formed in October 1970 and was followed by No 16. The South African Air Force has eight Buccaneer S.Mk 50s, this variant being fitted with an 8,000lb (3,630kg) st BS.605 twin-chamber auxiliary rocket engine.

Hawker Siddeley Vulcan

Great Britain

Five-seat medium bomber, in service.

Powered by: Four 20,000lb (9,072kg) st Rolls-Royce Bristol Olympus 301 turbojets.
Span: 111ft 0in (33.83m).
Length: 99ft 11in (30.45m).
Gross weight: Over 180,000lb (81,650kg).
Max cruising speed: Over Mach 0.94 (625mph; 1,006km/h) at 50,000ft (15,250m).
Combat radius: 1,725–2,875 miles (2,780–4,630km).
Armament: No guns. Mk 2 can carry nuclear free-fall weapons or 21 × 1,000lb high-explosive bombs.

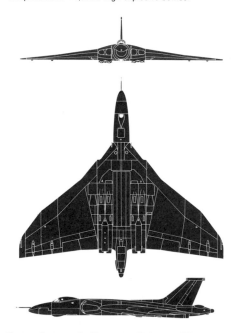

The prototype Avro 698 (VX770) made its first flight on August 30, 1952, and was powered by Rolls-Royce Avons. The second prototype (VX777) flew on September 3, 1953, and had Olympus 100 engines and the later-standard visual bomb-aiming station under the nose. Production Vulcan B.Mk 1s (45 built, commencing XA889) began to appear in February 1954, with Olympus 101, 102 or 104 engines. Deliveries to the RAF began in mid-1956, and Mk 1 and 1A (with electronics in bulged tail-cone) eventually equipped three operational squadrons of RAF Bomber Command. On August 31, 1957, VX777 flew as the aerodynamic test vehicle for the Mk 2, with enlarged and modified wing. The first production Mk 2 (XH533) flew in August 1958 and deliveries to the RAF began on July 1, 1960, the first squadron equipped being No 83. Following transfer of responsibility for Britain's nuclear deterrent to the Royal Navy's Polaris submarine force, the Vulcans of Strike Command were assigned primarily to the low-level penetration and strike role. Six squadrons were operating these Vulcans in 1978 (Nos 9, 35, 44, 50, 101 and 617), plus the OCU (No 230).

Conversion of some Vulcans for the strategic reconnaissance role began in 1973 and, with the designation SR.Mk 2, these were issued to No 27 Squadron in 1974, to replace the Victors of No 543 Squadron.

Data, photo and silhouette: Vulcan B.Mk 2.

Ilyushin Il-28
(NATO code names: Beagle and Mascot)

USSR

Four-seat tactical bomber, reconnaissance and ECM (electronic countermeasures) aircraft, in service.

Powered by: Two 5,950lb (2,700kg) st Klimov VK-1 turbojets.
Span: 64ft 0in (19.50m).
Length: 58ft 0in (17.68m).
Gross weight: 46,300lb (21,000kg).
Max speed: 560mph (900km/h) at 15,000ft (4,575m).
Range: 1,355 miles (2,180km) with max. bomb-load.
Armament: Two 23mm cannon in nose; two 23mm cannon in tail turret; 4,500lb (2,050kg) of bombs.

Russia's counterpart to the Canberra (which it preceded chronologically), the Il-28 was first shown publicly on May Day, 1950, when it took part in fair numbers in the Aviation Day fly-past over Moscow. Several thousand were built and Il-28s served as light attack/reconnaissance aircraft in the air forces of Russia, Poland, Bulgaria, Czechoslovakia, Hungary, East Germany, Afghanistan, Algeria, Iraq, North Korea, Morocco, Nigeria, Syria, North Vietnam, South Yemen, Indonesia, Yemen and Egypt. Replacement of the bomber version with Su-7 fighter-bombers has taken place in most countries. The main exception is China, where about 400, built in that country, are in first-line service. Elsewhere, versions adapted for electronic warfare and other support duties remain in use. Finland has two which are used primarily for target-towing.

The Il-28 is powered by two VK-1 turbojets, which are developed versions of the Rolls-Royce Nene, and has the straight wing/swept tail layout that characterised the first generation of Soviet jet-bombers. The blister under the front fuselage houses the scanner of a radar navigation and blind-bombing system of limited value. The torpedo-carrying version used by the Soviet Naval Air Force, and by the Chinese Navy, is designated Il-28T; the tactical reconnaissance version is the Il-28R.

In addition, there is an operational trainer version designated Il-28U (NATO code-name *Mascot*) which has a second pilot's cockpit below and forward of the standard fighter-type canopy. China is the major operator in the late seventies.

Ilyushin Il-38
(NATO code-name: May)

USSR

Maritime reconnaissance and anti-submarine aircraft, in production and service.

Powered by: Four Ivchenko AI-20 turboprops.
Span: 122ft 8½in (37.4m).
Length: 129ft 10in (39.6m).
Weights: Probably similar to those of Il-18.
Max crusing speed: 400mph (645km/h).
Max range: 4,500 miles (7,250km).

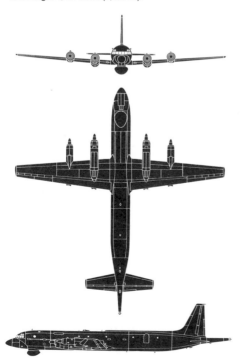

This Soviet maritime patrol aircraft bears the same relationship to the Il-18 (page 174) as does the Lockheed P-3 Orion to the Electra transport. To fit it for its important role it has an MAD tail "sting", an undernose radome, other ASW (anti-submarine warfare) electronics and weapon-carrying capability. The main cabin has few windows on each side. Concentration of equipment and weapons in the forward area changed the centre of gravity so much that the wing had to be moved forward and the rear fuselage lengthened considerably by comparison with the Il-18.

The Il-38 is the standard shore-based maritime patrol aircraft of the Soviet Naval Air Force, which was believed to have between 50 and 100 in service in 1978. In the early 'seventies, a few operated in the markings of the Egyptian Air Force but were thought to be flown by Soviet crews operating from bases in North Africa. Three Il-38s were ordered by the Indian Navy in 1975, these being the first genuine export examples of the type; they entered service with INAS 315 late in 1977 and were to be followed by sufficient additional aircraft to re-equip INAS 312, flying Super Constellations at that time.

During 1978, an electronic reconnaissance/ECM version of the Il-18 appeared in Soviet service and was given the NATO code-name Coot-A (see page 174).

Ilyushin Il-76
(NATO code-name: Candid)

USSR

Medium/long-range strategic freighter, in production and service.

Powered by: Four 26,455lb (12,000kg) st Soloviev D-30KP turbofans.
Span: 165ft 8in (50.50m).
Length: 152ft 10½in (46.59m).
Gross weight: 374,785lb (170,000kg).
Max payload: 88,185lb (40,000kg).
Cruising speed: 466–497mph (750–800km/h) at 29,500–39,350ft (9,000–12,000m).
Range: 3,100 miles (5,000km) with max payload.
Accommodation: Basic flight crew of three.
Armament: Gun turret at tail (not shown in illustrations).

This Soviet counterpart to the C-141A StarLifter was first flown on March 25, 1971, and the prototype was displayed only two months later at the Paris Air Show. Its nominal task was described as

the transport of 40 tonnes of freight for a distance of 5,000km in under six hours, after take-off from short, unprepared airstrips. The entire accommodation is pressurised, and advanced mechanical handling systems are installed in the freight hold for loading and unloading containerised cargoes via the rear ramp-door. There is a large ground-mapping radar under the navigator's station in the glazed nose, and a computer is fitted for use with the automatic flight control and automatic landing approach systems. The main eight-wheel bogies of the undercarriage retract inward into large blister fairings under the fuselage; two more large blister fairings cover the actuating mechanism. During development the rear fuselage has been modified, to increase the depth of the aft clamshell loading doors and so permit the entry of wider loads.

Production is under way on a large scale for both Aeroflot and the Soviet Air Force, as a replacement for the An-12. Military versions differ from the commercial model in having a tail gun turret. In addition, development of a version of the Il-76 as a flight refuelling tanker for the *Backfire* bomber force was confirmed in 1976, and it is likely that this aircraft will serve as a replacement for the M-4 *Bisons* used hitherto in that role. A series of flights in 1975 showed that, under the conditions laid down for record attempts, the Il-76 could lift a payload of 154,590lb (70,121kg) and could reach an altitude of 38,960ft (11,875m) with this load. Speeds of up to 533mph (857km/h) were recorded over closed circuits, with similar payloads. The first export deliveries of Il-76s were reported in mid-1978, when a small batch went to Iraq.

Israel Aircraft Industries Kfir

Israel

Single-seat close support and air superiority fighter, in production and service.

Powered by: One 11,870lb (5,385kg) st dry and 17,900lb (8,120kg) st with afterburning General Electric J79-GE-17 turbojet.
Span: 26ft 11½in (8.22m).
Length: 51ft 0¼in (15.55m).
Gross weight: 32,190lb (14,600kg).
Max speed: Mach 1.1 at 1,000ft (305m) and Mach 2.3 above 36,000ft (10,970m).
Radius of action: 323 miles (520km) for air superiority, 745 miles (1,200km) for ground attack.

Data, photo and silhouette: Kfir-C2.

The Kfir (Young Lion) is an Israeli-developed derivative of the Dassault Mirage, a total of 75 examples of which (Mirage IIICJ and IIIBJ) had been acquired by the Heyl Ha'Avir (Israeli Air Force) from 1962 onwards. These were to have been followed, from 1967 onwards, by 50 Mirage 5J close-support versions, but delivery of these later aircraft was embargoed by France. To help fill the gap which this decision left in the Heyl Ha'Avir inventory, IAI set about building a version of the Mirage 5J in Israel, helped by production drawings procured clandestinely in France. Powered by an Atar 9C engine, the prototype Israeli-built fighter flew in September 1969, named Nesher (Eagle), and deliveries began in 1972. As many as 100 are believed to have been built, of which about 40 saw operational service during the Yom Kippur war of October 1973. In parallel with the Nesher programme, IAI undertook the marriage of a Mirage airframe with a US-supplied J79 engine. Under the code-name Black Curtain, a prototype installation in a French-built airframe flew on October 19, 1970, and a full Israeli-built prototype flew in September 1971. The name Kfir was adopted for the production version which replaced the Nesher on the production lines in 1975, and is in service with the Heyl Ha'Avir in several versions. With different radar and equipment fits, early Kfirs were optimised either for air superiority or air-to-ground operations; subsequently, the Kfir-C2 appeared, featuring fixed canard surfaces above and aft of the engine intakes, and dogtooth extensions on the outer wing leading edges. These modifications improve the dogfighting characteristics of the Kfir-C2, which was the standard production version by 1977. An attempt to sell a batch of Kfirs to Ecuador early in 1977 was blocked by the US government (involved because of the J79 engines), but the possible purchase of 50 of these fighters for the Nationalist Chinese Air Force (Taiwan) was being discussed in 1978 and had received US approval.

Kawasaki C-1

Japan

Twin-turbofan troop and freight transport, in production and service.

Powered by: Two 14,500lb (6,575kg) st Pratt & Whitney (Mitsubishi) JT8D-M-9 turbofans.
Span: 100ft 4¾in (30.60m).
Length: 95ft 1¾in (29.00m).
Empty weight: 51,410lb (23,320kg).
Gross weight: 85,320lb (38,700kg).
Max speed: 501mph (806km/h) at 25,000ft (7,620m).
Range: 2,084 miles (3,353km) with 5,070lb (2,300kg) payload.
Accommodation: Crew of five, 60 troops, 45 paratroops, 36 litters and attendants, or 17,640lb (8,000kg) of freight.
Armament: None.

This medium-size troop and cargo transport was developed by Nihon Aeroplane Manufacturing Company (NAMC) to replace the Air Self-Defence Force's veteran fleet of Curtiss C-46s, the last of which was retired in 1977. Design work began in 1966 and the first of two XC-1 prototypes made its first flight on November 12, 1970, followed by the second on January 16, 1971. Two C-1 pre-production aircraft were ordered in the 1971 Fiscal Year, with Kawasaki now designated as prime contractor for the programme. Eleven production C-1s were ordered initially, in the 1972 Fiscal Year, followed by 13 more in FY 1975 and two in FY 1978, with plans for six more to be ordered in FY 1979 and six in FY 1980. Delivery of the first 24 aircraft was to be completed in 1977. Kawasaki builds the front fuselage and wing centre-section, and is responsible for final assembly and flight testing. The outer wings are built by Fuji; the centre and rear fuselage and tail unit by Mitsubishi, the flaps, ailerons, engine pylons and pods by Nihon Hikoki; the undercarriage by Sumitomo; and the cargo loading system by Shin Meiwa. Standard freight loads include a 2½-ton truck, 105mm howitzer two ¾-ton trucks, three jeeps, or three pre-loaded freight pallets, each 7ft 4in (2.24m) wide by 90ft 0in (2.74m) long.

Kawasaki P-2J Japan

Twelve-seat anti-submarine and maritime patrol bomber, in production and service.

Powered by: Two 2,850shp General Electric T64-IHI-10 turboprops and two 3,085lb (1,400kg) st Ishikawajima-Harima J3-IHI-7C auxiliary turbojets.
Span: 101ft 3½in (30.87m).
Length: 95ft 10¾in (29.23m).
Empty weight: 42,500lb (19,277kg).
Gross weight: 75,000lb (34,019kg).
Max cruising speed: 250mph (402km/h).
Max range: 2,765 miles (4,450km).
Armament: Attachments for sixteen 5in rockets under wings. Internal stowage for 8,000lb (3,630kg) of bombs, depth charges or torpedoes.

The P-2J is a development of the P-2H Neptune (see page 71), of which Kawasaki manufactured 48 for the Japanese Maritime Self-Defence Force in 1959–65. Work on the prototype began in 1965, after four years of design effort, and it flew for the first time on July 21, 1966. Although produced by conversion of a standard P-2H, only the wings and tail unit remained substantially unchanged, apart from an increase in rudder chord. The fuselage was lengthened by 50in (1.27m) forward of the wing to accommodate improved electronic equipment, almost up to the standard of that carried by the P-3 Orion. The undercarriage was redesigned to have twin-wheel main units. Biggest change of all was to the power plant, with the original piston-engines replaced by T64 turbo-props built under licence by Ishikawajima-Harima. These give less take-off power than the piston-engines, but make possible a saving of 10,000lb (4,535kg) in the aircraft's weight by comparison with the P-2H, and take-off performance is maintained by use of underwing jet engines, as on later models of the P-2 itself. Fuel capacity is increased, and an additional crew member, known as the combat co-ordinator, is carried. The first of an initial series of 46 production P-2Js flew on August 8, 1969, and was delivered to the JMSDF on October 7 that year. The first P-2J squadron had 10 aircraft in service by February 1971, and all 46 of the first series had been delivered by March 31, 1974. Further orders were placed in annual increments that brought the total delivered to 70 by March 1977; another 12 were then on order for delivery by March 1979.

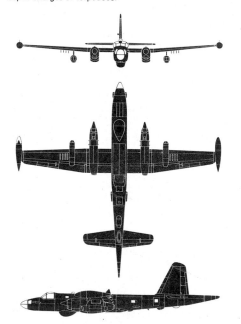

Lockheed C-5A Galaxy

USA

Heavy strategic transport, in service.

Powered by: Four 41,000lb (18,600kg) st General Electric TF39-GE-1 turbofans.
Span: 222ft 8½in (67.88m).
Length: 247ft 10in (75.54m).
Operating weight empty: 337,937lb (153,285kg).
Gross weight: 769,000lb (348,810kg).
Max speed: 571mph (919km/h) at 25,000ft (7,600m).
Range: 6,529 miles (10,505km) with 112,600lb (51,074kg) payload.
Armament: None.

The design of the massive Lockheed C-5A began in 1963 when the Military Air Transport Service (now Military Airlift Command) issued to industry a requirement for an outsize logistics transport which could carry a 125,000lb (56,700kg) load for 8,000 miles (12,875km), and could operate from the same airfields as those used by the C-141 StarLifter (see page 69). Development contracts went to Boeing, Douglas and Lockheed in May 1964, and to Pratt & Whitney and General Electric for engine development. During 1965, Lockheed's L500 design–the work of the company's Georgia Division was selected, together with General Electric GE1/6 engines, to meet the requirement. An initial contract for 58 aircraft was placed with Lockheed, with first and second options for 57 and 85 more. First flight of the first C-5A was made on June 30, 1968; the first operational model (the ninth C-5A built) was delivered to MAC on December 17, 1969. Production plans were limited subsequently to a total of 81 aircraft, because of rising costs; these equip four squadrons, one at Charleston AFB, one at Dover AFB and two at Travis AFB. During development, a C-5A took off at the then world record weight of 798,200lb (362,064kg). In service, loads such as two M-48 tanks, each weighing 99,000lb (45,000kg), or three CH-47 Chinook helicopters, have been airlifted over trans-oceanic ranges. During 1978, Lockheed developed and tested a major wing modification programme designed to extend the fatigue life of the Galaxy, and it is expected that all 77 remaining C-5As will be modified in this way by Lockheed in 1982–87.

Lockheed C-130 Hercules   USA

Multi-purpose transport, in production and service.

Powered by: Four 4,508eshp Allison T56-A-15 turboprops.
Span: 132ft 7in (40.41m).
Length: 97ft 9in (29.78m).
Empty weight: 75,621lb (34,300kg).
Max gross weight: 175,000lb (79,380kg).
Max cruising speed: 386mph (621km/h).
Range: 2,487-5,135 miles (4,002-8,264km).
Accommodation: Crew of four and 92 troops or 64 paratroops or 74 stretchers or freight.

First flight of the YC-130 Hercules was made on August 23, 1954 and delivery of the C-130A tactical transport began in December 1956. It was followed by the C-130B with higher weight and better range, production of the two versions totalling 461. The C-130E, first flown on August 25, 1961, was developed as an interim turbine transport for MAC, with more underwing fuel. On December 8, 1964, Lockheed flew the first of 66 HC-130Hs, with uprated T56-A-15 engines and special recovery equipment on the nose; 20 of these became HC-130Ps with provision to air-refuel helicopters and to recover parachute-borne loads in mid-air. KC-130H tankers have been supplied to Israel and Spain. Fifteen HC-130Ns are similar to the HC-130H, with advanced direction-finding equipment. The current production C-130H is basically an E with T56-A-15 engines instead of 4,050eshp T56-A-7s. The C-130K, similarly powered, was selected for the RAF; delivery began in 1967, and about 48 remained in service in 1978 in four squadrons. Thirty of these are to be lengthened by 15ft (4.57m), to the standard of the commercial L-100-30 version, to increase capacity to 128 troops, 92 paratroops, 99 stretchers or seven (instead of five) cargo pallets. Four EC-130Gs and ten improved EC-130Qs are operated by the US Navy for command communications, including worldwide relay of emergency action messages to ballistic missile submarines. Some Hercules were modified as AC-130A/H Gunships for the interdiction role in Vietnam and now fly with the Air Force Reserve. Special versions of the Hercules have included DC-130A/E/H drone carriers; 10 JC-130Bs and four JHC-130Hs for air-snatch satellite recovery; 12 C-130Ds with skis for Arctic operations. Also in service are 12 HC-130Bs for USCG search and rescue duties; the EC-130E of the USCG; 19 weather reconnaissance WC-130B/E/Hs used by the USAF; 46 KC-130Fs and 16 KC-130R tankers, used by the Marine Corps; seven US Navy C-130Fs; and four LC-130R ski-planes (converted from C-130H) used by the Navy in the Antarctic. Orders totalled 1,536 aircraft, for service in 42 nations, by January 1978, when Lockheed was actively promoting new military versions, including the L-400 Twin Hercules (with only two engines) and an advanced STOL variant.

Data, photo and silhouette: C-130H (Spain).

Lockheed C-141 StarLifter

USA

Long-range strategic freighter, in service.

Powered by: Four 21,000lb (9,525kg) st Pratt & Whitney TF33-P-7 turbofans.
Span: 159ft 11in (48.74m).
Length: 145ft 0in (44.20m).
Empty weight: 133,773lb (60,678kg).
Gross weight: 323,100lb (146,555kg).
Max cruising speed: 564mph (908km/h).
Max range: 6,140 miles (9,880km).
Accommodation: Crew of four-six plus 154 troops, 123 paratroops, 80 stretchers and 16 sitting casualties, or freight.

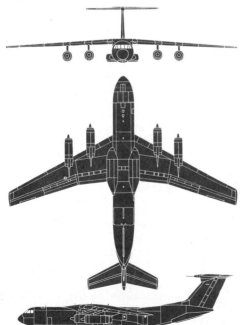

Lockheed won a hotly contested design competition in March 1961 with this design, laid out to meet the USAF's Specific Operational Requirement 182. The requirement was for a jet freighter to modernise the MAC fleet of piston-engined and turboprop transports. On March 16, 1961, following selection of the Lockheed design, procurement authorisation was issued to allow production of the new freighter to begin, and this was followed on August 16 by the contract for the first five aircraft. The original requirement was for 132 aircraft and later orders brought the total built to 284 by the time production ended late in 1967. The first of the evaluation aircraft flew on December 17, 1963 and delivery of operational aircraft to USAF began in 1965. The StarLifter is the flying element of the Logistics Support System 476L, and is built round an 81ft (24.7m) long cargo compartment, 10ft by 9ft (3.12m by 2.77m) in cross-section, with straight-in rear loading at truck-bed height and provision for air-dropping. Some aircraft have been modified to carry the Minuteman ICBM in a container, and have structural strengthening for the 86,207lb (39,103kg) weight of this load.

To increase the versatility of the StarLifter, Lockheed developed, under USAF contract, the C-141B configuration with fuselage lengthened by 23ft 4in (7.11m) and provision for in-flight refuelling. A prototype YC-141B conversion first flew on March 24, 1977 and in June 1978 the USAF contracted with Lockheed to convert all 270 StarLifters to this standard by 1983, increasing the usable space inside each aircraft by 30 per cent.

Data, photo and silhouette: C-141A

Lockheed F-104 Starfighter　　　　　　USA

Single-seat all-weather tactical strike and reconnaissance fighter, in service.

Powered by: One 17,900lb (8,120kg) st (with afterburning) General Electric J79-GE-19 turbojet.
Span: 21ft 11in (6.68m) without tip-tanks.
Length: 54ft 9in (16.69m).
Empty weight: 14,900lb (6,760kg).
Gross weight: 31,000lb (14,060kg).
Max speed: Mach 2.2 (1,450mph; 2,330km/h) at 36,000ft (11,000m).
Combat radius: 775 miles (1,247km) with max fuel.
Armament: One 20mm M61 Vulcan rotary-barrel cannon and up to 4,000lb (1,815kg) of external stores. Normally, two AIM-7 Sparrow and two AIM-9 Sidewinder air-to-air missiles for interceptor role.

Data: F-104S.
Photo: F-104A (Jordan).
Silhouette: F-104G.

Lockheed's Model 83 Starfighter was built in limited quantities for the USAF Tactical and Air Defense Commands after protracted development, following the first flight of the prototype on February 7, 1954. The single-seat F-104A and two-seat F-104B were used by ADC for North American air defence, and some were supplied to China and Pakistan; the F-104C and F-104D were TAC equivalents. A major re-design produced the F-104G multi-mission version with a 15,800lb (7,167kg) st (with afterburning) J79-GE-11A engine, which became the subject of an intra-European production programme, with assembly lines in Germany, Italy, Holland and Belgium which produced 977 aircraft plus a further 50 ordered by the Luftwaffe late in 1968; similar versions were built in Canada (for the CAF and export) and in Japan. Lockheed built another 179 F-104Gs, including one each for Italy and Belgium, 96 for Germany and 81 under USAF contract for supply under MAP to other nations. European nations which received F-104Gs from US and Canadian production comprised Denmark, Greece Norway, Spain and Turkey. Lockheed also built the two-seat F-104DJ for Japan, F-104F for Germany and TF-104G for Germany, Belgium, Italy, Netherlands, Denmark and other European air forces. Final production version was the F-104S, with nine external stores points and provision for Sparrow missiles. The Italian Air Force ordered 205 of this version, and the first of two prototypes built by Lockheed flew in 1966. Production was initiated by Aeritalia at Turin, where the first production model was flown on December 30, 1968. Deliveries were continuing during 1978 on 60 F-104S Starfighters ordered in addition by the Turkish Air Force, whilst earlier versions continued in service with the air forces of those nations mentioned above.

Lockheed P-2 Neptune

USA

Maritime patrol bomber, in service.

Powered by: Two 3,500hp Wright R-3350-32W piston-engines and two 3,400lb (1,540kg) st Westinghouse J34 turbojets.
Span: 103ft 10in (31.65m).
Length: 91ft 8in (27.94m).
Empty weight: 49,935lb (22,650kg).
Gross weight: 79,895lb (36,240kg).
Max speed: 403mph (648km/h).
Range: 3,685 miles (5,930km) with ferry tanks.
Accommodation: Crew of up to seven, comprising two pilots, navigator/bombardier, radar operator and gunners.
Armament: Optional dorsal turret with two 0.50in machine-guns. Sixteen 5in rocket projectiles under wings. Internal stowage for 8,000lb (3,630kg) of bombs, depth charges or torpedoes.

Work on the Lockheed Model 26 began in September 1941 to produce an aeroplane to meet US Navy requirements for an anti-submarine and anti-shipping patrol bomber. Design proposals were accepted by the US Navy in 1944 and orders for two prototypes and 15 production aircraft were placed. Production continued for 20 years, bringing the total built to more than 1,000 by the time the Lockheed production line closed in April 1962. The Neptune was initially designated P2V, and variants from P2V-1 to P2V-7 were produced. Progressive modifications accounted for the changes in designation, with the P2V-7 (later P-2H) introducing two jet engines under the wing to boost its performance. This became a retrospective modification on several earlier Neptune models. Only a few USN Reserve squadrons now use SP-2H Neptunes with Julie/Jezebel detection gear. Several overseas Services operate the Neptune, including the Royal Netherlands Navy, using 13 SP-2Hs; the Argentine Navy with six P-2Hs; the French Navy, using one Flotille equipped with 14 SP-2Hs; the Japanese MSDF with 45 P-2Hs and the Portuguese Air Force, which has eight ex-Dutch SP-2Es. In Japan, Kawasaki built 48 P-2H Neptunes under licence and then evolved the P-2J which has 2,850shp General Electric T64-IHI-10 turboprops in place of piston-engines, and 3,085lb (1,400kg) st IHI J3-7C underwing jets (see page 66).

Data and silhouette: P-2H.
Photo: SP-2H (French Navy).

Lockheed P-3 Orion and CP-140 Aurora   USA

Shore-based anti-submarine reconnaissance aircraft, in production and service. Crew of ten.

Powered by: Four 4,910eshp Allison T56-A-14 turboprops.
Span: 99ft 8in (30.37m).
Length: 116ft 10in (35.61m).
Empty weight: 61,491lb (27,890kg).
Gross weight: 142,000lb (64,410kg).
Max speed: 473mph (761km/h) at 15,000ft (4,570m).
Mission radius: 1,550 miles (2,494km) with 3 hours on station at 1,500ft (450m).
Armament: Torpedoes, mines, depth charges and bombs (including nuclear weapons) in internal weapons bay; wing-mounted weapons on ten pylons. Max total weapons load 20,000lb (9,070kg).

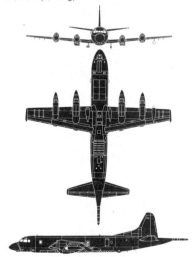

Data and photo: P-3C (RAAF).
Silhouette: CP-140 Aurora.

The Orion was designed to the US Navy's Type Specification 146, calling for an anti-submarine aircraft derived from an existing production type. Thus, an Electra transport modified as an aerodynamic prototype of the Orion flew on August 19, 1958. An operational prototype, the YP3V-1, flew on November 25, 1959, and the first production P3V-1 on April 15, 1961. The designation was changed to P-3A in July 1962, and on August 13 Navy Squadron VP-8 formally accepted the first three P-3A Orions, with 4,500eshp T56-A-10W engines. After 157 P-3As had been built, production switched to the P-3B with 4,910eshp T56-A-14 engines; a total of 125 P-3Bs were built for the US Navy. In addition, the RAAF acquired ten P-3Bs, the RNZAF five and the Royal Norwegian Air Force five. Three P-3As were delivered to the Spanish Air Force. Current US Navy production version is the P-3C, with A-NEW data processing system, which flew for the first time on September 18, 1968; over 200 were to be acquired by the USN, and the RAAF ordered 10 for 1977/78 delivery. A version of the P-3C ordered by Canada in 1976 uses avionics similar to those in the S-3A and is called the CP-140 Aurora; 18 will be delivered in 1980/81. Japan plans to acquire 45 P-3Cs between 1978 and 1987, of which 42 will be built by Kawasaki. Six P-3Fs for Iran differ in having some equipment deleted, including MAD and active sonar. Four WP-3As equipped for weather reconnaissance are operated by the US Navy, as are 12 EP-3E special reconnaissance aircraft with radomes above and below the fuselage, converted from P-3As (10) and EP-3Bs (2). A single RP-3D is operated by the US Naval Oceanographic Office for mapping the Earth's magnetic field. Two WP-3Ds are used by the US National Oceanic and Atmospheric Administration.

Lockheed S-3A Viking

USA

Four-seat carrier-borne anti-submarine aircraft, in service.

Powered by: Two 9,275lb (4,207kg) st General Electric TF34-GE-2 turbofans.
Span: 68ft 8in (20.93m).
Length: 53ft 4in (16.26m).
Empty weight: 26,650lb (12,088kg).
Gross weight: 52,539lb (23,831kg).
Max speed: 518mph (834km/h).
Combat range: more than 2,300 miles (3,705km).
Armament: Torpedoes, depth charges, mines, missiles, rockets and special weapons in internal bomb-bays and under wings.

This carrier-based anti-submarine aircraft was developed to replace the S-2 Tracker in service with the US Navy. Lockheed-California was awarded an initial $461 million contract for the S-3A in August 1969, after a design competition, and flew the first of eight research and development aircraft ahead of schedule on January 21, 1972. All eight were flying by the Spring of 1973, and delivery of production S-3As to the Fleet began officially on February 20, 1974. A total of 187 was built, to provide 12 squadrons, one on each USN multi-purpose carrier; the last S-3A was delivered in 1978.

The crew of the S-3A consists of a pilot, co-pilot, tactical operator and acoustic sensor operator. The co-pilot is responsible for non-acoustic sensors, such as radar and infra-red devices. Improved sonobuoys and MAD equipment enhance the capability of finding the quieter, deeper-diving submarines now in service. The fuselage will take a 50 per cent expansion of the present electronics, and the basic design could be adapted easily to provide variants for other tasks. One S-3A was used as a flight refuelling tanker during the flight trials of the Viking, to extend the endurance of other trials aircraft, and a KS-3A version has been projected by Lockheed. The USN planned to procure a US-3A version for COD use, and a prototype flew on July 2, 1976; but this version has now been dropped, and no funds have yet been made available for the ES-3A special electronics version.

Lockheed SR-71 USA

Two-seat strategic reconnaissance aircraft, in service.

Powered by: Two 32,500lb (14,740kg) st (with afterburning) Pratt & Whitney J58 turbojets.
Span: 55ft 7in (16.95m).
Length: 107ft 5in (32.74m).
Gross weight: 170,000lb (77,110kg).
Max speed: More than Mach 3.0 (2,000mph; 3,220km/h).
Range: 2,982 miles (4,800km) at Mach 3.0 at 78,750ft (24,000m).
Accommodation: Crew of two.
Armament: Unarmed.

Data, photo and silhouette: SR-71A.

Developed in strict secrecy and with remarkable speed, the basic Lockheed A-11 flew for the first time on April 26, 1962, but was not revealed publicly until February 1964. The original requirement is believed to have been for a "U-2 replacement", an aircraft capable of flying at sufficient altitude and speed to be virtually un-interceptable if used on long-range strategic reconnaissance flights. Three A-11s were modified during 1964 for evaluation as YF-12As in the role of air defence fighters, carrying eight Hughes AIM-47A missiles in internal bays. The similar but longer SR-71A was first flown on December 22, 1964 and at least 27 were built to equip the 9th Strategic Reconnaissance Wing of SAC, which received its first SR-71s in January 1966. Since then, its aircraft have seen extensive worldwide use, as the fastest military aircraft ever put into service, able to photograph 100,000 sq. miles (259,000 km^2) in one hour. Two SR-71Bs each had a raised rear cockpit and were used as trainers by the 9th Wing. When one crashed, it was replaced by one of the YF-12As converted for the training role and designated SR-71C. Before the fully-operational SR-71s entered service, an initial batch of A-11s is reputed to have been used to launch GTD-21 reconnaissance drones on operational missions. The GTD-21, also built by Lockheed, was of similar wing configuration to the A-11, but had only a single engine.

World records set up by a YF-12A on May 1, 1965, included a speed of 2,070mph (3,331km/h) over a 15/25-km course and a sustained height of 80,258ft (24,462m). These stood as absolute records until July 1976, when they were bettered by an SR-71A which reached an altitude of 85,069ft (25,929m) and a speed of 2,193mph (3,529km/h). Two important point-to-point records set up by a USAF SR-71A in 1974 comprised a New York to London transatlantic record of 1 hour 55 min 32 sec, and a London to Los Angeles time of 3 hours 47 min 39 sec at an average speed of 1,480mph (2,382km/h).

McDonnell F-101 Voodoo

USA

Two-seat long-range interceptor fighter, in service.

Powered by: Two 14,880lb (6,750kg) st (with afterburning) Pratt & Whitney J57-P-55 turbojets.
Span: 39ft 8in (12.09m).
Length: 67ft 5in (20.55m).
Gross weight: 46,500lb (21,100kg).
Max speed: Mach 1.85 (1,220mph; 1,963km/h) at 40,000ft (12,200m).
Max range: 1,550 miles (2,495km).
Armament: Two Genie missiles in internal weapon bay plus two Falcon missiles under fuselage.

The Voodoo was derived from an earlier McDonnell design, the XF-88, only two prototypes of which were built. A production order for the developed design, the F-101, was placed in 1951 to provide Strategic Air Command with a single-seat escort fighter for its B-36s. This requirement was later dropped and production of the F-101 was continued for Tactical Air Command. The first flight was made on September 29, 1954 and three squadrons were equipped with F-101As (77 built) before the F-101C (47 built) succeeded it, with improved load-carrying ability. During 1967 and 1968, many of these aircraft were converted to reconnaissance fighters for ANG squadrons, with nose-mounted cameras, as RF-101Gs and RF-101Hs respectively. The RF-101A and RF-101C also carried cameras in a lengthened nose, production totals being 35 and 166 respectively. For service with Air Defense Command, the F-101B was developed as a two-seat long-range interceptor, with all-weather capability; this version first flew on March 27, 1957. Production totalled 480, including some with full dual control, designated TF-101B. The Voodoo is out of service with the active USAF, but three ANG units fly F-101Bs and one flies RF-101Cs. Fifty-six Voodoo two-seaters were supplied to the RCAF after service with ADC, plus ten with dual control, these being designated F-101F and TF-101F respectively by the USAF, and CF-101B and CF-101F by the Canadian Armed Forces. In the early 'seventies, the 58 remaining CF-101B/F aircraft were exchanged for 66 refurbished aircraft of similar type with updated electronics and other refinements. These remain operational in four squadrons.

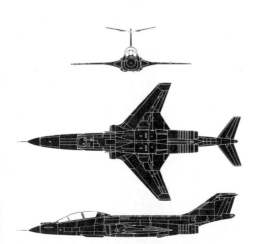

Data and silhouette: F-101B.
Photo: RF-101C.

McDonnell Douglas A-4 Skyhawk   USA

Single-seat carrier-based light attack bomber, in service.

Powered by: One 11,200lb (5,080kg) st Pratt & Whitney J52-P-408A turbojet.
Span: 27ft 6in (8.38m).
Length: 40ft 3¼in (12.27m).
Empty weight: 10,465lb (4,747kg).
Gross weight: 24,500lb (11,113kg).
Max speed: 645mph (1,038km/h) with 4,000lb (1,814kg) bombs.
Range: 2,055 miles (3,307km) with external fuel.
Armament: Two 20mm cannon in wings; fuselage crutch and four wing strong points carry maximum 10,000lb (4,535kg) load of assorted bombs, rockets or other stores.

Data: A-4M.
Photo: A-4K (foreground) and TA-4K.
Silhouette: TA-4J.

The prototype XA4D-1 flew on June 22, 1954, with a Wright J65-W-2 engine. The 166 initial production A-4As had J65-W-4 engines and entered service in October 1956. They were followed by the A-4B, first flown on March 26, 1956, with a J65-W-16A and other improvements. Equipment for all-weather operation, including terrain-clearance radar in a lengthened nose, produced the A-4C, first flown on August 21, 1958. Douglas built 542 A-4Bs and 638 A-4Cs. The A-4E, first flown on July 12, 1961, had more payload and range, with a J52-P-6A engine; 499 were built. The TA-4E trainer, with lengthened fuselage for tandem seating and a J52-P-8A engine, flew on June 30, 1965; production models were redesignated TA-4F. On August 31, 1966, Douglas flew the prototype A-4F, and deliveries of 146 of this version began in June 1967, with a J52-P-8A turbojet, avionics in a saddle bay behind the pilot and other changes. The TA-4J is a simplified trainer for the US Navy with P-6 engine. A-4Cs modified to A-4F equipment standard, for service with USN Reserve carrier air wings, are designated A-4L. The A-4M (data above), first flown on April 10, 1970, is a USMC derivative of the A-4F with J52-P-408A and other improvements. About 170 are being procured to maintain a five-squadron force, and these are being updated to A-4Ys with HUD and ARBS. The RAN purchased 12 A-4Gs and 4 TA-4Gs; the RNZAF bought 10 A-4Ks and 4 TA-4Ks; Argentina acquired 75 A-4B Skyhawks, redesignated A-4Q (Navy, 15) and A-4P (Air Force, 60) after modification; and Singapore has 40 A-4s, converted from A-4Bs, and seven TA-4S tandem two-seat trainers. Kuwait has ordered 30 A-4KUs and six two-seat TA-4KUs. The A-4N Skyhawk II, with P-408A engine, uprated avionics and 30mm guns, first flown on June 8, 1972, is in production for Israel, following the delivery of substantial quantities of A-4Es, A-4Hs and TA-4Hs; the total number of Skyhawks supplied to Israel exceeds 250.

McDonnell Douglas F-4 Phantom II USA

Two-seat multi-mission land and carrier-based fighter and fighter-bomber, in production and service.

Powered by: Two 17,900lb (8,120kg) st (with afterburning) Pratt & Whitney J79-GE-17 turbojets.
Span: 38ft 5in (11.70m).
Length: 63ft 0in (19.20m).
Empty weight: 30,073lb (13,641kg).
Gross weight: 57,400lb (26,037kg).
Max speed: Mach 2.2 (1,450mph; 2,330km/h) at 36,000ft (11,000m).
Max range: 1,860 miles (3,000km).
Armament: Basic armament of four Sparrow missiles on semi-submerged mountings under fuselage and two Sparrow or four Mitsubishi AAM-2 or Sidewinder missiles on two wing pylons. Alternative armament includes bombs exceeding 16,000lb (7,250kg) in weight, gun pods, rocket pods, etc.

Development of the Phantom II began in September 1953 under the designation AH-1 as a high-performance attack two-seater for the USN. The

Data: Phantom F-4EJ.
Photo: FGR.Mk 2.
Silhouette: F-4E.

designation was changed to F4H after the specification had been altered to include air-to-air armament, and the first XF4H-1 was flown on May 27, 1958. US Navy Squadron VF-101 received its first production aircraft in December 1960. Trials in the ground attack role led to USAF adoption, and basic Navy and USAF versions became the F-4B and F-4C respectively. The first F-4C flew on May 27, 1963, the first YRF-4C (reconnaissance version) on August 9, 1963 and the first production RF-4C on May 18, 1964. The RF-4B reconnaissance version for the USN flew on March 12, 1965. Production totalled 696 F-4A/Bs, 46 RF-4Bs, 583 F-4Cs and 505 RF-4Cs; some F-4As have become TF-4As for land-based training duties and several F-4Bs have been converted as QF-4B drones. Later USAF versions are the F-4D (flown December 8, 1965; 825 built) with improved avionics, and F-4E with nose-mounted M61 gun. The Navy acquired one squadron of F-4Gs with improved avionics, followed by full production F-4Js with J79-GE-10 engines and many improvements. Total of 170 F-4Ks and F-4Ms are Spey-engined Phantom FG.Mk 1s and FGR.Mk 2s respectively. The RN received 24 Phantom FG.Mk 1s, and has one operational squadron. The other aircraft are operated by the RAF in the UK and Germany for air defence and reconnaissance roles. Iran is receiving 261 F-4D/Es, and delivery of 36 F-4Ds to South Korea began in mid-1969, followed by about 40 F-4Es. Israel received the first of over 200 F-4Es and RF-4Es in the latter half of 1969. Germany received 88 RF-4E reconnaissance fighters and 175 F-4Fs (modified to have leading-edge slats, also retro-fitted to all F-4Es); and Japan bought 158 F-4EJs, built by Mitsubishi. Other operators of the F-4E and RF-4E include the Turkish and Greek Air Forces, which received 80 and 64 respectively. Spain has 36 F-4Cs in service as C-12s. The USN has updated 178 F-4Bs as F-4Ns and has a similar programme to update F-4Js to F-4S standard, while the USAF plans to acquire 116 F-4G (Wild Weasel) electronic warfare conversions to equip four squadrons. Total F-4 production reached 5,000 during 1978.

McDonnell Douglas F-15 Eagle   USA

Single-seat and two-seat air superiority fighter, in production and service.

Powered by: Two 25,000lb (11,340kg) st Pratt & Whitney F100-PW-100 afterburning turbofans.
Span: 42ft 9¾in (13.05m).
Length: 63ft 9¾in (19.45m).
Gross weight: 56,000lb (25,401kg).
Max speed: More than Mach 2.5.
Ferry range: more than 2,875 miles (4,630km); 3,450 miles (5,560km) with "Fast Pack" flush-fitting lateral fuel tanks.
Armament: One internally-mounted M61 20mm multi-barrel gun in fuselage. AIM-9L advanced Sidewinder air-to-air missiles on wing stations. Four AIM-7F advanced Sparrow air-to-air missiles on lower corners of air intake trunks. Provision for carrying electronic warfare pods on outboard wing stations. Max external weapon load 12,000lb (5,443kg).

When Russia's MiG-25 was first shown in public in 1967, the USAF began the urgent development

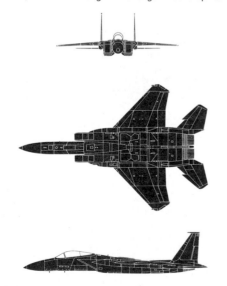

Data, photo and silhouette: F-15A.

of an air superiority fighter capable of fighter sweep, escort and combat air patrol duties in areas where the Soviet fighter might be met. McDonnell Douglas was selected to design and build the new aircraft, as the F-15, in December 1969, and received an initial order for 20 aircraft for development testing. Emphasis was placed on high manoeuvrability, rate of climb and acceleration. This led to selection of engines that would give the aircraft a thrust-to-weight ratio of better than one-to-one, and the same kind of twin-tail configuration as the MiG-25 and Grumman F-14. Close-range destructive power was planned around the use of new "dogfight" versions of the Sidewinder missile and a multi-barrel cannon.

The first single-seat F-15A, named Eagle, flew for the first time on July 27, 1972, and was subsequently joined in the flight test programme by 17 more F-15As and two F-15B (originally TF-15A) two-seat trainers, with full combat capability. Production of the first 30 aircraft for Tactical Air Command was authorised in 1973. Subsequent annual increments brought the total on order to 501 by 1978, out of a planned procurement of 729 Eagles for 19 squadrons. Deliveries to TAC began on November 15, 1974, when the first F-15B was delivered to the 555th Squadron, 58th TF Training Wing; the 1st TF Wing at Langley AFB subsequently became the first fully equipped with Eagles. A second unit was operational by 1977, when it moved to USAFE in Germany, and deliveries totalled 254 production aircraft by the beginning of 1978. From 1980, the F-15A and B will be superseded in production by the F-15C and D respectively, with improved radar, more internal fuel and ability to carry Fast Pack (Fuel and Sensor Tactical Package) pallets on the sides of the air intake trunks. Twenty-five F-15As, including refurbished flight development aircraft, have been bought by Israel, deliveries starting in 1977, with 15 more expected to follow in 1981–82. Japan is to have 100 F-15Js, licence-built by Mitsubishi, including 12 two-seaters; and the US government has offered Saudi Arabia 60 F-15s for 1981–84 delivery.

McDonnell Douglas F-18 and A-18 Hornet   USA

Single-seat carrier-borne multi-mission fighter, under development.

Powered by: Two 16,000lb (7,264kg) st General Electric F404-GE-400 turbofan engines.
Span: 37ft 6in (11.43m).
Length: 55ft 7in (16.94m).
Gross weight: Over 44,000lb (19,960kg).
Max speed: Over Mach 1.8.
Combat radius: Over 460 miles (740km) with internal fuel.
Armament: Seven weapon stations under wings and fuselage, plus wingtip missile shoes, with combined capacity for 13,700lb (6,215kg) of ordnance.

The F-18, under development by McDonnell Douglas at its St Louis plant under contract to the US Navy and in collaboration with Northrop, is the outcome of a competitive evaluation by the USN of the two fighter prototypes produced for USAF evaluation in 1964 by General Dynamics and Northrop. Since neither of those companies was a prime supplier of combat aircraft to the USN, they teamed, respectively, with Vought and McDonnell Douglas to submit versions of the lightweight fighters for naval use. Although the General Dynamics F-16 had meanwhile gained USAF backing, it was the Northrop YF-17 that provided the basis for the USN selection and around which a full-scale development programme was launched in January 1976. The designation F-18 was adopted to avoid the impression that the Navy was buying a USAF cast-off, and McDonnell Douglas influence subsequently led to an overall scaling up of the original design, with more fuel capacity in the fuselage, radar in the nose and greater wing area. Procurement of the first five F-18s was planned for FY 1979, leading to service introduction in FY 1983. Purchase of up to 800 in F-18 and A-18 versions is planned, by the end of the 1980s, to replace F-4 Phantom IIs, A-7 Corsair IIs, A-4M Skyhawks and AV-8As in USN and US Marine Corps service. A reconnaissance derivative is also under consideration. Initial contracts cover 11 F-18s for full-scale development, including a two-seat operational training version, and the first of these flew in October 1978. Northrop is offering a land-based variant, the F-18L, without folding wings, deck hook and naval equipment.

Data, photo and silhouette: F-18.

Mikoyan/Gurevich MiG-17 (NATO code-name: Fresco. Chinese designation: F-4)

USSR

Single-seat fighter, in service.

Powered by: One 6,990lb (3,170kg) st (with afterburning) Klimov VK-1A turbojet.
Span: 31ft 0in (9.45m).
Length: 36ft 4in (11.10m).
Gross weight (clean): 12,500lb (5,670kg).
Max speed: 700mph (1,125km/h) at sea level.
Max range with external tanks and bombs: 750 miles (1,205km).
Armament: Three 23mm NR-23 cannon; four eight-rocket pods or two 550lb (250kg) bombs.

Data and photo: *Fresco-C* (Cuba).
Silhouette: *Fresco-D*.

The MiG-17 was developed from the pioneer Soviet swept-wing MiG-15, which it began to supersede in production in 1953. In an effort to achieve supersonic performance, the design was considerably refined, with a thinner wing section, increased wing sweep and lengthened rear fuselage; but the MiG-17 remained subsonic in level flight. The initial production model, known to NATO as *Fresco-A*, had a 5,950lb (2,700kg) st VK-1 turbojet, without afterburner, narrow dive-brakes at the tail like the MiG-15 and an armament of one 37mm and two 23mm cannon. In *Fresco-B*, the dive-brakes were enlarged and moved to just aft of the wing trailing-edge. This was probably unsuccessful, as the next version, *Fresco-C*, retained the larger brakes but had them repositioned at the tail; it also introduced an afterburner, an additional 23mm cannon in place of the 37mm gun, and underwing armament. *Fresco-D* is a limited all-weather fighter version of the *C* with radar in a central bullet in its air intake, and sometimes carries four air-to-air missiles instead of cannon. *Fresco-E* is similar but without afterburner. Of an estimated 300 MiG-17s still equipping Soviet combat squadrons in less-critical areas, 80 are home defence *Fresco-Ds*, the rest *Fresco-Cs*.

Fresco-C was built in Czechoslovakia (as S-104), Poland (as LiM-5) and China (as F-4), as well as in Russia. Many remain in service, especially with air forces in Asia and Africa which receive aid from the USSR and China. Reported Soviet designations are MiG-17P for *Fresco-B*, MiG-17F for *Fresco-C*, MiG-17PF for *Fresco-D* and MiG-17PFU for *Fresco-E*.

Mikoyan MiG-19 (NATO code-name: Farmer. Chinese designation: F-6

USSR

Single-seat fighter, in production and service.

Powered by: Two 7,165lb (3,250kg) st (with afterburning) Klimov RD-9B turbojets.
Span: 29ft 6½in (9.00m).
Length: 48ft 10½in (14.90m).
Empty weight: 12,700lb (5,760kg).
Gross weight: 19,180lb (8.700kg).
Max speed: 902mph (1,450km/h) at 33,000ft (10,000m).
Combat radius: 426 miles (685km) with external tanks.
Armament: Three 30mm cannon and underwing pylons for two fuel tanks and either two 500lb (or 250kg) bombs, two 212mm rockets or two pods, each containing eight air-to-air rockets.

Data and photo: F-6 (MiG-19PF).
Silhouette: MiG-19S.

With the MiG-19, Mikoyan finally achieved supersonic performance in level flight. He retained the basic layout of the MiG-15 and 17, but mounted two small-diameter turbojets side-by-side in the rear fuselage, more than doubling the thrust of the earlier types. The initial version (*Farmer-A*) entered service early in 1955, armed with one 37mm and two 23mm cannon, plus underwing rockets, missiles and drop tanks. *Farmer-B* was similar, but with radar in a bullet radome in the air intake for limited all-weather operations. The most widely-used version (*Farmer-C*) introduced an underfuselage air-brake, supplementing the original air-brakes on the sides of the rear fuselage, and was fitted with three improved cannon of 30mm calibre. *Farmer-D* is the limited all-weather counterpart of the *C*, with radar in a nose bullet and only two guns. Some *Farmer-Ds* are armed with four underwing missiles (code-name *Alkali*) and no guns. Soviet designations are MiG-19S for early *Farmer-Cs* with Klimov AM-5 turbojets, MiG-19SF for later RD-9B-powered *Farmer-Cs*, MiG-19PF for *Farmer-D* and MiG-19PM for the *D* with *Alkali* missiles. Before its break with the USSR, China received full manufacturing data for the MiG-19 and put both *Farmer-C* and *D* versions into production, under the designation F-6. Manufacture continued, on a diminishing scale, up to 1978, and F-6s equip the Chinese, Albanian and Pakistan Air Forces. Some East European air forces still fly a few Soviet-built MiG-19s, as well as countries such as Iraq and Cuba which received Soviet military aid.

The Chinese have developed from the F-6 a somewhat larger and higher-performance fighter designated F-9, which is in squadron service and has been given the Western reporting name of *Fantan*.

Mikoyan MiG-21
(NATO code-names: Fishbed and Mongol.
Chinese designation: F-8)

USSR

Single-seat lightweight fighter and two-seat trainer, in production and service.

Powered by: One 14,550lb (6,600kg) st (with afterburning) Tumansky R-13-300 turbojet.
Span: 23ft 5½in (7.15m).
Length: 51ft 8½in (15.76m).
Gross weight: 20,725lb (9,400kg).
Max speed: Mach 2.1 (1,385mph; 2,230km/h) at 36,000ft (11,000m).
Range (clean): 683 miles (1,100km).
Armament: One twin-barrel 23mm cannon. Four underwing pylons for K-13A (*Atoll*) and/or *Advanced Atoll* missiles, packs of 16 rockets or drop tanks.

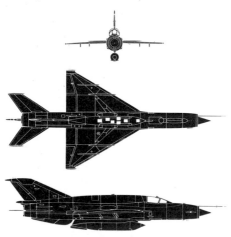

Data: MiG-21MF.
Photo: MiG-21bis *Fishbed-N.*
Silhouette: *Fishbed-K* with reconnaissance pod.

First seen in prototype form in the 1956 Aviation Day fly-past over Moscow, the MiG-21 is the most widely used fighter in the world, serving with some 30 air forces. The original MiG-21F production version (*Fishbed-C*) was built in Czechoslovakia and, probably in modified form without licence rights, in China as the F-8. It is a short-range clear-weather fighter, with armament of one 30mm gun and two rocket pods or *Atoll* infra-red homing missiles. With a wider-chord fin and optional underbelly twin-barrel 23mm gun pack it became *Fishbed-E*. The MiG-21PF (*Fishbed-D*) introduced a lengthened nose of larger diameter, housing more effective radar to give limited all-weather capability. Cannon armament is deleted, the pitot boom repositioned above the nose, and the R-11 turbojet uprated from the former 12,676lb (5,750kg) st to 13,120lb (5,950kg). Late MiG-21PFs and subsequent versions also have provision for flap-blowing (SPS) to reduce landing speed. A wider-chord fin, improved radar, optional underbelly gun pack, 13,668lb (6,200kg) st R-11-300 engine, but no SPS, identifies the MiG-21FL, of which 200 were produced in India by HAL. The MiG-21PFM (*Fishbed-F*) differs from the late-model PF in having the broader fin, a sideways-hinged canopy instead of the original one-piece windscreen/canopy, and the same radar as the FL, and was built in both the Soviet Union and Czechoslovakia. MiG-21PFMA (*Fishbed-J*) was the first of a new multi-role family, with two additional underwing pylons, able to carry, among other things, new *Advanced Atoll* radar-homing missiles. The dorsal spine fairing is deepened back to the fin, and late PFMAs can have the 23mm gun buried inside the fuselage with only the barrels visible, so that an underbelly

drop tank can also be carried. Variants are the MiG-21MF (*Fishbed-J*), with more powerful R-13-300 engine; MiG-21SMT (*Fishbed-K*), with the deep dorsal spine extended rearward as far as the parachute brake housing, and optional wingtip ECM pods; and the MiG-21M, similar to the PFMA but built by HAL. The MiG-21R and RF (*Fishbed-H*) are reconnaissance versions of the PFMA and MF respectively, with external pod for cameras and infra-red sensors, and wingtip ECM pods. *Fishbed-L* is the first variant of the third-generation MiG-21bis, with updated electronics, wider and deeper dorsal fairing and generally improved construction standards. It has been followed by

Fishbed-N, now standard in the Soviet Air Force, with 16,535lb (7,500kg) st Tumansky R-25 engine and further-enhanced electronics. Tandem two-seat training versions of the MiG-21 have the NATO code-name *Mongol*.

Top: Mongol, *a tandem two seat training version of the MiG*-21, *in service with the Czechoslovak Air Force*
Bottom: *MiG*-23 (*Flogger-E*) *export standard interceptor. Note smaller radome compared with Flogger-B of Soviet Air Force (overleaf), and absence of undernose laser rangefinder.*

Mikoyan MiG-23
(NATO code-name: Flogger-A, B, C, E and F)

USSR

Single-seat variable-geometry tactical fighter, in production and service.

Powered by: One turbojet, believed to give about 20,500lb (9,300kg) st with afterburning.
Span (estimated): 46ft 9in (14.25m) spread; 26ft 9½in (8.17m) swept.
Length (estimated): 55ft 1½in (16.80m).
Gross weight (estimated): 28,000-33,050lb (12,700-15,000kg).
Max speed (estimated): Mach 2.3 (1,520mph; 2,450km/h) at 36,000ft (11,000m) with external stores.
Combat radius (estimated): 600 miles (960km).
Armament: One 23mm GSh-23 twin-barrel cannon in belly. One pylon under centre fuselage, one under each air intake trunk, and one under each fixed inboard wing panel for air-to-air missiles (NATO *Apex* and *Aphid*) or other stores.

Data and silhouette: MiG-23S.
Photo: MiG-23S.

The prototype of this "swing-wing" tactical fighter, allocated the code-name *Flogger-A* by NATO, made its first public appearance in the 1967 Aviation Day display at Domodedovo Airport, Moscow, but did not land there. The commentator announced that it could fly at supersonic speed at ground level and Mach 2 at medium and high altitudes. Deliveries to the Soviet Air Force were reported to be under way in 1971. When photographs became available, it was clear that the basic single-seat MiG-23S (*Flogger-B*) differed considerably from the prototype, with the tail surfaces moved further aft (except for the ventral fin), and a fixed section inboard of the leading-edge flap on each pivoted outer wing panel. The lower half of the ventral fin is hinged to fold sideways during take-off and landing, to provide ground clearance. Initially, the dorsal fin was much enlarged by comparison with the prototype; but aircraft seen in 1978 have little more than a modest increase of leading-edge sweep on the lower part of the fin. Two regiments of MiG-23s and MiG-27s (see page 86) have been in service with Soviet fighter-bomber units at Kolberg in East Germany since early 1974, including tandem two-seat MiG-23U (*Flogger-C*) dual-role trainer/combat versions. The MiG-23U differs from the MiG-23S only in having an additional, slightly raised rear seat, with separate canopy, periscopic sight, and deepened fairing behind it. More than 1,000 MiG-23Ss and Us and MiG-27s are thought to have been delivered to the Soviet and Czechoslovak tactical air forces. Export models, delivered to Egypt, Iraq, Libya and Syria, and equipped to a lower standard, are the *Flogger-E* interceptor (equivalent to *Flogger-B*) and ground attack *Flogger-F*, which has a nose-shape similar to that of the MiG-27 and low-pressure tyres but is generally similar to other MiG-23s.

Mikoyan MiG-25
(NATO code-name: Foxbat)

USSR

Single-seat interceptor and reconnaissance aircraft, in production and service.

Powered by: Two 24,250lb (11,000kg) st Tumansky R-31 afterburning turbojets.
Span: 45ft 9in (13.95m).
Length: 73ft 2in (22.30m).
Gross weight: 79,800lb (36,200kg).
Max speed: Mach 2.8 with underwing missiles.
Max combat radius: 805 miles (1,300km).
Armament: Four air-to-air missiles (NATO *Acrid*) on underwing pylons.

Data and silhouette: *Foxbat-A.*
Photo: *Foxbat-B.*

The existence of a new Soviet aircraft designated E-266 was revealed in April 1965, when an aircraft of this type set a 1,000km closed-circuit speed record of 1,441.5mph (2,320km/h) carrying a 2,000kg payload. Four examples of the E-266 took part in the Aviation Day flypast over Moscow in July 1967, but the service designation MiG-25 was not confirmed until several years later. By that time, even more spectacular records had been set, including a still-unbeaten speed record of 1,852.62mph (2,981.5km/h) around a 500km closed circuit. A reconnaissance version (*Foxbat-B*), equipped with five cameras and side-looking airborne radar, was soon identified, in addition to the basic interceptor (*Foxbat-A*). Four "Bs" were ferried to Egypt on board An-22 transports in 1971, subsequently making flights off the coast of Israel and over Israeli-occupied Sinai at speeds which made them impossible to intercept. On September 6, 1976, a defecting Soviet pilot landed a *Foxbat-A* in Japan, where it was inspected thoroughly by Japanese and US intelligence teams. Construction was confirmed as being virtually all-steel, with extremely powerful radar and effective ECM. When carrying missiles, *Foxbat-A* is limited to Mach 2.8, whereas *Foxbat-B* can attain Mach 3.2 at height. The wing of the "B" also lacks the compound sweep of that on *Foxbat-A* and has a span of only 44ft (13.40m). Other versions in service are *Foxbat-D*, a reconnaissance variant with larger SLAR but no cameras, and the tandem-cockpit MiG-25U (*Foxbat-C*) two-seat trainer. The latest E-266M, with uprated (30,865lb; 14,000kg st) engines, has set an absolute height record of 123,523ft (37,650m) and climbed to 114,829ft (35,000m) in 4 min 11.3sec. Over 400 MiG-25s are believed to be in service with the Soviet air forces.

Mikoyan MiG-27
(NATO code-name: Flogger-D)

USSR

Single-seat variable-geometry ground attack aircraft, in production and service.
All data estimated.

Powered by: One turbojet, believed to give about 24,250lb (11,000kg) st with afterburning.
Span: 46ft 9in (14.25m) spread, 26ft 9½in (8.17m) swept.
Length: 55ft 1½in (16.80m).
Gross weight: 39,130lb (17,750kg).
Max ferry range: 1,550 miles (2,500km) with three external fuel tanks.
Armament: One six-barrel 23mm cannon. Five under-fuselage and underwing attachments for 4,200lb (1,900kg) of external stores, including tactical nuclear weapons and *Kerry* air-to-surface guided missiles.

Although much of the airframe of the MiG-27 is similar to that of the MiG-23, this aircraft has been optimised for high-speed attack, with heavy armament, at tree-top height. Instead of housing a large search radar, its nose slopes down sharply for optimum forward vision, and houses both electronics for low-level navigation and special-ised target-seeking aids such as a laser range-finder and marked target seeker. A Gatling-type gun adds to the attack potential of its external weapons. The cockpit is heavily armoured for pro-tection against ground fire. The variable-geometry air intakes and nozzle of the MiG-23 have given way to the fixed intakes and nozzle more ap-propriate to an aircraft intended to fly at just below the speed of sound at sea level. The engine, different from that of the MiG-23, may be related to the Tumansky R-31 fitted in the MiG-25 *Foxbat*.

Significantly, although the *Flogger-F* export ground attack aircraft resembles the MiG-27 outwardly, it is basically a MiG-23, with only the nose shape and low-pressure tyres of the Soviet Air Force's *Flogger-D*.

Mitsubishi F-1   Japan

Single-seat close-support fighter, in production and service.

Powered by: Two 7,070lb (3,207kg) st Ishikawajima-Harima TF40-IHI-801A (licence-built Rolls-Royce/Turboméca Adour) afterburning turbofans.
Span: 25ft 10¼in (7.88m).
Length: 58ft 6¾in (17.85m).
Empty weight: 14,017lb (6,358kg).
Gross weight: 30,146lb (13,674kg).
Max speed: Mach 1.6 (1,056mph; 1,700km/h) at 36,000ft (11,000m).
Combat radius: 173 miles (278km) with four Sidewinders and internal fuel only; 346 miles (556km) with two ASM-1s and an external tank.
Armament: One JM61 multi-barrel 20mm cannon. One underfuselage and four underwing attachments for twelve 500lb bombs, ASM-1 air-to-ship missiles, rockets or external fuel tanks. Two or four Sidewinder-class air-to-air missiles on wingtips.

The basic airframe, engines and systems of this efficient little fighter are similar to those of the Mitsubishi T-2 supersonic trainer (page 187). The F-1 prototypes were, in fact, conversions of the second and third production T-2s, making their first flights in single-seat form on June 7 and 3, 1975, respectively. Unlike the production F-1, the prototypes retained the rear cockpit and canopy of the T-2, but carried fire control equipment and test instrumentation instead of a second crew member. Only other external difference by comparison with the trainer was the installation of a passive warning radar antenna at the tip of the tail-fin. The initial production contract, for 18 F-1s, was placed in March 1976; eight more were ordered a year later. The first production aircraft flew on June 16, 1977, and the JASDF plans to acquire a total of 80 to equip four squadrons. The first squadron was formed in the spring of 1978, when deliveries began to the 3rd Squadron, JASDF, at Misawa AB in northern Japan. This squadron is a unit of the 3rd Air Wing, together with the 8th Squadron, which is scheduled to relinquish its F-86Fs for F-1s by 1980. Each squadron has an establishment of 18 aircraft.

Myasishchev M-4 (NATO code-name: Bison)

USSR

Four-jet long-range reconnaissance-bomber, in service.
The following data are estimated:

Powered by: Four 19,180lb (8,700kg) st Mikulin AM-3D turbojets.
Span: 165ft 7½in (50.48m).
Length: 154ft 10in (47.20m).
Loaded weight: 350,000lb (158,750kg).
Max speed: 560mph (900km/h) at 36,000ft (11,000m).
Unrefuelled range: 7,000 miles (11,265km) at 520mph (837km/h) with 10,000lb (4,535kg) of bombs.

Data: *Bison-B.*
Photo and silhouette: *Bison-C.*

This huge bomber, which was designed by V. M. Myasishchev, was described for many years as Russia's answer to the American B-52 Stratofortress. It was designed for the same task of carrying thermonuclear weapons over intercontinental ranges, with the help of flight refuelling in extreme cases. But it was probably contemporary with, rather than an "answer" to, the B-52, because it first put in an appearance over Moscow in May 1954, only two years after the first flight of the prototype Stratofortress.

In contrast with the B-52's four pairs of podded turbojets, the M-4 has only four engines in a buried wing-root installation. Its service ceiling is believed to be little more than 45,000ft (13,700m), which explains the heavy defensive armament. On the original bomber version (*Bison-A*), of which more than 40 are in service as flight refuelling tankers, this included ten 23mm cannon in twin-gun turrets in the tail, above the fuselage fore and aft of the wing and under the fuselage fore and aft of the bomb-bays. A modified version (*Bison-B*), with refuelling probe on a "solid" nose and new electronic equipment, appeared in the maritime reconnaissance role in 1964. A further maritime development (*Bison-C*) had a large radar in a lengthened nose, as shown in the photograph. A testbed version was powered by 28,660lb (13,000kg) st D-15 turbojets when used to set a series of payload-to-height records in 1959. Armament on these later versions is reduced to six 23mm guns. They appear to have been retired from maritime reconnaissance duties, but 40 *Bisons* still formed part of the 140-bomber fleet of the Soviet Long-Range Aviation force in 1978.

Nord 2501/2504 Noratlas

France

Twin-engined medium-range transport, in service.

Powered by: Two 2,040hp SNECMA (Bristol) Hercules 738 or 758 piston-engines.
Span: 106ft 7in (32.50m).
Length: 72ft 0in (21.96m).
Gross weight: 45,415lb (20,600kg).
Max speed: 273mph (440km/h).
Range: 1,550 miles (2,500km) with a $4\frac{1}{2}$-ton payload.
Armament: None.

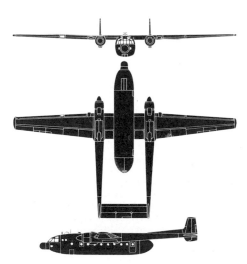

The original prototype Nord 2500 (first flown September 10, 1949) had 1,600hp Gnome-Rhone 14R engines. The second prototype, designated Nord 2501 and first flown on November 28, 1950, switched to Hercules engines and 200 aircraft of this type were built for the French Air Force; 30 were acquired by Israel and more than 20 by the Portuguese Air Force, including some bought second-hand. Twenty-five were built for Federal Germany, where a further 161 were produced under licence by Flugzeugbau Nord. None remain in Luftwaffe service. Four were transferred to the air force of Niger, six to Nigeria, about 50 to Greece, and others to commercial operators. Some of the French aircraft were fitted subsequently with a nose radome to serve with the Air Force as flying classrooms.

Maximum payload of the Nord 2501 is about $7\frac{1}{2}$ tons of cargo or 45 passengers, including paratroops. Other military variants were the 2504, of which five were supplied to the French Navy as flying classrooms for anti-submarine crews, with wingtip Marboré turbojets; and the 2508 transport, of which two were built with 2,500hp Pratt & Whitney R-2800 engines and wingtip-mounted Marborés, and were taken over by the German Air Force in 1963 to flight test equipment then under development for the Transall C-160 transport.

Data and photo: Nord 2501.
Silhouette: Nord 2501 flying classroom.

North American F-86 Sabre USA

Single-seat tactical fighter and fighter-bomber, in service.

Powered by: One 5,970lb (2,708kg) st General Electric J47-GE-27 turbojet.
Span: 39ft 1in (11.91m).
Length: 37ft 6½in (11.44m).
Empty weight: 11,125lb (5,046kg).
Max gross weight: 20,610lb (9,350kg).
Max speed: 687mph (1,105km/h) at sea level.
Range: 925 miles (1,488km) at 530mph (853km/h).
Armament: Six 0.50in machine-guns, plus two Sidewinder missiles, two 1,000lb bombs or eight rockets.

The Sabre first flew on October 1, 1947, and was produced as the USAF's first sweptwing fighter. It was widely used in the Korean War and was licence-built in Australia, Canada, Italy and Japan. North American built more than 6,000 of the F-86A, D, E, F, H and K versions. Of these, the F-86A, E, F and H were day fighters and fighter-bombers. The F-86D was an allweather interceptor with radar in a nose radome above the air intake and an afterburning engine. The F-86K, built by Fiat in Italy, was similar, for service with NATO air forces in Europe; and the F-86L, of which 981 were completed, was a conversion of the D with more advanced electronics. Although no longer operational with the USAF, versions of the Sabre still serve with nearly ten air forces, and surplus USAF Sabres are being converted to QF-86 target drones.

Canadair built 1,815 Sabres under licence between 1950 and 1958, for the RCAF, RAF and foreign air forces. The last version built was the Sabre Mk 6 with Orenda 14 turbojet; this remains in service as an interceptor in the Pakistan Air Force and as a trainer in South Africa.

A version of the F-86 with Rolls-Royce Avon engine was ordered by the RAAF from the Commonwealth Aircraft Corporation in 1951, and a prototype flew on August 3, 1953. This was followed by 111 production aircraft known as Sabre 30, 31 and 32. They were superseded in the RAAF by Mirage IIIs, but sufficient Avon-Sabre 32s to equip a single fighter-bomber squadron were transferred to the Indonesian Air Force, with which they continued to serve in 1978.

Data and silhouette: F-86F.
Photo: F-86K (Venezuela).

90

North American F-100 Super Sabre USA

Interceptor and fighter-bomber, in service.

Powered by: One 17,000lb (7,710kg) st Pratt & Whitney J57-P-21A afterburning turbojet.
Span: 38ft 9in (11.81m).
Length: 54ft 3in (16.53m).
Empty weight: 21,000lb (9,525kg).
Gross weight: 34,832lb (15,800kg).
Max speed: Mach 1.3 (864mph; 1,390km/h) at 36,000ft (11,000m).
Range: 1,500 miles (2,410km) with two external tanks.
Accommodation: Pilot only.
Armament: Four 20mm cannon in fuselage; six underwing pick-up points for bombs, rockets, air-to-air or air-to-surface missiles, etc.

First of the USAF's "Century Series" of fighters (so called because the "F" designations were 100 and above), the Super Sabre began life, as the name suggests, as a development of the F-86 Sabre. An official contract was placed in November 1951 and the prototype YF-100A flew on May 25, 1953. The first production model F-100A flew on October 29, 1953, and three aircraft were delivered to the USAF in the following month. The three principal variants were the F-100A interceptor, the F-100C fighter-bomber with a strengthened wing and the F-100D, also a fighter-bomber, with improved equipment and other changes. The F-100F was a two-seater with lengthened fuselage, capable of use as a trainer or an operational fighter. F-100s played a prominent part in the war in Vietnam in its early years and about 400 still served in 1978 with 11 Air National Guard units assigned to USAF Tactical Air Command; all were scheduled to be replaced with F-4s, A-7s, F-105s and A-10s by the end of FY 1979. Examples of all production variants were supplied under MDAP to other NATO nations, including Denmark and Turkey, which continue to operate the type. Others serve with the Nationalist Chinese Air Force, and the French Air Force still had a single squadron based in Djibouti in 1978.

Data and silhouette: F-100D.
Photo: F-100F (Denmark).

North American RA-5C Vigilante   USA

Carrier-based reconnaissance aircraft, in service.

Powered by: Two General Electric J79-GE-10 turbojets, each rated at 17,859lb (8,118kg) st with afterburning.
Span: 53ft 0in (16.15m).
Length: 76ft 7¼in (23.35m).
Empty weight: 40,900lb (18,552kg).
Gross weight: 66,800lb (30,300kg).
Max speed: Mach 2.1 (1,385mph; 2,230km/h) at 40,000ft (12,200m).
Range: 3,000 miles (4,825km).
Accommodation: Crew of two in tandem.
Armament: Four underwing pylons for nuclear or conventional bombs, missiles or external fuel tanks.

First flown on August 31, 1958 (as the XA3J-1), the Vigilante was designed primarily to deliver any type of bomb after operating from the deck of an aircraft carrier and to have a Mach 2 speed. A unique feature was the "linear" bomb bay, comprising a tunnel running the length of the fuselage, from which bombs were ejected at the aft end. As originally designed, the A3J-1 was to have had an XLR46-NA-2 rocket motor in addition to the jet engines but this scheme was abandoned. The A-5A Vigilante (57 delivered) entered service with VAH-7 in 1961, and was first operational at sea on board the USS *Enterprise* in February 1962. The A-5B Vigilante (six built, prototype first flown on April 29, 1962) was a long-range version of the A-5A with additional fuel in a "saddleback" fairing on the fuselage, but the attack role was abandoned before this version entered production and the RA-5C was adopted instead in a reconnaissance role. The RA-5C (55 originally ordered) is externally similar to the A-5B, with four underwing attachments for 333-gallon (1,515 litre) fuel tanks, bombs or missiles, and carries cameras, side-looking radar and other reconnaissance equipment in a long ventral fairing. The first RA-5C flew on June 30, 1962, and deliveries to the USN began in 1964. In addition to new production, 49 A-5As and Bs were converted to RA-5C standard. Then, in 1969, the type was re-instated in production to meet Vietnam needs, a total of 36 additional aircraft being completed, to which the above data apply. Earlier RA-5Cs have 17,000lb (7,710kg) st J79-GE-8 engines.

RA-5Cs still in USN service are to be replaced by 1980, on an interim basis, by F-14 Tomcats carrying reconnaissance pods.

North American T-28 Trojan and Sud-Aviation Fennec

USA; France

Two-seat basic trainer and light ground attack aircraft, in service.

Powered by: One 1,425hp Wright R-1820-56S piston-engine.
Span: 40ft 7½in (12.38m).
Length: 32ft 10in (10.00m).
Empty weight: 6,521lb (2,958kg).
Gross weight: 8,495lb (3,853kg).
Max speed: 380mph (611km/h).
Range: Over 500 miles (805km) with full weapon load.
Armament: Two 0.50in machine-gun packs, plus bombs, rockets, napalm, etc., on six underwing racks.

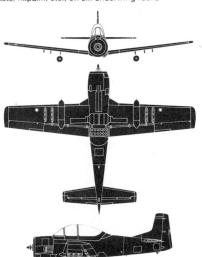

The North American NA-159 design, winner of a USAF competition in 1948 for a new trainer, bridged the gap between the earlier primary trainers of considerably lower power and the *ab initio* jet trainers now in use. At the time of its introduction into service, the T-28 was the most powerful aircraft ever used for primary training and was adopted by both the USAF and the US Navy. Production trainers for the USAF, with an 800hp Wright R-1300 engine, were designated T-28A; the prototype flew on September 26, 1949. With a 1,425hp R-1820 engine, the US Navy's T-28B was similar; the T-28C had deck landing arrester gear for training purposes. Trainer versions continue in service with many foreign air forces. In addition, several hundred surplus T-28s were adapted for ground attack duties. Carrying bombs, rockets and gun packs under the wings, the T-28D was evolved as a US version for operation in South Vietnam and the Congo, and still serves with several air forces, some designated AT-28D as attack trainers. A similar variant produced by Sud-Aviation in France was called the Fennec and was used in Algeria; Fennecs continue in service in the Argentine Navy, with the ability to operate from its carriers. A version of the T-28 with a turboprop engine, developed in Taiwan for the Nationalist Chinese Air Force, is described on page 130.

Data, photo and silhouette: T-28D.

93

Northrop F-5 and F-5E/F Tiger II — USA

Lightweight fighter, in production and service.

Powered by: Two 5,000lb (2,267kg) st General Electric J85-GE-21A afterburning turbojets.
Span: 26ft 8in (8.13m).
Length: 48ft 2in (14.68m).
Empty weight: 9,683lb (4,392kg).
Gross weight: 24,664lb (11,187kg).
Max speed: Mach 1.64 (1,082mph; 1,742km/h) at 36,000ft (11,000m).
Max range: 1,784 miles (2,871km).
Accommodation: Pilot only.
Armament: Two 20mm cannon in nose. One Sidewinder air-to-air missile on each wingtip; five pylons under fuselage and wings for assorted stores up to a total of 7,000lb (3,175kg).

Data and photo: F-5E Tiger II (Brazil).
Silhouette: F-5A.

The F-5 was the outcome of a project begun by Northrop in 1954 to develop a low-cost lightweight supersonic fighter. Construction of three N-156Fs began in May 1958, and the first of these flew on July 30, 1959. Production contracts were placed by the Department of Defense for N-156s to be supplied as the F-5A and RF-5A (single-seat) and F-5B (two-seat), mainly under mutual aid programmes, to Greece, Turkey, Morocco, Nationalist China, the Philippines, Thailand, South Vietnam, Iran, Ethiopia, Libya, Pakistan and South Korea. The Royal Norwegian AF ordered 108, including F-5Gs, camera-equipped RF-5Gs and F-5Bs for training. Spain acquired 36 SF-5As and 34 SF-5Bs, assembled by CASA and operated by the Spanish Air Force as C-9s and CE-9s respectively. Canadair built 89 CF-5A single-seaters and 44 two-seat CF-5Ds for the Canadian Armed Forces, plus 75 NF-5As and 30 NF-5Bs for the RNethAF. Eighteen of the CF-5As and two CF-5Ds were transferred to Venezuela. Following flight trials of a YF-5B-21 prototype, with uprated engines, manoeuvring flaps and other improvements, the USAF ordered a production version for supply to America's allies under the designation F-5E Tiger II. The first F-5E flew on August 11, 1972. Deliveries have been made to many countries, including South Korea, Kenya, Singapore, Thailand, Jordan, Saudi Arabia, Chile, Brazil, Malaysia and Iran, and F-5Es are built under licence in Taiwan and Switzerland for the airforces of these countries. Delivery of 50 Tiger IIs to the Egyptian Air Force was approved by the US government in the spring of 1978, by which time orders totalled 1,021, of which 778 had been delivered, including camera-carrying reconnaissance-fighters and two-seat F-5Fs (first flown September 25, 1974). The USAF bought 112 F-5Es as 'aggressors' to simulate hostile aircraft in air combat training; the US Navy has 10 F-5Es and 3 F-5Fs.

Panavia Tornado   Great Britain/Germany/Italy

Two-seat multi-role combat aircraft, in production.

Powered by: Two 16,000lb (7,264kg) st Turbo-Union RB.199-34R Mk 101 afterburning turbofans.
Span: 45ft 7¼in (13.90m) spread, 28ft 2½in (8.60m) swept.
Length: 54ft 9½in (16.70m).
Max weapon load carried by spring 1978: 16,000lb (7,257kq).
Max T-O weight: over 58,000lb (26,332kg).
Max speed: approx Mach 2.2 (1,452mph; 2,336km/h) at 36,000ft (11,000m).
Armament: Guided and semi-active homing air-to-air missiles, "scatter-weapons", and many types of nuclear and conventional air-to-surface weapons, according to version, on seven pylons under the fuselage and wings. Built-in armament comprises two 27mm Mauser cannon.

Data, photo and silhouette: Tornado GR.Mk 1.

Panavia Aircraft GmbH was set up in Munich in March 1969 to design and build a multi-role combat aircraft (MRCA) for service with the air forces of Great Britain, West Germany and Italy from 1977. Shareholders were British Aircraft Corporation (now British Aerospace) (42½%), Messerschmitt-Bölkow-Blohm (42½%) and Aeritalia (15%). A second company named Turbo-Union was established by Rolls-Royce (40%), MTU (40%) and Fiat (20%) to supply engines for the MRCA, which is a compact swing-wing aircraft able to fulfil six major duties: close air support/battlefield interdiction, interdictor strike, air superiority, interception, naval strike, and reconnaissance. In addition, all three member nations in the project require a trainer version. Nine prototypes were completed initially, four of them assembled in the UK, three in Germany and two in Italy. First to fly, on August 14, 1974, was the P-01 aircraft assembled by MBB. The ninth prototype flew in February 1977, as did the first of six pre-series aircraft. The name Tornado has been selected for the MRCA, and two batches of production aircraft, totalling 150, had been ordered by 1978. The RAF will eventually receive at least 385 Tornadoes, of which 220 will be interdictor/strike GR.Mk 1s to replace Vulcans and Buccaneers for overland strike, maritime strike and reconnaissance; the other 165 will be air defence F.Mk 2s to replace Phantoms, with longer fuselage, extended-chord wing roots, new fire control radar, extra fuel, and Sky Flash and AIM-9L Sidewinder air-to-air missiles. The German Air Force and Navy will receive 324 aircraft to replace F-104G Starfighters. The 100 Italian Air Force Tornadoes will replace F-104Gs and G91Rs for air superiority, ground attack and reconnaissance duties. Deliveries are scheduled to begin in 1979.

95

Republic F-105 Thunderchief

USA

Single-seat long-range tactical fighter-bomber, in service.

Powered by: One 26,500lb (12,030kg) st Pratt & Whitney J75-P-19W afterburning turbojet.
Span: 34ft 11¼in (10.65m).
Length: 67ft 0¼in (20.43m).
Empty weight: 27,500lb (12,475kg).
Gross weight: 52,838lb (23,967kg).
Max speed: Mach 2.1 (1,385mph; 2,230km/h) at 36,000ft (11,000m).
Max range: Over 2000 miles (3,220km).
Armament: One General Electric 20mm Vulcan multi-barrel gun, plus more than 14,000lb (6,350kg) of stores under fuselage and wings.

Development of the F-105 was started in 1951. Two prototypes, designated YF-105A, had J57-P-25 turbojets, and the first of these flew on October 22, 1955. A switch to the more powerful J75-P-3 or -5 engine changed the designation to F-105B on the next 75 aircraft, these being the first to feature the Thunderchief's unique swept-forward air intakes. Three trials aircraft were laid down in the reconnaissance role as RF-105Bs, but this version was not developed. Principal production version was the F-105D (600 built) with many improvements. A proposed two-seat version, the F-105E, was dropped, but 143 F-105Fs were ordered in 1962 for use as operational trainers. These had a 31-inch longer fuselage, second cockpit with dual controls, and taller fin; the first F-105F flew on June 11, 1963. The F-105D and F-105F played a major part in the air war in Vietnam. Continuous updating enabled them to carry the latest missiles and equipment, including advanced electronic countermeasures devices. About 30 F-105Ds were modified to have the T-Stick II bombing system, including electronics in a "saddle-back" fairing above the fuselage; the first of these flew with the new equipment on August 9, 1969. F-105Gs were Fs converted for the suppression of surface-to-air missile sites in Vietnam, with an ECM pod mounted on the lower sides of the fuselage, and four Shrike or two Standard ARM anti-radar missiles, and were known as Wild Weasels. Two squadrons of F-105Gs were still operational in TAC in 1978, but were to be replaced by F-4G Wild Weasels and these aircraft were then to be transferred to the ANG. In 1978, the ANG and AF Reserve had five groups or wings of F-105D/Fs and one of F-105Bs.

Data: F-105D. Photo and silhouette: F-105G.

Rockwell International OV-10 Bronco

USA

Observation and COIN aircraft, in production and service.

Powered by: Two 715eshp Garrett AiResearch T76-G-416/417 turboprops.
Span: 40ft 0in (12.19m).
Length: 41ft 7in (12.67m).
Empty weight: 6,969lb (3,161kg).
Gross weight: 14,466lb (6,563kg).
Max speed: 281mph (452km/h) clean at sea level.
Combat radius: 228 miles (367km) with max weapon load, no loiter.
Armament: Four 0.30in machine-guns in sponsons, which also carry maximum of 2,400lb external ordnance; provision for one Sidewinder AAM under each wing, and for 1,200lb load under fuselage. Max weapon load 3,600lb (1,633kg).

Data and silhouette: OV-10A.
Photo: OV-10D.

The North American NA300 won a design competition for a light multi-purpose counter-insurgency aircraft against entries from eight other companies. Seven prototypes were ordered, under the designation YOV-10A; and the first of these flew on July 16, 1965. These early aircraft had 660shp T76-GE-6/8 (handed) engines, span of 30ft (9.14m), max weight of 12,364lb (5,608kg) and "straight" sponsons. The sixth YOV-10A was modified in 1967 to production configuration with a 10ft increase in wing span, uprated engines as shown above, anhedral on the sponsons and a number of smaller modifications. The first production contracts were placed in October 1966 and deliveries began early in 1968. The USAF acquired 157 OV-10As for forward air control and secondary ground support duties; the US Marine Corps received 114 similar aircraft, of which 18 were loaned to the US Navy, for light armed reconnaissance, helicopter escort and forward air control duties in Vietnam. Production for the US services ended in April 1969; but the Thai Air Force ordered 32 OV-10Cs, while the Federal German government ordered 24 OV-10Bs for target towing duties. Eighteen of the latter have a General Electric J85 auxiliary turbojet mounted above the fuselage to boost their max speed to 393mph (632km/h), in which form they are redesignated OV-10B(Z) (first flown on September 21, 1970). Two YOV-10Ds (converted OV-10As) were armed night observation gunships for the US Marines, and are expected to be followed by 18 to 24 OV-10D conversions with 1,040ehp T76 engines, and an undernose sensor (FLIR and laser) designator. The first full-system OV-10D flew for the first time in February 1978. Sixteen OV-10Es ordered by Venezuela are similar to the OV-10A, as are 16 OV-16Fs supplied to Indonesia and 24 OV-10Gs ordered by South Korea in 1977.

Saab-35 Draken   Sweden

Single-seat fighter, reconnaissance aircraft and two-seat trainer, in service.

Powered by: One 17,650lb (8,000kg) st Volvo Flygmotor R.M.6C (Avon 300-series) afterburning turbojet.
Span: 30ft 10in (9.40m).
Length: 50ft 4in (15.35m).
Normal gross weight: 33,070lb (15,000kg).
Max speed: Mach 2 (1,320mph; 2,125km/h) at 36,000ft (11,000m).
Armament: Two 30mm cannon (optional). Racks under fuselage and wings for four Sidewinder air-to-air missiles, 9,000lb (4,080kg) of bombs, or rockets.

Data: Saab-35XD. Photo: S-35XS.
Silhouette: J35F.

Like the earlier Lansen, the Draken was designed to operate from auxiliary airstrips formed by sections of Sweden's main roads. The large area of its "double delta" wing helps to give it short take-off and landing runs. The first of three prototypes flew on October 25, 1955, with an imported Avon. The first production J35A interceptor for the Swedish Air Force flew on February 15, 1958, with a 15,200lb (6,895kg) st Swedish-built R.M.6B (200-series Avon) and this version entered service in 1960. It was followed by the J35B (first flown on November 29, 1959) with a more advanced fire-control system for collision-course tactics. This version entered service in 1961, but most J35As and Bs were converted subsequently to J35D standard, with 17,200lb (7,800kg) st R.M.6C engine, an improved autopilot and extra fuel. The prototype J35D flew on December 27, 1960, and this version became operational in 1964. Some J35As were also converted into SK35C two-seat dual-control trainers, to supplement new production. The S35E is a reconnaissance version with cameras in its nose.

Final production version for the Swedish Air Force was the J35F, basically similar to the D but with improved fire-control system and armament of one 30mm gun and two or four Falcon air-to-air missiles. The F was manufactured in greater numbers than any of its predecessors, and 17 Swedish allweather fighter squadrons, plus two reconnaissance squadrons, operated Drakens in 1978.

First export customer for the Draken was Denmark, which took delivery of 51 Saab-35XDs, with greatly increased weapon load and range, including 20 F-35 fighter-bombers, 20 RF-35 reconnaissance/fighters and 11 TF-35 trainer/fighters. They were followed by six Saab-35Bs supplied to Finland and 12 Saab-35Xs assembled by Valmet for the Finnish Air Force. Overload take-off weight of these export single-seaters, with nine 1,000lb bombs, is 35,275lb (16,000kg).

Saab-37 Viggen

Sweden

Single-seat multi-mission combat aircraft and two-seat trainer, in production and service.

Powered by: One 25,970lb (11,780kg) st Volvo Flygmotor R.M.8A (P. & W. JT8D-22) afterburning turbofan.
Span: 34ft 9¼in (10.60m).
Length: 53ft 5¾in (16.30m).
Normal gross weight: approx. 35,275lb (16,000kg).
Max speed: Mach 2 (1,320mph; 2,125km/h) at 36,000ft (11,000m).
Combat radius: 310–620 miles (500–1,000km).
Armament: Three attachments under fuselage and two under each wing, for RB04 or RB05 air-to surface missiles, or alternative 30mm gun packs, bombs, rockets or mines.

Data: AJ37.
Photo: SF37.
Silhouette: JA37.

The Viggen is a multi-mission combat aircraft, intended to replace the whole range of A32A Lansens, J35 and S35E Drakens and S32C Lansens used at present by the Swedish Air Force for attack, interception, and reconnaissance duties. Having pioneered the double-delta configuration with the Draken, Saab turned to an even more advanced aerodynamic shape for the Viggen, which uses a foreplane, fitted with flaps, in combination with a main delta wing. This, together with the great power of its engine, gives it STOL capability and it is able to operate from roads and runways only 550 yards (500m) long. The first of seven prototypes flew on February 8, 1967, and all were completed by July 2, 1970, when the SK37 tandem two-seat trainer version made its first flight. The initial production contracts, announced in 1967–68, were for a total of 175 of the AJ37 single-seat attack version, which has secondary interception capability, SK37 trainer, and SF/SH37 armed reconnaissance aircraft for overland and maritime operations respectively. The other major version is the JA37 single-seat interceptor, which can be used also for attack. An initial batch of 30 production JA37s was ordered in 1974, and approval for production of a further 119 was given in 1978, to re-equip at least eight Draken squadrons in 1978–85. The first production AJ37 flew on February 23, 1971, and deliveries to F7 Wing of the Swedish Air Force began in June 1971. Two squadrons of this Wing and one squadron of F15 were equipped with AJ37s by early 1978.

Following the first flight of an SF37 Viggen on May 21, 1973, deliveries to F21 Wing began in April 1977. The SH37 Viggen, first flown on December 10, 1973, already equipped one squadron of F13 and was being delivered to F17 in 1977. The prototype of the SK37 two-seat trainer flew on July 2, 1970 and production deliveries began in June 1972.

Saab-105   Sweden

Two-seat basic trainer and light attack aircraft, in service.

Powered by: Two 2,850lb (1,293kg) st General Electric J85-GE-17B turbojets.
Span: 31ft 2in (9.50m).
Length: 35ft 5in (10.80m).
Empty weight: 6,173lb (2,800kg).
Max gross weight: 14,330lb (6,500kg).
Max speed: 603mph (970km/h) at sea level.
Range: 1,820 miles (2,930km) at 43,000ft (13,100m) with external tanks.
Armament: Six underwing attachments for up to 4,410lb (2,000kg) of Minigun or 30mm gun packs, rockets, rocket packs, bombs, Sidewinder missiles, or reconnaissance packs.

Although it is operated mainly as a two-seater in its military roles, the Saab-105 is a multi-purpose light twin-jet aircraft capable of accommodating two more people on rear seats behind the crew. It was developed as a private venture, the first of two prototypes flying for the first time on June 29, 1963. Early in the following year, Saab received a Royal Swedish Air Board contract for 130 production models, each powered by two 1,640lb (743kg) st Turboméca Aubisque turbofans. Subsequently, a further 20 were ordered. The first production model flew on August 27, 1965, and deliveries of the basic SK60A trainer to the Swedish Air Force began in the spring of 1966. Some were returned to Saab to be fitted with attachments for weapons and a gunsight, in which form they are designated SK60B; although still used mainly for training, they are now capable of quick conversion to attack configuration. In addition, a small number of the As that were modified to B standard were fitted with a permanent panoramic reconnaissance camera installation in the nose, as shown in the silhouette drawings. The prototype of this version, the SK60C, flew on January 18, 1967; full attack capability is retained. Austria has 40 Saab-105Ös (developed from the prototype Saab-105XT) with General Electric J85 turbojets, higher performance and much increased weapon load. The first of these flew on February 17, 1970 and deliveries began soon afterwards. The Saab-105G was a further development with increased armament, more advanced avionics and refined controls. It first flew on May 26, 1972, but did not go into production.

Data: Saab-105Ö.
Photo and silhouette: SK60C.

SEPECAT Jaguar

Great Britain/France

Single-seat light tactical support aircraft, in production and service.

Powered by: Two 7,305lb (3,313kg) st Rolls-Royce/Turboméca Adour 102 afterburning turbofans.
Span: 28ft 6in (8.69m).
Length: 55ft 2½in (16.83m).
Max gross weight: 34,000lb (15,500kg).
Max speed: Mach 1.5 (990mph; 1,593km/h) at 36,000ft (11,000m).
Max range: 2,614 miles (4,210km) with external tanks.
Armament: Two 30mm Aden guns in lower fuselage. One attachment under fuselage and four under wings for up to 10,000lb (4,500kg) of stores (Martel missiles, 1,000lb bombs, napalm tanks, rocket pods, reconnaissance packs, etc).

Evolved from Breguet's Br 121 project, the Jaguar is a lightweight dual-role aircraft that has been

Data and silhouette: Jaguar GR Mk 1.
Photo: Jaguar International.

built in five main versions: Jaguar A is a single-seat tactical support aircraft for the French Air Force; its RAF counterpart is the Jaguar S; Jaguar E is a two-seat advanced trainer for the French services, its RAF counterpart being the Jaguar B. Jaguar International is the export version. Development and production were undertaken by an international company known as SEPECAT, formed by BAC (now British Aerospace) and Dassault/Breguet.

Development of the Jaguar began in 1965, and the first of the two prototypes of the Jaguar E was first flown on September 8, 1968. It was followed by the second E on February 11, 1969 and the two proto-type Jaguar As on March 29 and May 27, 1969. The two British single-seat prototypes flew on October 12, 1969 and June 12, 1970. The final prototype, a Jaguar B, flew for the first time on August 30, 1971. The first production Jaguar E flew on November 2, 1971, and deliveries of this version began in 1972. The RAF took delivery of 165 Ss, designated Jaguar GR.Mk 1 in service, sufficient for eight first-line squadrons, and the first of these flew on October 11, 1972. The first squadron, No 54, was formed in March 1974. The full production standard includes a laser rangefinder and marked target seeker in the nose and an electronic countermeasures pack near the tip of the fin. Two of the RAF squadrons operate Jaguars in a recon-naissance role, with an external camera/sensor pack. In addition, 37 Jaguar B (designated T.Mk 2) two-seaters were delivered for operational conversion and continuation training. France is acquiring 200 Jaguars (160 A, 40 E); and Jaguar Internationals have been delivered to Ecuador (12) and Oman (10 single-seat and two two-seat), with 8,600lb (3,900kg) st Adour 804 engines, and provision for night sensors and dog-fight missiles on overwing pylons.

Shin Meiwa PS-1 and US-1   Japan

Four-turboprop STOL anti-submarine flying-boat, in production and service.

Powered by: Four 3,060eshp Ishikawajima-Harima (General Electric) T64-IHI-10 turboprops.
Span: 108ft 9in (33.15m).
Length: 109ft 9¼in (33.46m).
Empty weight: 58,000lb (26,300kg).
Gross weight: 94,800lb (43,000kg).
Max speed: 340mph (547km/h) at 5,000ft (1,525m).
Ferry range: 2,948 miles (4,744km) at 196mph (315km/h).
Accommodation: Crew of ten, comprising two pilots, a flight engineer, two sonar operators, navigator, MAD operator, radio and radar operators, and a tactical co-ordinator.
Armament: Two underwing pods, between each pair of engine nacelles, each contain two homing torpedoes; six 5in rockets on attachments under wingtips; four 330lb anti-submarine bombs in weapon-bay.

Data and silhouette: PS-1.
Photo: US-1.

The big PS-1 flying-boat is a rarity at a time when most anti-submarine aircraft are land-based or carrier-borne. It has many novel features, including a built-in tricycle beaching gear which enables it to move on the ground under its own power. A 1,400shp General Electric T58-IHI-10 shaft-turbine is housed in the upper centre portion of the hull to provide compressed air for the "blown" flaps and tail surfaces which help to give the PS-1 STOL capability. It will take off from a calm sea in 820ft (250m) and land in 590ft (180m). It has been designed to operate in winds of up to 25 knots and waves 10ft (3m) high. The PS-1 is designed to alight and take off repeatedly, to dip its large sonar deep into the sea, while searching for submarines. Other operational equipment includes a searchlight, search radar in the nose, magnetic anomaly detector (MAD), sono-buoys and electronic countermeasures installation. The prototype, known as the PX-S, flew on October 5, 1967, and was followed by a second in mid-1968. They were delivered to a Maritime Self-Defence Force test squadron in 1968, and had been followed by 15 production aircraft by early 1978, most of them operated by No 51 Squadron of the JMSDF. Three US-1 amphibious search and rescue models have also been delivered, to No 71 SAR Squadron. Basically similar to the PS-1, the US-1 has a retractable tricycle undercarriage capable of use for conventional take-off and landing ashore, and a slightly less powerful (1,250shp) T58 engine for its STOL system. It is equipped normally to carry a crew of nine, and 12 survivors on stretchers. Alternatively, it could be equipped to carry 36 stretchers or 69 passengers. Current orders, in 1978, cover the manufacture of five more anti-submarine PS-1s.

Soko/CIAR Orao/IAR-93   Yugoslavia/Romania

Single-seat ground attack fighter, under development.

Powered by: Two 4,000lb (1,814kg) st Rolls-Royce Viper Mk 632-41 turbojets.
Span: 24ft 9¾in (7.56m).
Length: 42ft 3¾in (12.90m).
Empty weight: 9,480lb (4,300kg).
Gross weight: 19,840lb (9,000kg).
Max speed: Mach 0.95 (627mph; 1,009km/h) at 36,000ft (11,000m).
Service ceiling: 42,650ft (13,000m).
Combat radius: 124-248 miles (200-400km) with 4,410lb (2,000kg) external stores, depending on altitude flown.
Armament: Two 30mm cannon. One under-fuselage and four underwing attachments for 4,410lb (2,000kg) of external stores.

Identified originally as the Jurom (*Ju*goslavia-*Rom*ania), this Jaguar-like tactical fighter is being developed afterburners to give each turbojet a ments less dependent on combat aircraft provided by the super-powers. It is known as the Orao (Eagle) in Yugoslavia, and as the IAR-93 in Romania. Design and manufacture are being shared by the industries of these countries, with the engines and much of the equipment coming from western Europe. The first prototype is believed to have flown in August 1974, followed by two more prototypes and nine pre-production aircraft. Non-afterburning Vipers have been fitted initially, but press reports have suggested that production Orao/IAR-93s may have Rolls-Royce-developed afterburners to give each turbojet a maximum output of 5,950lb (2,700kg) st. This would increase the gross weight to 22,700lb (10,300kg), permitting a 50% greater weapon load. Max speed at altitude would increase to about Mach 1.6, with Mach 1.0 attainable at low altitude. First flight of a production aircraft was expected to take place in 1977/78, with the Romanian and Yugoslav Air Forces each likely to take about 100.

Data, photo and silhouette: Prototypes.

Soko J-1 and RJ-1 Jastreb   Yugoslavia

Single-seat light attack aircraft, in production and service.

Powered by: One 3,000lb (1,360kg) st Rolls-Royce Viper 531 turbojet.
Span: 38ft 4in (11.68m) with wingtip tanks.
Length: 35ft 8½in (10.88m).
Empty weight: 6,217lb (2,820kg).
Gross weight: 11,245lb (5,100kg).
Max speed: 510mph (820km/h) at 20,000ft (6,100m).
Max range: 945 miles (1,520km).
Armament: Three 0.50in Colt-Browning machine-guns in nose; eight underwing attachments for two bombs of up to 550lb each, and 57mm or 127mm rockets.

The Jastreb is a light attack version of the Galeb two-seat basic trainer described on page 208, with modified wings, more powerful engine and heavier armament provisions. Its electrical system has been augmented to make the aircraft independent of ground supply for engine starting. Optional equipment includes assisted take-off rockets. Two prototypes were flying by early 1968, when the type was already in production for the Yugoslav Air Force and available for export. Four Jastrebs were supplied to Zambia in 1971.

New versions are the export J-1-E with updated equipment, first flown in 1975, of which several have already been ordered; and the tandem two-seat TJ-1 Jastreb Trainer, with full operational capability, of which deliveries to the Yugoslav Air Force and export customers began in January 1975.

There are specialised tactical reconnaissance versions of both the J-1 and J-1-E, designated RJ-1 and RJ-1-E respectively. The RJ-1 for the Yugoslav Air Force has one camera in the fuselage and two further cameras in the noses of the wingtip tanks. The RJ-1-E can be supplied with three Vinten 360/140A cameras in similar locations for daylight reconnaissance, or a single Vinten 1025/527 camera at the fuselage station for night operations, with flash bombs or high-explosive bombs on the underwing attachments.

Data, photo and silhouette: J-1 Jastreb.

Sukhoi Su-7B
(NATO code-names: Fitter-A and Moujik)

USSR

Single-seat ground-attack fighter, in service.

Powered by: One 22,050lb (10,000kg) st Lyulka AL-7F-1 (TRD 31) afterburning turbojet.
Span: 29ft 3½in (8.93m).
Length: 57ft 0in (17.37m).
Max gross weight: 29,750lb (13,500kg).
Max speed: Mach 1.6 (1,055mph; 1,700km/h) at 36,000ft (11,000m); 530mph (850km/h) at sea level without afterburning.
Max range: 900 miles (1,450km).
Armament: Two 30mm cannon in wing roots; attachments under wings for bombs (usually two 750kg and two 500kg) or rocket pods. External load reduced to 2,200lb (1,000kg) when two underbelly fuel tanks are carried.

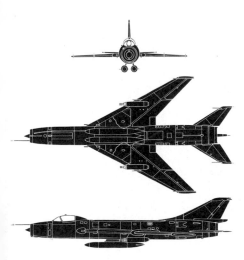

This sweptwing fighter was for many years standard equipment in Soviet ground attack squadrons and about 400 remain in Soviet service. Su-7s were also supplied to the Afghan, Algerian, Cuban, Czech, Peruvian, Polish, East German, Hungarian, North Korean, North Vietnamese, Egyptian, Iraqi, Romanian, Syrian and Indian air forces. The fuselage, power plant and tail unit appear to be almost identical with those of the delta-wing Su-11, with the same provision for carrying two external fuel tanks under the centre-fuselage. The Su-7 was one of four single-seat fighter aircraft seen for the first time, in prototype form, at the 1956 Tushino display, the others being the MiG-21, the Su-9 and a sweptwing counterpart of the MiG-21 which was allocated the NATO code-name *Faceplate*. It seems probable that the Su-7 and *Faceplate* were evaluated in competition to find a new fighter for close-support duties, and that the Sukhoi design was chosen, as *Faceplate* did not enter service. When first seen, the Su-7 had its pitot boom mounted centrally above the air intake; but current versions have the boom offset to starboard. Very large area-increasing wing-flaps are fitted, extending from the root to more than mid-span. Wing sweep is approximately 60°, with fences at about mid-span and just inboard of the tip of each wing. Major variants are the Su-7B and the Su-7BM which can be identified by the bulged doors which enclose its low-pressure nosewheel tyre when the undercarriage is retracted. A tandem two-seat version is used for training and has the NATO code-name *Moujik*.

Data and silhouette: Su-7B.
Photo: Su-7BM.

Sukhoi Su-9 and Su-11 (NATO code-names: Fishpot and Maiden)

USSR

Single-seat all-weather fighter, in service.
The following data are estimated:

Powered by: One 22,050lb (10,000kg) st Lyulka AL-7F-1 afterburning turbojet.
Span: 27ft 8in (8.43m).
Length: 56ft 0in (17.00m).
Gross weight: 30,000lb (13,600kg).
Max speed: Mach 1.8 (1,190mph; 1,915km/h) at 36,000ft (11,000m).
Armament: Two *Anab* infra-red and/or radar homing air-to-air missiles under wings. No guns.

In its prototype form, as seen in the 1956 Soviet Aviation Day display in Moscow, this delta-wing all-weather fighter had a small conical radome above its air intake and was allocated the NATO code-name *Fishpot-A*. On initial production aircraft (*Fishpot-B*), the radome forms a centre-body in the circular air intake. The resulting fighter bears a superficial resemblance to the MiG-21, but is considerably heavier and has a much more powerful (Lyulka AL-7F) engine, rated at 19,840lb (9,000kg) st with afterburning. It is a generally cleaner design, with a more sturdy-looking undercarriage and with no cut-out at the roots of the tailplane trailing-edge.

Fishpot-B probably has a better all-weather capability than the MiG-21. It is normally seen with a pair of external fuel tanks side-by-side under the centre-fuselage. A developed version, first seen at Tushino in 1961, has a new forward fuselage of longer and less-tapered form, with enlarged centrebody, and uprated engine; this is now known to be designated Su-11 (*Fishpot-C*). Both versions are in large-scale service, together with operational trainers (NATO *Maiden*) with tandem cockpits like those of the Su-7 trainer (NATO *Moujik*).

Up to the present, the Su-9 and Su-11 have been identified in service only with the Soviet Air Force, making up nearly 25 per cent of its 2,600-strong interceptor force.

Data and silhouette: Su-11.
Photo: Su-9.

Sukhoi Su-15
(NATO code-name: Flagon)

USSR

Single-seat interceptor, in production and service.

Powered by: Two turbojets with afterburning.
Span (estimated): 30ft 0in (9.15m).
Length (estimated): 68ft 0in (20.50m).
Gross weight: 35,275lb (16,000kg).
Max speed (estimated): Mach 2.5 (1,650mph; 2,655km/h) at 36,000ft (11,000m).
Combat radius: 450 miles (725km).
Armament: One radar-homing *Anab* missile and one infra-red homing *Anab* on underwing pylons. No guns.

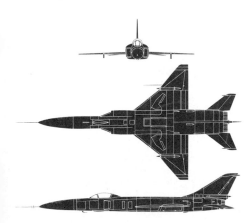

Data: *Flagon-A.*
Photo and silhouette: *Flagon-F.*

One of several types of Soviet aircraft making their first public appearance at the Domodedovo flying display in July 1967 was this high-performance interceptor, a product of the Sukhoi design bureau and now known to be designated Su-15. In addition to a single black-painted example, probably a prototype, in which Vladimir Ilyushin performed aerobatics, nine fighters of the same type appeared in formation, suggesting that the Su-15 had reached squadron service. Some carried an *Anab* air-to-air missile beneath each wing. The initial production fighter (NATO code-name *Flagon-A*), built in small numbers, had wings and tail surfaces almost identical to those of the Su-11. Also at Domodedovo in 1967 was a variant known as *Flagon-B*, which had STOL performance through the addition of lift-jets amidships. These engines were located aft of the cockpit and between the jet pipes of the two propulsion engines Doors in the top of the fuselage hinged up to form air intakes for the lift-jet engines when they were in use. *Flagon-B*, which was a development aircraft rather than a service type, had extended wing-tips with reduced sweepback on the leading-edge of the outer panels. In other respects, it appeared to be a standard *Flagon-A*.
The first major production version, *Flagon-D*, also has wings of compound sweep, produced by reducing the sweepback at the tips via a narrow unswept section. This increases the span to about 34ft 6in (10.53m). *Flagon-C* is similar, but has two seats in tandem and is probably a trainer with combat capability. Speed and range improvements came with the installation of new and more powerful engines in *Flagon-E*. Wings and conical radome were unchanged from the "D", but the electronics were uprated, and this became the major production version from 1973. The latest *Flagon-F* differs in having an ogival radome.

Sukhoi Su-17, Su-20 and Su-22 (NATO code-name: Fitter-C and D)

USSR

Single-seat ground-attack fighter, in production and service.

The following data are estimated:
Powered by: One 25,000lb (11,350kg) st Lyulka AL-21F-3 afterburning turbojet.
Span: 45ft 11¼in (14.00m) spread; 34ft 9½in (10.60m) swept.
Length: 61ft 6¼in (18.75m).
Empty weight: 22,050lb (10,000kg).
Max gross weight: 41,887lb (19,000kg).
Max speed: Mach 2.17 (1,430mph; 2,300km/h) at 36,000ft (11,000m); Mach 1.05 at sea level.
Combat radius: 224–391 miles (360–630km) with 4,410lb (2,000kg) of external stores.
Armament: Two 30mm cannon in wing roots. Max weapon load 11,023lb (5,000kg).

Data and photo: Su-17.
Silhouette: Su-20.

The prototype of this ground-attack fighter is believed to have been the first variable-geometry aircraft test-flown in the Soviet Union. When it appeared at the 1967 Aviation Day display at Domodedovo Airport it was regarded as a test-bed, built to evaluate the merits of a swing-wing as economically as possible. It differed from the standard Su-7 only in having the outer 13ft (4.0m) of each wing pivoted, with one very large fence and two smaller ones near the tip of each inner, fixed panel. There was a full-span leading-edge slat on each outer panel.

Photographs taken at Domodedovo suggested that this prototype had weapon attachments built into the bottom of its two large wing fences. The significance of these was made clear when one or two squadrons of similar aircraft were discovered to be in front-line service with the Soviet Air Force in 1972. Since then, several hundred have been delivered to Soviet tactical squadrons, all differing from the prototype in having a second nose-probe, a dorsal spine fairing between the cockpit canopy and fin, and a total of eight weapon attachments under the wings and fuselage. There are at least four different models. The basic Soviet Air Force Su-17 is most powerful, with a Lyulka AL-21F-3 afterburning turbojet, and has more advanced equipment than the Su-20 exported to Egypt and Poland. Both are known to NATO as *Fitter-C*. A Soviet Air Force variant is *Fitter-D*, identified by a small, flat radome under its nose and laser marked target seeker in the bottom of its intake centre-body. It is assumed that the Su-20 retains an engine similar to that of the Su-7. The Su-22, of which 36 examples have been delivered to Peru, is even less like the Su-17, with an earlier type of warning radar, mountings for veteran *Atoll* air-to-air missiles and virtually no navigation aids.

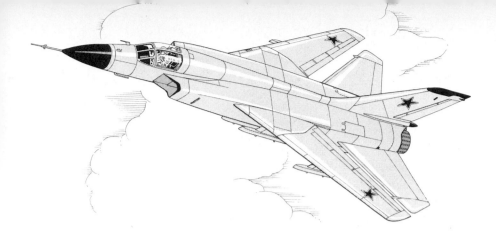

Sukhoi Su-19 (NATO code-name: Fencer)　　USSR

Two-seat variable-geometry attack aircraft, in production and service.

Powered by: Two afterburning turbojets, each probably rated at about 25,000lb (11,340kg) st.
Span: 56ft 3in (17.15m) spread, 31ft 3in (9.53m) swept.
Length: 69ft 10in (21.29m).
Gross weight: 68,000lb (30,850kg).
Max speed: Mach 2.5 (1,650mph; 2,655km/h) at 36,000ft (11,000m).
Combat radius: 200 miles (322km) at low altitude.
Armament: One GSh-23 twin-barrel 23mm cannon. Six underwing and underfuselage attachments for more than 10,000lb (4,535kg) of guided and unguided air-to-surface weapons.

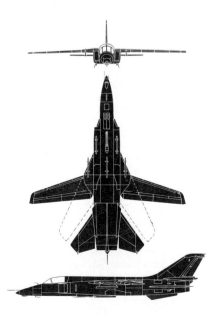

Nothing was known publicly about this Soviet counterpart of the F-111 and Tornado until 1974, when Admiral Thomas H. Moorer, then Chairman of the US Joint Chiefs of Staff, referred to it as "the first modern Soviet fighter to be developed specifically as a fighter-bomber for the ground attack mission". One year later, Su-19s were already based in western Russia, probably with an operational evaluation unit; but not a single good photograph of the type had become available by the Summer of 1978 and the accompanying illustrations must be regarded as provisional. Layout is known to be fairly conventional, with side-by-side seating for the crew of two, and a vertical tail unit of typical Sukhoi form. The air intake trunks probably derive from Su-15 technology, and the turbojets may well be similar to the Lyulka AL-21F-3s of the Soviet Air Force's Su-17. Wing sweep is believed to be about 23 degrees spread, 70 degrees fully swept; an interesting feature is the first known Soviet use of pivoting weapon pylons under the variable-geometry outer panels. At least 250 Su-19s were operational by early 1978, each able to carry about five times the weapon load five times as far as the aircraft they replaced. Such range would enable them to attack targets anywhere in England from bases in East Germany.

Transall C-160

France/Germany

Twin-turboprop medium-range transport, in production and service.

Powered by: Two 6,100shp Rolls-Royce Tyne R.Ty.20 Mk 22 turboprops.
Span: 131ft 3in (40.0m).
Length: 106ft 3½in (32.40m).
Empty weight: 63,400lb (28,758kg).
Gross weight: 108,250lb (49,100kg).
Max speed: 333mph (536km/h) at 15,000ft (4,500m).
Range: 2,832 miles (4,558km) with 8-ton payload.
Accommodation: Crew of four, 93 troops, 61–81 paratroops, 62 litters or 35,270lb (16,000kg) freight.
Armament: None.

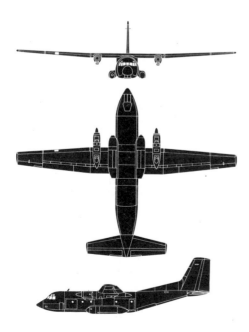

Photo: C-160F.

The Transall (Transporter Allianz) C-160 resulted from design collaboration between French and German companies which, in January 1959, undertook the joint production of a medium transport to meet the requirements of the Armée de l'Air and Luftwaffe, with possible commercial applications also. The Rolls-Royce Tyne engines were built by a British/French/Belgian/German consortium, and equipment includes a Smiths flight control system which was intended to be used as the basis of an automatic landing system. Operation from semi-prepared surfaces was one of the original requirements of the design, and there was provision (never utilised) for fitting two auxiliary turbojets under the outer wings to reduce the take-off run.

The first of three flying prototypes was assembled in France by Nord-Aviation (now part of Aérospatiale) and flew on February 25, 1963. The second, assembled in Germany by VFW (later VFW-Fokker), flew on May 25, 1963. The third, assembled in Germany by Hamburger Flugzeugbau (now part of Messerschmitt-Bölkow-Blohm), flew on February 19, 1964. Nord began flight testing the first of six C-160A pre-production aircraft, with a 20-inch longer fuselage, on May 21, 1965. The first production C-160s were completed in 1967. Subsequent deliveries totalled 52 C-160Fs for France, 108 similar C-160Ds to replace the Luftwaffe's Noratlas, and nine C-160Zs for the South African Air Force. Twenty of the C-160Ds were transferred to the Turkish Air Force, and four C-160Fs were modified into C-160Ps for the French night mail service. Production ended in October 1972, but was restarted in 1977 to meet an Armée de l'Air requirement for 25 additional aircraft. Four of these were funded in 1978, with 10 to follow in FY 1979 and the rest in FY 1980. The new-batch aircraft, which will be assembled only in France, do not have the forward cargo loading door; their avionics are updated and other small changes have been made.

Tupolev Tu-16 (NATO code-name: Badger)

USSR

Twin-jet medium bomber, in service.
The following data are estimated:

Powered by: Two 20,950lb (9,500kg) st Mikulin AM-3M turbojets.
Span: 110ft 0in (33.50m).
Length: 120ft 0in (36.50m).
Gross weight: 150,000lb (68,000kg).
Max speed: 587mph (945km/h) at 35,000ft (10,700m).
Range: 3,975 miles (6,400km) at 480mph (770km/h) with 3 tons of bombs.
Accommodation: Crew of six.
Armament: *Badger-A* has seven 23mm cannon, in pairs in dorsal, ventral and tail turrets and singly on starboard side of nose, plus nine tons of bombs in bomb-bay. *Badger-G* is similar except that two rocket-powered *Kelt* air-to-surface anti-shipping missiles are carried under wings. *Badger-C* has a large nose radome, precluding fitment of the nose cannon, and carries a *Kipper* air-to-surface missile under the fuselage.

First seen in a Moscow fly-past in 1954, the Tu-16 has been a standard Soviet medium-range reconnaissance-bomber ever since. It is the aircraft from which the Tu-104 airliner was evolved. Some 2,000 appear to have been built, of which about 300 are still in service with the Soviet Long-Range Aviation force, supported by a few Tu-16 flight refuelling tankers, and more than 100 reconnaissance and ECM variants. The Naval Air Fleet has nearly 300 Tu-16 missile-carriers, 80 tankers and 70 reconnaissance/ECM models. Nine of the basic *Badger-A*s were supplied to the Iraqi Air Force, and about 75 are operational with the Chinese Air Force, mostly built in China. Indonesia received about 24 early *Badgers*, with provision to carry a *Kennel* missile under each wing; these are no longer in use.

The Soviet Naval Air Fleet uses five versions of *Badger* as long-range reconnaissance-bombers. Of these, *Badger-C* was first shown in the 1961 Aviation Day flypast over Moscow, and has a large radome built into its nose, plus provision for carrying a *Kipper* anti-shipping missile. *Badger-D* (with nose radome) has under-fuselage electronic blisters. *Badger-E* has a glazed nose and windows in its bomb-bay doors for a battery of reconnaissance cameras; while *Badger F* has electronic pods on underwing pylons. *Badger-G* carries two rocket-powered *Kelt* missiles under its wings; most examples are flown by Soviet naval crews, but some were supplied to Egypt and were used operationally against Israeli targets in the 1973 Yom Kippur war. All versions can refuel in flight from other *Badgers*, using a unique wingtip-to-wingtip hose technique.

Photo: *Badger-D.*
Silhouette: *Badger-G.*

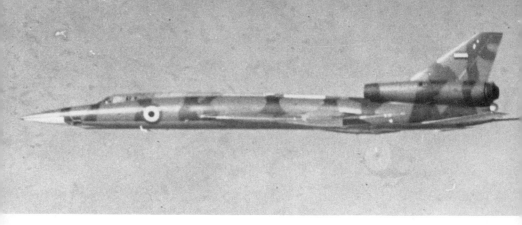

Tupolev Tu-22
(NATO code-name: Blinder)

USSR

Twin-jet supersonic bomber, in service.
The following data are estimated:

Powered by: Two unidentified turbojets with afterburners, rated at about 27,000lb (12,250kg) st each.
Span: 90ft 10½in (27.70m).
Length: 132ft 11½in (40.53m).
Gross weight: About 185,000lb (83,900kg).
Max speed: Mach 1.4 (920mph; 1,480km/h) at 40,000ft (12,000m).
Max range: 1,400 miles (2,250km).
Accommodation: Crew of three.
Armament: *Blinder-B* carries *Kitchen* missile semi-recessed in fuselage undersurface; radar-controlled tail gun.

This rear-engined bomber was first shown at the 1961 Tushino air display, prior to which time it was unknown to the West. Ten examples flew overhead on that occasion: of these, nine appeared to be reconnaissance-bombers, with a fairly small internal weapon-bay and a pointed nose radome. The tenth carried a *Kitchen* (NATO code-name) air-to-surface missile under its belly and was fitted with a considerably larger radome. In both cases there were large windows in the bottom of the fuselage, immediately aft of the radome, for visual bomb-aiming or cameras.
At the 1967 air display over Domodedovo, a total of 22 Tu-22s appeared, most of them carrying *Kitchen* missiles. All had flight refuelling probes and the wider radome of the single example seen previously. This version is now identified as *Blinder-B*, while the version carrying internally-housed free-fall weapons is *Blinder-A*. A total of about 140 of the two models remain operational with the Soviet Air Force, and 12 have been supplied to Libya. A third version, *Blinder-C*, can be identified by the six windows for reconnaissance cameras in its bomb-bay doors. There is also a trainer version (*Blinder-D*) with an extra pilot's cockpit above and to the rear of the standard position. Of the 250 Tu-22s thought to have been built, about 65 were transferred to the Naval Air Force, which continues to use about 50 as shore-based attack bombers and reconnaissance aircraft; an ECM version has also been reported.

Photo and silhouette: *Blinder-B*.

112

Tupolev Tu-26 (NATO code-name: Backfire) USSR

Supersonic variable-geometry strategic bomber, in production and service.

Powered by: Two afterburning turbofans, probably related to the 44,090lb (20,000kg) st Kuznetsov NK-144s used in the Tu-144 supersonic airliner.
Span: 113ft 0in (34.45m) spread, 86ft 0in (26.21m) swept.
Length: 132ft 0in (40.23m).
Gross weight: 270,000lb (122,500kg).
Max speed: Mach 2.25 to 2.5 (1,485-1,650mph; 2,390-2,665km/h).
Max combat radius: 3,570 miles (5,745km).
Armament: Single gun in radar-directed tail mounting. Nominal weapon load of 20,800lb (9,435kg), including *Kitchen* or *Kingfish* missile and the complete range of Soviet nuclear and conventional free-fall weapons.

Data: *Backfire-B* **(estimated).**
Photo and silhouette: *Backfire-B.*

Failure of the Tu-22 to fulfil its planned role as a supersonic strategic bomber, through inadequate range, required the Tupolev design bureau to try again, and the existence of a Soviet variable-geometry (swing-wing) medium bomber was acknowledged in the West by 1969. Apprehension was allayed a little when reports indicated that the original version of the bomber (known to NATO as *Backfire-A*) also seemed unlikely to achieve its intended range. However, this was soon remedied by redesign, including an extension of the wing span and deletion of the large main landing gear pods on the inner wings. It was soon apparent that, even without flight refuelling or staging from bases in the Arctic, the redesigned *Backfire-B* could attack virtually anywhere in the continental USA on a one-way mission, with recovery in a third country such as Cuba. Using Arctic staging and refuelling, it could achieve similar coverage and return to its base in the USSR. The nuclear-warhead *Kingfish* missile developed for *Backfire* is equally formidable if, as has been suggested, it is rocket-powered and extremely accurate, with a span of 8ft $2\frac{1}{2}$in (2.50m), length of 34ft 6in (10.50m) and range of 375 miles (600km) at high supersonic speed. This is but one of the weapons which caused an RAF Chief of Air Staff to comment that *Backfires* in Naval Aviation service may represent a greater danger to allied shipping than do the relatively slow-moving Russian submarines.

Up to twelve pre-production *Backfires* appear to have followed the prototypes. Production of *Backfire-A* was then limited to sufficient aircraft for a single Soviet Air Force squadron. By early 1978, more than 100 *Backfire-Bs* were operational with the Air Force and Naval Air Fleet, with production thought to be continuing at the rate of 36 per year towards an eventual force of at least 250, and perhaps as many as 400 aircraft.

Tupolev Tu-28P
(NATO code-name: Fiddler)

USSR

Two-seat all-weather fighter, in service.
The following data are estimated:

Powered by: Two unidentified turbojets with afterburners; rating about 27,000lb (12,250kg) st each.
Span: 65ft 0in (20.00m).
Length: 85ft 0in (26.00m).
Gross weight: About 100,000lb (45,000kg).
Max speed: Mach 1.75 (1,150mph; 1,850km/h) at 36,000ft (11,000m).
Range: 3,100 miles (4,990km).
Armament: Four large infra-red and/or radar-homing air-to-air missiles (NATO code-name *Ash*) under wings.

This very large long-range interceptor was first seen at the 1961 Tushino air display. Its evolution can be traced back to the Tu-16 (*Badger*) through the Tu-98 (*Backfin*) prototypes which were produced in 1955 to provide a long-range all-weather interceptor capable of defending the USSR against British and American strategic bombers. The examples of *Fiddler* seen in 1961 each carried two *Ash* missiles, but three Tu-28Ps displayed in 1967 each carried four of these missiles and dispensed with the large ventral fairing and ventral fins of the earlier versions.

According to the US Secretary of Defense in 1974, Tu-28Ps, MiG-25s, Su-15s and Yak-28Ps made up about 50 per cent of the Soviet Union's 2,500-strong interceptor fighter force at that time. However, there is good reason to believe that the number of Tu-28Ps in first-line service has never exceeded 150. Unconfirmed reports have suggested that these may have been replaced by an interceptor conversion of the Tu-22.

Tupolev Tu-95
(NATO code-name: Bear)

USSR

**Four-turboprop long-range bomber, in service.
The following data are estimated:**

Powered by: Four 14,795shp Kuznetsov NK-12MV turbo-props.
Span: 159ft 0in (48.50m).
Length: 155ft 10in (47.50m).
Gross weight: 340,000lb (154,220kg).
Max speed: 500mph (805km/h) at 41,000ft (12,500m).
Range: 7,800 miles (12,550km) with 11 tons of bombs.
Armament: Six 23mm cannon, in pairs in dorsal, ventral and tail turrets. *Bear-A* carries up to 25,000lb (11,340kg) of bombs in internal bay. *Bear-B/C* have nose radome and carry *Kangaroo* air-to-surface missile under fuselage. Some *Bears* also carry *Kitchen* missile.

Data: *Bear-A.*
Photo and silhouette: *Bear-D.*

The Tu-95 (NATO *Bear-A*) was first seen in the 1955 Aviation Day display, when seven flew over Moscow escorted by MiG-17 fighters. Four NK-12MV turboprops made it the fastest propeller-driven aircraft in service, with a cruising speed matching that of the twin-jet Tu-16 and a greater range and bomb-carrying capacity than the Myasishchev M-4. By 1961, a modernisation pro-gramme was under way, based on the employment of a long-range jet-powered air-to-surface missile (code-name *Kangaroo*). The updated aircraft (redesignated *Bear-B* by NATO) took part in the Tushino air display that year, and about 100 continue in service with the Soviet strategic bomber force. Others, in Naval service have been seen frequently, minus missile, on long-range reconnaissance flights to photograph NATO fleet movements at sea, and on electronic intelligence missions. *Bear-B* has a wide nose radome, instead of glazing, and a flight refuelling probe. Another maritime reconnaissance version is *Bear-C* with streamlined blister fairings on both sides of its rear fuselage. *Bear-D*, first seen in 1967, has an under-nose radome like that of the Canadair Argus and a huge under-belly radome; it is able to seek and pinpoint targets for anti-shipping missiles launched from other aircraft or ships. *Bear-E* is generally similar to the *A* but carries reconnais-sance cameras in its bomb-bay. *Bear-F* has enlarged fairings at the rear of its undercarriage pods, longer front fuselage, radar like that of *Bear-D* but further forward, a second stores bay in the rear fuselage, and only two (tail) guns. About 45 *Bear-Ds* and 15 *Bear-Fs* were opera-tional in 1978.

Tupolev Tu-126
(NATO code-name: Moss)

USSR

Airborne early warning and fighter control aircraft, in service.

Powered by: Four 14,795shp Kuznetsov NK-12MV turbo-props.
Span: 168ft (51.20m)
Length: 181ft 1in (55.20m)
Armament: None.

This AWACS (airborne warning and control system) aircraft caused quite a stir when it was first seen in a Soviet documentary film in 1968, because the USAF was at that time only beginning to consider development of a similar machine based on the Boeing 707 transport (see page 23). *Moss* is based on the Tu-114 transport, which was itself evolved from the Tu-95 bomber, and has a similar power plant of four Kuznetsov NK-12MV turboprop engines, driving contra-rotating propellers. Changes centre mainly on the fuselage, which has only a few windows in the electronics-packed cabin and a great number of added excrescences, including a flight refuelling nose-probe, ventral tail-fin and many external antennae and fairings. The 36ft (11m) diameter rotating "saucer" radome above the fuselage is intended to detect incoming attack aircraft over long ranges, so that *Moss* can direct interceptor fighters towards them. It might also assist Soviet attack aircraft, by helping them to elude fighters sent up to intercept them, although it is said to operate effectively only over water, where there is no ground "clutter" to affect its radar picture.

Aircraft of this type have been encountered frequently during NATO exercises, and the accompanying photograph was taken during an encounter between *Moss* and RN Phantom fighters from HMS *Ark Royal*. The Tu-126's specification should be similar to that of the Tu-114, which has a gross weight of 376,990lb (171,000kg), maximum speed of 540mph (870km/h) and maximum range of 5,560 miles (8,950km). About ten or twelve were operational in 1978.

Vought A-7 Corsair II   USA

Single-seat light attack aircraft, in production and service.

Powered by: One 14,250lb (6,465kg) st Allison TF41-A-1 (Rolls-Royce Spey) turbofan.
Span: 38ft 9in (11.80m).
Length: 46ft 1½in (14.06m).
Empty weight: 19,781lb (8,972kg).
Gross weight: 42,000lb (19,050kg).
Max speed: 698mph (1,123km/h) at sea level.
Max ferry range: 2,871 miles (4,621km).
Armament: One M-61 20mm multi-barrel cannon in fuselage. Two fuselage and six wing strong-points for external load of more than 15,000lb (6,805kg) of missiles, bombs, rockets, gun packs or fuel tanks.

Data and silhouette: A-7D.
Photo: A-7H

Winner of a 1963 design contest for a light-weight attack aircraft for the US Navy, the A-7A Corsair II was derived from the F-8 Crusader fighter. Differences included a shorter fuselage, a fixed (as opposed to variable-incidence) wing, revised control surfaces for subsonic operations, and the installation of an 11,350lb (5,150kg) st Pratt & Whitney TF30-P-6 non-afterburning turbofan for greater range and endurance. An initial contract for three prototypes was placed in March 1964, and the first of these aircraft flew on September 27, 1965. Deliveries to a Corsair II training unit began in October 1966 and the first operational unit, VA-147, was commissioned in February 1967: it was deployed to the Vietnam theatre in December 1967. LTV Aerospace built 199 A-7As. The first A-7B (196 built) flew on February 6, 1968, with a 12,200lb (5,534kg) st TF30-P-8 engine. In October 1966 the USAF ordered the A-7D, with more advanced avionics and an Allison TF41 (Rolls-Royce Spey) engine. The first Spey-powered A-7D flew on September 26, 1968, following earlier trials with two A-7D airframes powered by TF30 engines. Deliveries began in December 1968, and 459 were built. The US Navy's A-7E also has more advanced avionics and features of the A-7D. The first 67 had TF30-P-8 engines (first flown November 25, 1968) and were retrospectively designated A-7C to avoid confusion with subsequent A-7Es (over 470 ordered) which have a 15,000lb (6,805kg) st TF41-A-2. The YA-7E (originally YA-7H, first flown August 29, 1972) was a private-venture tandem two-seat training/combat conversion of an A-7E, with an overall length of 48ft 2in (14.68m). The US Navy ordered 65 similar trainers as TA-7Cs, converted from A-7Bs and A-7Cs, for 1977-79 delivery and 16 similar TA-7Ds were ordered in 1978 for ANG use. Sixty A-7Hs for Greece are similar to A-7Es; the first flew on May 6, 1975 and deliveries were completed by mid-1977. One A-7H is to be converted to TA-7H two-seat configuration in 1979, and five new-production TA-7Hs will follow in 1980.

Vought F-8 Crusader

USA

Single-seat carrier-based day fighter, in service.

Powered by: One 18,000lb (8,165kg) st Pratt & Whitney J57-P-20 turbojet.
Span: 35ft 8in (10.87m).
Length: 54ft 6in (16.61m).
Max gross weight: 34,000lb (15,420kg).
Max speed: Nearly Mach 2.
Armament: Four 20mm cannon. Four Sidewinder missiles on fuselage; wing racks for two 2,000lb bombs or two Bullpup A or B missiles or 24 Zuni air-to-ground rockets.

The Crusader was winner of a 1953 design competition for a deck-landing supersonic fighter. An unusual feature of the design was the high wing position, adopted to permit the

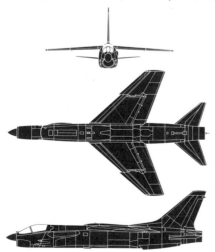

Data and silhouette: F-8E.
Photo: F-8H for Philippines.

wing incidence to be increased for low approach speeds without high angles of incidence on the fuselage. The original designation for the Crusader series was F8U, changed to F-8 in 1962. First flight of the prototype was on March 25, 1955 and deliveries of the F-8A (with 16,000lb; 7,257kg st J57-P-12) to VF-32 Squadron began in March 1957. Later As had a J57-P-4A of 16,200lb (7,327kg) st. The F-8B was similar with J57-P-4A and improved radar; production of these first two models totalled 318 and 130 respectively, plus 144 camera-equipped RF-8As. Distinguished by two ventral fins, the F-8C introduced the 16,900lb (7,665kg) st J57-P-16 and first flew on August 20, 1958. Production totalled 187 before the F-8D appeared. First flown on February 16, 1960, this introduced the P-20 engine and limited all-weather capability; 152 were built. With higher-performance radar and a three-inch longer nose radome, the F-8E prototype first flew on June 30, 1961 and this version went into service in February 1962. Production ended in mid-1964 when 286 F-8Es had been built. The French Navy purchased 42 F-8E(FN)s with provision for Matra 530 missiles; the first of these flew on June 26, 1964, and they still equip two *Flotilles*. In post-production modification and modernisation programmes, 73 RF-8As became RF-8G, and 89 F-8Ds and 136 F-8Es were updated to F-8H and F-8J respectively, with attack capability and other improvements. Subsequently, 87 F-8Cs were modified to F-8K and 61 F-8Bs to F-8L. Surviving F-8As are now designated TF-8A. By 1977, the F-8s were out of active USN service, but several squadrons of RF-8Gs were still operational, and the USN Reserves flew two squadrons of F-8Js and two of RF-8Gs. The Philippine Air Force acquired 35 ex-USN F-8H Crusaders for late-1978 delivery.

Yakovlev Yak-28, Yak-28P and Yak-28U   USSR
(NATO code-names: Brewer, Firebar and Maestro)

Two-seat multi-purpose tactical aircraft, all weather fighter and trainer, in service.

Powered by: Two 13,120lb (5,950kg) st Tumansky R-11 turbojets, with afterburning on current aircraft.
Span: 42ft 6in (12.95m).
Length: 71ft 0½in (21.65m).
Gross weight: 35,000lb (15,875kg).
Max speed: Mach 1.1 (733mph; 1,180km/h) at 36,000ft (11,000m).
Combat radius: 575 miles (925km).
Armament: Two *Anab* air-to-air missiles under wings, with alternative infra-red or semi-active radar homing heads.

These successors to the long-retired Yak-25/27 were first seen at the 1961 Tushino display and can be identified by their shoulder-mounted wing, compared with the mid-wing of the Yak-25/27 series. They have extended wingtips and pointed balancer wheel fairings, as on the Yak-26 (*Mangrove*) but the entire wing leading-edge in-board of the nacelle on each side is extended forward. Another major change is that the under-carriage of the Yak-28 series has two twin wheeled units in tandem, with the rear unit much further aft than on the earlier designs. The engine nacelles have intake centre-bodies.

The Yak-28P (*Firebar*) is a tandem two-seat all-weather fighter, with pointed radome and under-wing armament of two *Anab* air-to-air guided missiles. A new and longer radome has been fitted retrospectively to some aircraft.

The basic Yak-28 (*Brewer-A to C*) was a multi-purpose tactical aircraft, with glazed nose, and could be regarded as a "third generation" coun-terpart of *Mangrove*. It had one or two 30mm cannon submerged in the sides of the fuselage, an internal weapon-bay and, usually, an under-fuselage radar fairing. Few remain in service. *Brewer-D* has cameras in the weapon-bay. *Brewer-E* has an ECM pack protruding from its weapon-bay and a rocket pod under each outer wing. A further variant, the Yak-28U (*Maestro*), is a dual-control training version of *Firebar*, with an additional blister canopy forward of, and lower than, the rear canopy and a much larger nose-probe.

Data apply to Yak-28P and are estimated.
Photo and silhouette: Yak-28P.

119

Yakovlev Yak-36 (NATO code-name: Forger) USSR

Single-seat VTOL carrier-based combat aircraft, in production and service.

Powered by: One propulsion turbojet rated at about 17,000lb (7,710kg) st. Two lift-jets, each rated at about 5,600lb (2,540kg) st.
Span: 23ft 0in (7.00m).
Length: 49ft 3in (15.00m).
Gross weight: 22,050lb (10,000kg).
Max speed: Mach 1.3 at 36,000ft (11,000m).
Armament: Four underwing pylons for gun pods and rocket packs.

Data, photo and silhouette: Forger-A.

Alexander Yakovlev's first thoughts on V/STOL combat aircraft design were revealed at the 1967 Soviet Aviation Day display at Domodedovo Airport, Moscow. A pair of rather ungainly 'fighters' were sent to the airport, one of which took part in the flying programme; NATO allocated the code-name Freehand to the type, but nobody expected the aircraft to enter squadron service, even when one of the small batch of four or five development models was used for experimental operations from a platform installed on the helicopter cruiser Moskva.

Reports of a more refined Yakovlev design were confirmed when the first of the Soviet Navy's new 40,000 ton carrier/cruisers, the Kiev, entered the Mediterranean in July 1976, for a working-up cruise that took her on through the North Atlantic to Murmansk. En route, considerable flying was done by her complement of about a dozen Ka-25 ASW helicopters and a similar number of completely new VTOL fixed-wing aircraft which appeared to be designated Yak-36. Most were single-seaters (NATO Forger-A); but they were accompanied by a much-lengthened tandem two-seat training version, which received the NATO code-name of Forger-B. No attempt was made to hide their operations from Kiev. Take-off was seen to be made with the two vectored-thrust nozzles of the propulsion turbojet rotated about 10 degrees forward of vertical, and with the two lift-jets (inclined about 10 degrees rearward; immediately aft of the cockpit) switched on. Handling was precise; but STOL take-off would appear to be impossible with such a configuration, which must restrict the weapon/fuel load. The aircraft were assumed to be from a development squadron.

Part Two

Aeritalia/Aermacchi AM.3C   Italy

The three-seat AM.3 was developed as a potential replacement for the L-19s and other observation aircraft currently in service with the Italian Army. It was a joint product of the Aermacchi and Aeritalia companies and utilised the basic wing of the Aermacchi-Lockheed AL.60. The prototype flew for the first time on May 12, 1967, powered by a 340hp Continental GTSIO-520-C engine, and was followed by a second on August 22, 1968; both were subsequently re-engined with the Piaggio-Lycoming GSO-480-B1B6. A hard-point under each wing, immediately outboard of the bracing strut pick-up point, enables the AM.3 to be used for light tactical support duties, carrying a wide variety of armament, including two AS.11 or AS.12 wire-guided missiles, two 250lb bombs, twelve 2.75in rockets, two Minigun pods and 3,000 rounds of ammunition or two pods each containing a pair of 7.62mm machine-guns and 2,000 rounds. Production models are designated AM.3C and the last of 40 for the SAAF, which has named this type the Bosbok, was delivered in December 1974. The only other customer for the type was the Rwanda Air Force, which bought three. **Data:** Span 41ft 5½in (12.64m). Length 29ft 5½in (8.98m). Gross weight 3,860lb (1,750kg). Max speed 173mph (278km/h). Range 615 miles (990km).

Aermacchi-Lockheed AL.60C5   Italy

This all-metal utility aircraft was designed and built in prototype form (first flight September 15, 1959) by Lockheed-Georgia. Production was then entrusted to two Lockheed associates—Lockheed-Azcarate S.A. in Mexico and Aermacchi in Italy. The version built in Mexico is no longer in service. The air force of the Central African Empire has ten AL.60C5/F5 Conestogas, built by Aermacchi, with tailwheel undercarriage and 400hp Lycoming IO-720-A1A engine. A similar variant is used by the Mauritanian Islamic Air Force (1) and by the Rhodesian Air Force as the Trojan (10). **Data** (AL.60C5): Span 39ft 4in (11.99m). Length 28ft 10½in (8.80m). Gross weight 4,500lb (2,041kg). Max speed 156mph (251km/h). Range 645 miles (1,037km).

Aermacchi MB 339   Italy

Closely related to the MB 326 (page 6), the MB339 was evolved during 1973/74 after a close study of the future requirements of the Italian *Aeronautica Militare*, and of military users in general, for an advanced trainer with secondary close-support capabilities. The outward similarity between the MB 339 and the earlier Aermacchi product, with the exception of the forward fuselage, belies the extent of internal redesign to improve the structure and to introduce new equipment and systems. The front fuselage was redesigned to raise the rear (instructor's) seat, giving the MB 339 a profile similar to that of the BAe Hawk, Dassault–Bre-guet/Dornier Alpha Jet and other contemporary trainer designs. The engine is a 4,000lb (1,814kg) st Piaggio-built Rolls-Royce Viper 632–43 as used in the MB 326K, and the MB 339 has provision to carry an extensive range of ordnance under the wings in addition to a 7.62-mm multi-barrel gun pod under the fuselage. The first of two prototypes flew on August 12, 1976, and production of the first 15 of a planned series of 100 for the AMI was underway in early 1978. **Data:** Span 35ft 7½in (10.86m). Length 36ft 0in (10.97m). Gross weight 13,000lb (5,895kg). Max speed 558mph (898km/h). Range (internal fuel) 1,093 miles (1,760km).

Aero L-29 Delfin   Czechoslovakia
(NATO code-name: Maya)

The prototype of this tandem two-seat basic trainer flew for the first time on April 5, 1959, with a Bristol Siddeley Viper turbojet, but production machines have a locally designed M-701 VC-150 or S-50 engine of 1,960lb (890kg) st. The L-29 was designed to replace piston-engined trainers in service with the Czech Air Force and, after evaluation in competition with jet trainers built in other countries, was also chosen as the standard basic trainer of the Soviet Air Force. Other nations which have L-29s are reported to include Bulgaria, East Germany, Egypt, Guinea, Hungary, Indonesia, Iraq, Nigeria, Romania, Syria and Uganda, and more than 3,000 had been delivered by the time production ended in 1974. Two underwing attachments can be used to carry external fuel tanks, 100kg bombs, 7.62mm machine-gun pods or up to eight rockets. The L-29A Akrobat single-seater for specialised aerobatics did not enter series production. **Data** (L-29): Span 33ft 9in (10.29m). Length 35ft 5½in (10.81m). Gross weight 7,804lb (3,540kg). Max speed 407mph (655km/h). Range 555 miles (894km).

Aero L-39 Albatros

Czechoslovakia

Powered by a 3,192lb (1,722kg) st Ivchenko AI-25-TL engine built in Czechoslovakia as the Walter Titan, the L-39 is a subsonic trainer with capability for development in the light strike role, carrying bombs, rocket-pods or air-to-air missiles on up to four underwing pylons. The first flight was made on November 4, 1968 and four more prototypes had joined the flight test programme by mid-1970. An initial production batch of 10 was put in hand in 1971 and full production deliveries began in 1974, initially to the Czech and Soviet Air Forces. The L-39 was chosen as the standard advanced flying and armaments trainer for all the Warsaw Pact nations except Poland. Exports have also been made to Iraq. **Data:** Span 31ft 0½in (9.46m). Length 40ft 5in (12.32m). Gross weight 10,141lb (4,600kg). Max speed 435mph (700km/h) at sea level. Range 565 miles (910km) without tip tanks.

Aero Commander Shrike Commander (and Turbo Commander)

USA

First major foreign customer for the twin-engined Shrike Commander for military use was the Argentinian Air Force, which placed an order for 14 of these aircraft in March 1968. The Shrike Commander (known originally as the Model 500U) is used also by the Iranian Army (5), and in small numbers elsewhere, for liaison, training and general transport duties, carrying six people. The engines are 290hp Lycoming IO-540-E1A5s. During 1972, three similar Turbo Commanders, with Garrett AiResearch TPE 331 turboprops, were acquired by the Imperial Iranian Air Force; five were delivered to the Argentine Army in 1975–76. Examples of the earlier Commander Model 500U with 340hp Lycoming GSO-480 engines were acquired by the USAF and US Army, and were operated respectively as the U-4 and U-9. **Data** (Shrike Commander): Span 49ft 0½in (14.95m). Length 36ft 7in (11.15m). Gross weight 6,750lb (3,062kg). Max speed 215mph (346km/h) at 10,000ft (3,050m). Photo: Turbo Commander 681B.

Aerospace Airtrainer CT4   New Zealand

This primary trainer was designed 25 years ago in its basic form, and won a design competition for two-seat light aircraft organised by the Royal Aero Club of Great Britain. Its designer was an Australian, Henry Millicer, and it eventually went into production as the Airtourer, first by Victa Ltd in Australia and then by NZAI in New Zealand. Four Airtourer T6/24s were delivered to the RNZAF in 1970. The Air-trainer CT4, first flown on February 23, 1972, is derived from the Airtourer by way of

the four-seat Aircruiser. It is aerodynamically similar, but with completely new structure, and is powered by a 210hp Continental IO-360-D engine. Provision is made for bombs, or rocket pods or gun pods, beneath the wings. Deliveries totalled 19 for the RNZAF (CT4B version), 24 for the Royal Thai Air Force and 37 for the RAAF. **Data:** Span 26ft (7.92m). Length 23ft 2in (7.06m). Gross weight 2,350lb (1,066kg). Max speed 188mph (303km/h). Endurance about 5hr.

Aérospatiale/Potez CM 170 Magister,   France
Super Magister and CM 175 Zephyr

The first of three prototypes of the Magister tandem two-seat jet trainer flew on July 23, 1952. Eleven months later, the French Air Force placed a pre-production order for ten (first flown July 7, 1954) followed by production orders for a total of 387 (first flown February 29, 1956). The original design and manufacturing company, Fouga, became part of the Potez group, which continued production until the Magister was taken over by Sud-Aviation (now Aérospatiale) in 1967. Magisters built by these companies continue to serve in Algeria, France, Belgium, Cameroun, Kampuchea, Ireland, Morocco, Lebanon, Libya, Rwanda, El Salvador and Togo. Others, built under licence by Valmet of Finland and Israel Aircraft Industries,

serve in Finland and Israel. The standard CM 170 Magister has two 880lb (400kg) st Turboméca Marboré IIA turbojets and can carry two machine-guns, plus underwing racks for two 50kg bombs, four 25kg rockets, up to 36 smaller rockets or two AS.11 guided missiles. The last 130 aircraft for the French Air Force were Super Magisters with 1,058lb (480kg) st Marboré VI engines. Thirty-two CM 175 Zephyrs for the French Navy (first flown May 30, 1959) are equipped for carrier operation. **Data** (Magister): Span 39ft 10in (12.14m). Length 33ft (10.06m). Gross weight 7,055lb (3,200kg). Max speed 444mph (714km/h). Range 735 miles (1,200km). Photo: Israeli-built Magister.

Aérospatiale Fouga 90 France

The phototype of this modernised version of the CM 170 Magister was produced by conversion of an existing airframe and flew for the first time on August 20, 1978. The basic wing and tail unit remain. The centre fuselage has been redesigned and deepened, so that the rear seat can be raised to give the instructor a view forward over the head of the pupil. The original turbojets are replaced by 1,520lb (690kg) st Turboméca Astafan IIG turbofans, for reduced fuel consumption and noise, and the electronics and equipment are to the latest standards. Armament can be carried, as on the Magister, for weapons training or light attack missions. **Data:** Span 39ft 10¼in (12.15m) with tip-tanks. Length 34ft 0½in (10.38m). Gross weight 9,259lb (4,200kg). Max speed 398mph (640km/h). Range 1,150 miles (1,850km).

Aérospatiale N262/Frégate France

The original N262 was developed by Nord-Aviation as a 26/29-seat transport powered by two Turboméca Bastan turboprops. Layout is conventional, with a pressurised cabin and fairings to house the main undercarriage when it is retracted. Many N262s were sold for commerical operation, and in June 1967 the French Navy ordered 15 of the Srs. A version, with 1,065eshp Bastan VIC engines, for use as aircrew trainers and light transports. It subsequently acquired six more, including five previously operated by the French Air Force. The latter had six Srs. A transports and 24 Frégates, with 1,145eshp Bastan VIIs, for training and liaison duties, taking delivery of the first of these in November 1968. Another Frégate was sold to the Congo Air Force. **Data** (Frégate): Span 74ft 1¾in (22.60m). Length 63ft 3in (19.28m). Gross weight 23,810lb (10,800kg). Max speed 260mph (418km/h). Range 1,135 miles (1,825km) at 247mph (397km/h). Photo: N262 Srs A.

Aérospatiale SE313B Alouette II Artouste, SA315 Lama and SA318C Alouette II Astazou

France

The five-seat SE313B, with 360hp Turboméca Artouste IIC turboshaft, first flew on March 12, 1955. The total of 1,305 built included about 363 for the French Services and others for military and civilian customers in 33 different countries, including 267 for the West German Services and 17 for the British Army (as Alouette AH.Mk 2). Also included in the total were some SA318C Alouette IIs with 360hp (derated) Turboméca Astazou IIA turboshafts, giving higher performance. The SA315B Lama combines the airframe of the Alouette II with a 550shp (derated) Artouste IIIB and dynamic components of the Alouette III.

Production totalled 207 by January 1978; the Argentine Air Force has six, the Chilean Air Force six, the Ecuadorian Air Force four (with gun and rocket armament) and India 40, followed by others manufactured in India by HAL with the local name of Cheetah. The first HAL-built SA315 was delivered in November 1972. **Data** (SA318C): Rotor diameter 33ft 5½in (10.20m). Length 31ft 11¾in (9.75m). Gross weight 3,630lb (1,650kg). Max speed 127mph (205km/h). Range 447 miles (720km). Photo: Indian-built Lama (Cheetah).

Aérospatiale SA316/319 Alouette III

France

The Alouette III, a larger and more powerful development of the Alouette II, is available for military use as a tactical troop transport or assault helicopter, and can carry a variety of armament. The basic version, with 570shp Artouste IIIB engine, first flew on February 28, 1959, and serves as the SA316A and SA316B, the latter having a strengthened transmission and increased weights. By the beginning of 1978 production totalled 1,362, including 218 for French military and civil operators, and exports to 70 countries. Sixty are being built in Switzerland and 130 in Romania. In addition, 200 Alouette IIIs are being built in India by HAL with the name Chetak; some serve with the Indian Navy carrying Mk 44 torpedoes. During 1974, the French Aéronavale also adopted an anti-submarine version, known as the Alouette III/ASM, and *Flotille* 34F was formed at BAN de Lanveoc–

Poulmic to provide detached flights for service on board anti-submarine corvettes and frigates. The SA319 variant has a 600shp Astazou XIV engine, gross weight of 4,960lb (2,250kg), max speed of 137mph (220km/h), and max range of 375 miles (600km). **Data:** (SA316) Rotor diameter 36ft 1¾in (11.02m). Length: 32ft 10¾in (10.03m). Empty weight 2,474lb (1,122kg). Gross weight 4,850lb (2,200kg). Max speed 130mph (210km/h) at sea level. Max range 335 miles (540km). Photo: SA316, Jordan.

Aérospatiale SA321 Super Frelon

France

The first of two prototypes of the Super Frelon, largest helicopter yet built in France, flew on December 7, 1962, with 1,320hp Turmo engines, and subsequently set a helicopter speed record of 217.77mph (350.47km/h) over a 15/25-km course which stood until 1971. The second prototype was representative of the naval anti-submarine version, with crew of four, sonar, search radar in the stabilising floats and provision for other special equipment and weapons. Four pre-production Super Frelons followed the prototypes, with 1,500hp engines; the first of these flew on January 31, 1964. Orders include 24 SA321G anti-submarine versions for the French Navy, operated by *Flotille* 32F, 16 SA321L transports for the South African Air Force, 12 SA321K transports for the

Israeli Defence Force, 10 for Iraq, 16 for the Imperial Iranian Army, and nine transports for Libya. During 1974, deliveries began of 13 SA321J utility versions of the Super Frelon ordered by the Chinese People's Republic, and sales totalled 98 by September 1978. **Data**: Rotor diameter 62ft 0in (18.90m). Fuselage length 65ft 10¾in (20.08m). Empty weight (Naval version) 14,600lb (6,625kg). Gross weight 28,660lb (13,000kg). Max speed 171mph (275km/h) at sea level. Endurance 4 hrs. Photo: SA321L, SAAF.

Aérospatiale/Westland SA330 Puma France/GB

Development of the SA330 to meet a French Army requirement for a "hélicoptère de manoeuvre" was authorised in June 1963, with a contract for two prototypes and six pre-production aircraft. The first of these flew on April 15, 1965. The SA330 became one of three helicopters in the joint Anglo-French programme agreed early in 1968, with Westland becoming responsible for production of certain components and for assembly of 40 Pumas ordered by the RAF. The first British production SA330E Puma HC Mk 1 flew on November 25, 1970. Deliveries of French-built SA330Bs began in 1969 and the first French army unit became operational in June 1970. The first RAF unit, No 33 Squadron, formed on the type a year later; a second squadron, No 230, equipped with the Puma subsequently and production of additional

Pumas for the RAF was planned in 1978. French army orders total 140 and the French Air Force has acquired about 10. Military users of the export model SA330C (Turmo IVA) and SA330H (Turmo IVC) include Algeria, Chile, Portugal, South Africa, Belgium (Police air arm), Kuwait, Morocco, Pakistan, Zaïre, Ivory Coast, Congo Republic, Nigeria, Indonesia and Abu Dhabi. The SA330F and SA330G are civil versions and the SA330J and SA330L are respectively civil and military variants with Turmo IVC engines, composite rotor blades and increased take-off weight. Over 500 Pumas have been built. **Data:** Rotor diameter 49ft 2½in (15.00m). Fuselage length 46ft 1½in (14.06m). Empty weight 7,795lb (3,536kg). Gross weight 15,430lb (7,000kg). Cruising speed 159mph (257km/h) at sea level. Max range 360 miles (580km) with standard fuel.

Aérospatiale/ France/Great Britain
Westland SA341/342 Gazelle

The five-seat SA341 was conceived as a modernised development of the Alouette II, utilising the same transmission system and a 590shp Astazou III engine. The semi-rigid three-blade rotor has glassfibre blades and the tail rotor is of the "fenestron" fan-in-fin type. The SA340-01 prototype, fitted initially with an Alouette II tail rotor, flew on April 7, 1967, and was followed by a second prototype and four pre-production SA 341s. British variants, assembled by Westland, are the Gazelle AH.Mk1 (164 for the Army and Marines), HT.Mk2 (30 for the Navy), HT.Mk3 (19 for the RAF) and HCC.Mk4 (planned RAF communications version). The SA341H export model is licence-built in Yugoslavia. To meet Middle East-

ern requirements, Aérospatiale developed the uprated SA342 during 1973, with an 870shp Astazou XIVH engine to improve take-off and climb under "hot and high" conditions. Deliveries of the SA 342K military export model to Kuwait began in 1974; others have gone to Egypt and Libya. An armed version is offered, with gyro-stabilised sight above the cabin and provision for two or four air-to-surface missiles such as Hot, TOW or AS.12, or rocket or gun pods. Production of all models totalled 751 by January 1978. **Data** (SA342): Rotor diameter 34ft 5½in (10.50m). Length 31ft 3¼in (9.53m). Gross weight 4,190lb (1,900kg). Max speed 192mph (310km/h). Range 469 miles (755km). Photo: Gazelle HT.Mk3.

Aerotec T-23 Uirapuru

Brazil

The prototype of this side-by-side two-seat all-metal light aircraft flew on June 2, 1965, powered by a 108hp Lycoming O-235-C1 engine. A second Uirapuru followed, this time with a 150hp Lycoming O-320-A engine, and was offered to the Brazilian Air Force as a replacement for its locally-built Fokker S.11 and S.12 Instructor basic trainers. Seventy Uirapurus were ordered for this purpose in 1968–69, under the military designation T-23,

with a further batch of 30 ordered later. Eight Uirapurus were acquired by the Paraguayan Air Force and 18 by the Bolivian Air Force. All have a 160hp Lycoming O-320-B2B and differ from the civilian model in having fully-adjustable seats, stick-type controls and a modified cockpit canopy. **Data:** Span 27ft 10¾in (8.50m). Length 21ft 8in (6.60m). Gross weight 1,825lb (840kg). Max speed 140mph (225km/h). Range 495 miles (800km).

Agusta A 109A

Italy

The first of three prototypes of the basic A 109 helicopter, with seats for one or two pilots and six passengers, flew on August 4, 1971. Deliveries, initially to customers in the USA, began in 1976, powered by two 420shp Allison 250-C20B turboshaft engines. In early 1977, the Italian Army began evaluating the A 109 as an anti-tank helicopter, armed with four TOW missiles; as a result, it decided to start development of the specialised Agusta A 129 Mangusta anti-tank helicopter, using A 109 dynamic components. Meanwhile, standard general-purpose A 109s have been ordered by a number of foreign armed services, including those of the Argentine. A special naval version is also in production for anti-sub-

marine, anti-surface vessel, electronic warfare, search and rescue, and utility duties with several navies. **Data:** Rotor diameter 36ft 1in (11.00m). Fuselage length 35ft 1¾in (10.71m). Gross weight 5,400lb (2,450kg). Max cruising speed 165mph (266km/h). Range 351 miles (565km). Photo: Anti-tank version.

Agusta Bell 206B JetRanger
(and Bell OH-58A Kiowa and TH-57A SeaRanger)

Italy/USA

Agusta added the five-seat Bell Model 206 to its range of licence-built helicopters in 1967, since which time more than 500 examples have been built in Italy for commercial and military use. Of the latter, those for the Swedish Navy (HKP 6) are equipped for anti-submarine and anti-shipping patrol and attack, carrying assorted weapons beneath the fuselage, and feature the high-skid landing gear (originally developed by Bell for use in rough terrain) to permit clearance for these weapons. The AB-206A and AB-206B differ only in engine variant—respectively the 317shp Allison 250-C18 and 400shp (derated to 317shp) 250-C20—and the basic models have a rotor diameter of 33ft 4in (10.16m). Some military models have a

larger rotor and carry the Agusta designation AB-206A-1. In the USA, Bell built 2,200 Model 206As for the US Army as OH-58A Kiowa observation helicopters, and the US Navy has 40 similar TH-57A SeaRangers for training duties. Other users of the type in its unarmed versions include the Canadian Armed Forces (74 CH-136), Australian Army (56, built by CAC as CA-36), Brazilian Navy (18), Austria, Brunei, Spain, Turkey, Iran, Italy and Saudi Arabia. **Data** (206B): Rotor diameter 33ft 4in (10.16m). Fuselage length 31ft 2in (9.50m). Gross weight 3,200lb (1,451kg). Max speed 140mph (226km/h). Max range 418 miles (673km). Photo: Bell 206B JetRanger II, Brazil.

AIDC T-CH-1

Taiwan

The T-CH-1 is a product of the Aero Industry Development Center of the Chinese Air Force on Taiwan (Nationalist China), and is a tandem two-seat trainer similar in overall concept and size to the North American T-28, but with a turboprop engine. Construction of two prototypes began early in 1972 and the first of these, as the XT-CH-1A, made its first flight on November 23, 1973. The second prototype, flown on November 27, 1974,

incorporated modifications to permit its use as a weapons trainer and for counter-insurgency missions; this prototype is designated XT-CH-1B. A batch of T-CH-1s was put into production at the AIDC in 1976. **Data:** One 1,450ehp Lycoming T53-L-701 turboprop. Span 40ft 0in (12.19m). Length 33ft 8in (10.26m). Gross weight 11,150lb (5,057kg). Max speed 368mph (592km/h). Range 1,250 miles (2,010km).

AIDC T-C-2

Taiwan

As its second major design project, the Chinese Air Force's Aero Industry Development Center in Taiwan undertook the development of a light twin-turboprop transport, on which work began in early 1973. Powered by two 1,451ehp Lycoming T53-L-701A turboprops, this T-C-2 is able to seat 38 passengers in the cabin, which has quick-change provisions and a rear ramp to allow the rapid loading of supplies and the dropping of para-troops. The T-C-2 has a high wing and a retract-able tricycle undercarriage, the main units of which retract into fuselage-side fairings. A proto-type, designated XC-2, was scheduled to fly before the end of 1978. **Data:** Span 81ft 8½in (24.90m). Length 64ft 9in (19.74m). Gross weight 25,000lb (11,340kg). Max speed 265mph (426km/h). Range 1.324 miles (2,131km). No photo available.

Antonov An-2 (NATO code-name: Colt)

USSR

First flown in 1947, the An-2 was designed as a rugged and versatile replacement for aircraft like the little Po-2, particularly for agricultural work in "outback" areas. Its ability to operate from short strips, thanks to its large wing area, and to carry a payload of around 1¼ tons, made it an ideal utility transport for the Soviet Air Force, and more than 12,000 have been built in the Soviet Union and Poland. Examples were supplied for military use in nearly 20 other countries, including Afghanistan, Bulgaria, Cuba, Czechoslovakia, East Germany, Hungary, Iraq, North Korea, Romania, Somalia and Tanzania. The An-2 was built under licence also in China; production in Poland continued into 1978, by which time that country alone had built over 7,000 mostly for export to the USSR, with many for civil use. Powered by a 1,000hp Shvetsov ASh-62IR engine, it carries 14 troops, six stretchers or freight, and can operate on wheels, skis or floats. **Data:** Span 59ft 8½in (18.18m). Length 40ft 8¼in (12.40m). Gross weight 12,125lb (5,500kg). Max speed 157mph (253km/h). Range 562 miles (900km) at 124mph (200km/h).

Antonov An-14
(NATO code-name: Clod)

USSR

First flown on March 15, 1958, the An-14 underwent a lengthy period of flight development, during which major changes were made to the wing and tail design and more powerful engines were introduced. Production aircraft have 300hp Ivchenko AI-14RF engines and normally seat 6 passengers in the cabin. Since 1967, examples of the An-14 have been seen in service with the Soviet Air Force and some Communist bloc countries, including Bulgaria and East Germany. A turboprop derivative, the 15/19-passenger An-28 (NATO code-name *Cash*), appeared in 1972 and has entered production for Aeroflot. A version may also be used for military duties in due course. **Data** (An-14): Span 72ft 2in (21.99m). Length 37ft 6½in (11.44m). Gross weight 7,935lb (3,600kg). Max cruising speed 118mph (190km/h). Range 404 miles (650km) with 1,590lb (720kg) payload. Photo: An-14, Bulgaria.

Armstrong Whitworth
Sea Hawk

Great Britain

Of 555 Sea Hawks produced by Armstrong Whitworth and Hawker, only about 30 remain in frontline service. These equip the fighter squadron which serves, together with Breguet Alizés, aboard the Indian Navy's aircraft carrier *Vikrant*. India purchased 24 Sea Hawk FGA Mk6s, to the same production standard as the final version for the Royal Navy, which acquired a total of 434 in six marks. Other export orders were from Germany (64 Mk100 and Mk101) and the Netherlands (36 Mk50). India later acquired 12 more Sea Hawks ex-Royal Navy and 28 from Germany. All versions were powered by a Rolls-Royce Nene turbojet, with the 5,400lb (2,450kg) st Nene 103 in the Sea Hawk F. (GA) Mk6. **Data:** Span 39ft 0in (11.89m). Length 39ft 8in (12.09m). Gross weight 16,200lb (7,348kg). Max cruising speed 590mph (950km/h) at sea level.

Atlas C4M   South Africa

The C4, known in civil guise as the Kudu, was evolved by the Atlas Aircraft Corporation, in the Transvaal, out of its experience in assembling the Aeritalia/Aermacchi AM.3C Bosbok for the SAAF (page 121). The wings, tail assembly, undercarriage and 340hp Piaggio-built Lycoming GSO-480-B1B3 power plant are all virtually identical with those of the Bosbok, while the fuselage is derived from the original design of the Lockheed AL.60, a utility transport for which Aermacchi was responsible in Europe. A six/eight-seat light transport, the C4M can be converted quickly to operate in the freighting role and can be flown into and out of semi-prepared strips. A civil prototype Kudu first flew on 16 February 1974 and was used to obtain certification, granted on 16 June 1975, two days before the first flight of the military prototype C4M, which was subsequently evaluated by the SAAF. Production was begun to re-equip No 43 Squadron, one of the South African Active Citizen Force squadrons. **Data:** Span 42ft 10$\frac{3}{4}$in (13.08m). Length 30ft 6$\frac{1}{2}$in (9.31m). Gross weight 4,497lb (2,040kg). Max speed 161mph (259km/h). Range 806 miles (1,297km).

Avro Canada CF-100   Canada

The CF-100 is the only fighter of original Canadian design to have reached production status, a total of 692 having been built for the RCAF (now Canadian Armed Forces) and 53 for export to Belgium. First flown in January 1950, the prototype CF-100 Mk1 was powered by Avon engines; but the 10 pre-production Mk2s had Orenda engines, also designed and built in Canada, and these engines were used also in 70 Mk3s, 137 Mk4As, 194 Mk4Bs and 279 Mk5s produced as all-weather fighters. The CF-100s had been retired as front-line equipment by 1963, but a small number of Mk5s was retained to serve with the Electronic Warfare Unit to provide electronic countermeasures training and radar targets to exercise Canadian air defence forces. This role has now been taken on by No 414 (Black Knight) Squadron, which had 13 CF-100s on strength in 1978 and was expected to continue using the type until 1980. **Data:** Two 7,275lb (3,700kg) st Orenda Mk11 or 14 turbojets. Span 60ft 10in (18.54m). Length 54ft 2in (16.50m). Gross weight 33,600lb (18,254kg). Max speed 650mph (1,045km/h) at 40,000ft (12,200m). Range 2,300 miles (3,700km). Photo: CF-100 Mk5D.

BAe (BAC) One-Eleven

Great Britain

First military Service to purchase BAC One-Elevens was the Royal Australian Air Force, which took delivery of two for VIP transport duties. They are used by No 34 (VIP) Squadron, which operates from Fairbairn, Canberra, on transport and liaison work for the Australian government. Basically Series 200 aircraft, they are each powered by two 10,410lb (4,722kg) st Rolls-Royce Spey-2 Mk506 engines. Two others fly in British military markings at the RAE Bedford. Three Srs 475s were ordered in 1974 by the Sultan of Oman's Air Force, and these were subsequently modified to have a large freight door in the port side of the fuselage. **Data:** Span 88ft 6in (26.97m). Length 93ft 6in (28.50m). Gross weight 78,500lb (35,610kg). Max speed 541mph (871km/h). Typical range 1,155 miles (1,860km). Photo: Srs 475, Oman.

BAe HS.125, and Dominie T.Mk1

Great Britain

The Hawker Siddeley 125 Srs 2 was ordered for the RAF in September 1962, as a navigational trainer, under the name Dominie T.Mk 1. The first of 20 production models flew on December 30, 1964, and deliveries to No 1 Air Navigation School at Stradishall, Suffolk, began in the Autumn of 1965. They are now used by No 6 FTS at Finningley. The Dominie T.1 is similar to the commercial twin-jet executive versions of the HS.125, with 3,000lb (1,360kg) st Rolls-Royce Viper 520 turbojets, but is equipped to carry a pilot, pilot assister, two students and an instructor. The RAF also has five HS.125 CC.Mk1s and two lengthened CC.Mk2s (Srs 600) for communication duties, serving with No 32 Squadron. Other air forces using the HS.125 include those of Malaysia (2), Brazil (8, as VC-93) and South Africa (4, named Mercurius). **Data** (Srs 600): Span 47ft 0in (14.32m). Length 50ft 5$\frac{3}{4}$in (15.37m). Gross weight 25,000lb (11,340kg). Max speed 359mph (578km/h). Range 1,876 miles (3,020km). Photo: Mercurius, SAAF.

BAe HS Hawk

Great Britain

This design was selected by the RAF during 1972 as its new basic trainer to replace the Gnat, the Hunter and eventually the Jet Provost for pilot training. Powered by a Rolls-Royce/Turboméca RT.172-06 Adour 151 turbofan, without reheat, the Hawk seats two in tandem and, as a weapons trainer or in a secondary ground-attack role, it can carry a 30mm Aden gun pod beneath the fuselage and some 5,000lb (2,268kg) of weapons on four underwing pylons. First flight of a pre-production prototype was made on August 21, 1974 and deliveries of a batch of 175 ordered by the RAF began towards the end of 1976, with the first student course training on the type in July 1977 at No 4 FTS, Valley. First export customers for the Hawk are Finland (50) and Indonesia (6). **Data:** Span 30ft 10in (9.4m). Length 33ft 11in (11.96m). Gross weight 10,250lb (4,650kg). Max speed approx. 560mph (1,046km/h).

BAe (Scottish Aviation) Bulldog

Great Britain

This two-seat primary trainer was developed originally by Beagle Aircraft as the B.125 Series 1. Its all-metal airframe was basically similar to that of the civil Pup, with structural and equipment changes to suit it for military use. In particular, the Bulldog has a large rearward-sliding jettisonable canopy over its side-by-side seats and is powered by a 200hp Lycoming IO-360-A1B6 engine. The Beagle prototype flew for the first time on May 19, 1969 and the Scottish Aviation prototype Bulldog 100 Series on February 14, 1971. Deliveries began in July 1971, to meet orders from Sweden (58 Model 101 for Swedish Air Force and 20 for Swedish Army; designation SK 61), Malaysia (15 Model 102) and Kenya (5 Model 103). First flown on January 30, 1973, the Series 120 has a strengthened centre-section and increased aerobatic gross weight. The RAF bought 130 as Bulldog T.Mk1 (Model 121), the Ghana Air Force 13 (Model 122/122A), the Nigerian Air Force 20 (Model 123), the Jordanian Royal Academy of Aeronautics 13 (Model 125), the Lebanese Air Force 6 (Model 126), the Kenya Air Force 9 (Model 127) and the Royal Hong Kong Auxiliary Air Force 2 (Model 128). **Data** (Series 120): Span 33ft (10.06m). Length 23ft 3in (7.09m). Gross weight 2,350lb (1,065kg). Max speed 150mph (240km/h). Range 621 miles (1,000km). Photo: Model 128, Hong Kong.

BAe (Scottish Aviation) Jetstream

Great Britain

After a chequered history, the Jetstream was given a new surge of life by its choice as the type to replace RAF Varsity multi-engined pilot training aircraft. The order was for 26 Jetstream T.Mk1s, for delivery in 1973–75. Power plant comprises two 940shp Turboméca Astazou XVI turboprops, permitting higher operating weights and performance than the Astazou XIIs and XIVs fitted in the prototype (first flown August 18, 1967) and early Mk1 aircraft built by Handley Page, before the company ceased operations. In 1972 full responsibility for the programme was taken over by Scottish Aviation (now British Aerospace), and the 26 aircraft had all been delivered by Spring 1976. After a period in store, eight have been delivered to the RAF for multi-engine training. Sixteen are being converted to T.Mk2 standard, to replace the Royal Navy's Sea Princes in an observer training role, with weather/mapping radar in a nose "thimble". Deliveries were to begin in 1978. **Data** (T.Mk1): Span 52ft 0in (15.85m). Length 47ft 1½in (14.37m). Gross weight 12,566lb (5,700kg). Max speed 282mph (454km/h). Max range 1,380 miles (2,224km). Photo: Jetstream T.Mk2.

Beechcraft Bonanza

USA

The prototype Bonanza flew for the first time on December 22, 1945, and the type has now been in continuous production, in progressively improved versions, for more than 30 years. The 10,000th example of the basic V-tailed Model 35 Bonanza was flown in early 1977. Since 1959, variants have included a conventional-tail family of lightplanes, known originally as Debonairs, but currently designated F33 series Bonanzas. The first military order for Bonanzas, placed by the Imperial Iranian Air Force in 1972, was for F33As for training and liaison duties. Contracts for F33Cs, approved for aerobatic flying, have followed, and in 1978, the IIAF had a total of 49 of these two variants in service. All are basically four/five-seaters, with a 285hp Continental IO-520 engine. Other operators are the Mexican Air Force and Naval Aviation, with 23 Bonanza F33Cs, and the Spanish Air Force, with 25 F33Cs and 29 F33Es. **Data** (F33C): Span 33ft 6in (10.21m). Length 26ft 8in (8.13m). Gross weight 3,400lb (1,542kg). Max speed 209mph (338km/h). Range 1,023 miles (1,648km). Photo: F33A (E.24A), Spain.

Beechcraft C-12 Huron and RU-21J   USA

Both the USAF and the US Army adopted the Beech Super King Air 200 during 1974, to meet a long-outstanding requirement for a liaison and staff transport. The commercial prototype had first flown on October 27, 1972. By the beginning of 1978, the USAF had taken delivery of 30 C-12As, for use by US attaches overseas and by military missions; the US Army had received 40 C-12A Hurons for utility transport and liaison duties. Orders placed in December 1977 covered 20 more for the Army and a first batch of 22 for the US Navy, which has a requirement for a total of 66, each equipped to carry two pilots and eight passengers or cargo. These military versions have less power than the commercial model, with two 750shp Pratt & Whitney (Canada) PT6A-38 turboprops. In 1974, the US Army also took delivery of three RU-21Js. These are Super King Airs fitted with standard 850shp PT6A-41 engines and extensive aerial arrays for electronic reconnaissance. **Data** (C-12A): Span 54ft 6in (16.60m). Length 43ft 9in (13.16m). Gross weight 12,500lb (5,670kg). Max cruising speed 262mph (421km/h). Range 1,824 miles (2,935km). Photo: C-12A.

Beechcraft C-45 Expeditor   USA

A total of 5,204 Beechcraft twin-engined military transports/trainers were delivered in World War II. Examples remain in service with more than a dozen air forces. Most numerous are C-45G and C-45H six-seat utility transports, which were produced originally for the post-war USAF by conversion of T-7 and T-11 Kansan trainers. Some T-11s also remain in service, particularly in South America. **Data**(C-45G): Two 45hp P. & W. R985- AN-3 piston-engines. Span 47ft 7in (14.50m). Length 33ft 11½in (10.34m). Gross weight 9,000lb (4,082kg). Max speed 225mph (362km/h). Range 1,200 miles (1,931km). Photo: Model D-18, Venezuela.

Beechcraft Musketeer USA

The Musketeer and its successors have been in production since 1962 and by 1977 more than 3,500 had been sold for service throughout the world. The majority were delivered for private or club use, in two-, four or six-seat variants. During January 1970, the *Fuerza Aérea Mexicana* took delivery of 20 two-seat Musketeer Sport models to be used as instrument trainers, each with a 150hp Lycoming O-320-E2C engine and fixed tricycle undercarriage. During 1971, the Canadian Armed Forces took delivery of 25 Musketeers (CAF designation CT-134) to replace Chipmunk primary trainers; the Royal Hong Kong Auxiliary Air Force has two. **Data:** Span 32ft 9in (9.98m). Length 25ft 0in (7.62m). Gross weight 2,250lb (1,020kg). Max speed 140mph (225km/h). Range 880 miles (1,420km). Photo: Musketeer Sport, Mexico.

Beechcraft T-34 Mentor USA

Derived from the civil Bonanza lightplane, as a private venture, the Mentor first flew on December 2, 1948. Three YT-34s were ordered by the USAF for evaluation in 1950. Subsequently, 350 T-34As were built for the USAF, and the US Navy took delivery of 423 similar T-34Bs before production ended in October 1957. The Mentor was also built by Canadian Car and Foundry for the USAF (100) and RCAF (25); by Fuji Industries in Japan (140 for JASDF, 36 for Philippine Air Force) and at Cordoba in the Argentine (75). Mentors were supplied to several other nations through MAP, and continue to fly with about 15 air forces. Production ended in October 1957. **Data:** One 225hp Continental O-470-13 engine. Span 32ft 10in (10.0m). Length 25ft 11¼in (7.90m). Gross weight 2,950lb (1,338kg). Max speed 189mph (304km/h). Range 735 miles (1,183km). Photo: T-34.

Beechcraft T-34C Turbo Mentor   USA

In 1973 Beech received a US Navy contract to modify two T-34B Mentor trainers to YT-34C Turbo Mentor standard. This involved installing the 715shp (derated to 400shp) Pratt & Whitney PT6A-25 turboprop engine and the latest electronics. The first YT-34C flew on September 21, 1973. By March 1975 the two prototypes had completed 700 flying hours, including 300 hours of Navy evaluation, as a result of which the type was ordered into production as a replacement for the piston-engined T-34B and T-28. Total procurement of more than 200 is planned, of which 116 had been ordered by early 1978, when 48 had been delivered. In addition, orders have been placed by Morocco (12), Argentina (16), Ecuador (20), Indonesia (16) and Peru (6), some of these being for the armed version known as the T-34C-1. **Data:** Span 33ft 3⅞in (10.15m). Length 28ft 8½in (8.75m). Gross weight 4,274lb (1,939kg). Max cruising speed 247mph (397km/h). Max range 749 miles (1,205km). Photo: T-34C-1, Peru.

Beechcraft T-42A Cochise   USA

In February 1965, the USAF chose the Beech B55 Baron to meet its requirement for a twin-engined instrument trainer, following a design competition limited to "off-the-shelf" types. Subsequently, Beech received contracts for 65 aircraft, to be designated T-42A. In 1971, five more T-42As were sold, to Turkey, and in 1972 the Spanish Air Force ordered seven B55 Barons (since supplemented by a further 12). The B55 is a four/six-seat light transport, powered by two 260hp Continental IO-470-L engines. **Data:** Span 37ft 10in (11.53m). Length 27ft 0in (8.23m). Gross weight 5,100lb (2,313kg). Max speed 236mph (380km/h). Range 1,225 miles (1,971km).

Beechcraft U-8 Seminole and Queen Air　　USA

Final version of the U-8 Seminole series supplied to the US Army was a variant of the commercial Queen Air designated U-8F, with a fuselage seating up to six passengers, and 340hp Lycoming IGSO-480 engines. Three pre-production and 68 production U-8Fs were delivered. The standard Queen Air is used by the Japan Maritime Self-Defence Force as a transport and navigation trainer, and others are used by the air forces of Israel, Peru, Venezuela and Uruguay. Earlier Seminoles in US Army service had included the U-8D, with 340hp GSO-480 engines, and the U-8E, with 295hp GO-480 engines, similar to the commercial Model F50 and D50 Twin Bonanzas respectively; some of these earlier models have been modified to U-8Gs. **Data** (U-8F); Span 45ft 10½in (13.98m). Length 35ft 6in (10.82m). Gross weight 7,700lb (3,493kg). Max speed 239mph (384km/h). Range 1,220 miles (1,963km). Photo: Queen Air B80 Venezuela.

Beechcraft U-21 Ute, T-44A and King Air　　USA

During 1963, Beech converted a Queen Air airframe to have Pratt & Whitney PT6A-6 turboprops, and this aircraft was evaluated by the US Army as the NU-8F. In production guise, with the designation U-21A, the same basic airframe has a double freight-loading door, extensive avionics and an interior layout for 10 troops, 6–8 command personnel or 3 stretchers. Delivery of the U-21As began in May 1967 and subsequent contracts brought the total by late 1973 to 184. These include U-21A, RU-21A and RU-21D variants with 550hp PT6A-20 engines and RU-21B, RU-21C and RU-21E variants with 620hp PT6A-29s and 10,900lb (4,994kg) gross weight. Many of these aircraft have extensive aerial arrays for electronic reconnaissance duties. Five U-21Fs acquired by the US Army in 1971 are similar to the commercial, pressurised King Air A100 and 17 U-21Gs are updated USAF versions of the U-21A. The single VC-6B is a VIP transport similar to the King Air 90, and about ten foreign air forces have bought King Airs. In 1976, the US Navy also ordered a version of the King Air 90 as a new advanced trainer, designated T-44A. Deliveries of 61 began in August 1977, to replace piston-engined Grumman TS-2As and Bs.
Data (U-21F): Span 45ft 10½in (13.98m). Length 39ft 11¼in (12.17m). Gross weight 11,500lb (5,216kg). Max cruising speed 285mph (459km/h). Range 1,395 miles (2,245km). Photo: RU-21E.

Beechcraft 99 USA

The first purchase of Beechcraft 99As for military use was announced early in 1970, when the Chilean Air Force ordered nine to replace Beech C-45s. Deliveries were completed in August 1970. Powered by two 680shp Pratt & Whitney PT6A-27 engines, the Beechcraft 99A is basically a 15-seat third-level airliner, about 150 examples of which are in service. The prototype first flew in July 1966, and deliveries of the refined production version began in May 1968. **Data:** Span 45ft 10½in (14.00m). Length 44ft 6¾in (13.58m). Gross weight 10,400lb (4,717kg). Max cruising speed 284mph (457km/h) at 12,000ft (3,650m). Range up to 1,000 miles (1,610km). Photo: Beechcraft 99A, Chile.

Bell AH-1 HueyCobra USA

Bell developed the HueyCobra from the UH-1 Iroquois (also known as the Huey), initially as a private venture, against US Army requirements for an armed helicopter. The prototype Bell 209 HueyCobra flew on September 7, 1965, and two pre-production aircraft and an initial production batch of 110 were ordered in April 1966, with the designation AH-1G, powered by the 1,100shp Lycoming T53-L-13B. Operational service in Vietnam began in Autumn 1967. Early Army AH-1Gs had a TAT-102A nose turret with a six-barrel 7.62mm Minigun. Later aircraft have the XM-28 armament system with two Miniguns or two XM-129 40mm grenade launchers, or one of each; production totalled 1,078, plus 20 for the Spanish Navy. In 1973, the Army began a programme to convert AH-1Gs to AH-1Q standard, with provision to carry eight Hughes TOW (Tube-launched Optically-tracked Wire-guided) missile containers and associated equipment, including a helmet sight sub-system. Only 63 remain converted to AH-1Q standard; the remainder became AH-1S when fitted with the 1,800hp T53-L-703 and upgraded gearbox and transmission. The Army also ordered 297 new-build AH-1S helicopters, some with a 20mm turret cannon, plus conversion of many AH-1Gs to the same standard or to AH-1R standard with the new engines but without TOW provision. **Data** (AH-1S): Rotor diameter 44ft 0in (13.41m). Gross weight 10,000lb (4,535kg). Max speed 141mph (227km/h). Max range 315 miles (507km). Photo: AH-1Q.

Bell AH-1J/1T SeaCobra USA

The SeaCobra was originally ordered by the US Marine Corps in May 1968 as an improved version of the AH-1G HueyCobra, the principal difference being the use of a Pratt & Whitney T400-CP-400 coupled free-turbine turboshaft, flat rated to give a continuous output of 1,100shp, or 1,250shp for take-off. Armament comprised an electrically-driven turret system in the nose with a 20mm General Electric XM-197 three-barrel cannon, plus four external weapon points under stub-wings carrying rockets, Minigun pods, etc. Delivery of 69 AH-1Js to the USMC began in mid-1970, but the last two were converted before delivery to AH-1T standard with 1,970shp T400-WV-402 engine, larger main rotor, lengthened fuselage and other new features. Fifty-seven of these AH-1Ts had been ordered by the Marine Corps by early 1978.

Through the US government, the Imperial Iranian Army Aviation service has acquired 202 Bell 209s similar to the AH-1Js. **Data** (AH-1J): Rotor diameter 44ft 0in (13.41m). Fuselage length 44ft 7in (13.59m). Gross weight 10,000lb (4,535kg). Max speed 207mph (333km/h). Max range 359 miles (577km). Photo: AH-1J, Iran.

Bell H-13 Sioux USA

At least 30 air forces have used the Bell 47 helicopter in different versions and many examples remain in use for miscellaneous duties. The US Army's OH-13G and US Navy's TH-13M were based on the civil 47G, with 200hp Franklin 6V4-200-C32 engine. The OH-13H was based on the 47G-2 with 240hp Lycoming VO-435 engine. Late production models included the three-seat OH-13S, a standard 47G-3B with 260hp TVO-435-25 engine, and the TH-13T two-seat instrument trainer version of the 47G-3B-1, with 270hp TVO-435-25, of which 415 were supplied to the US Army; and the 47J-3, with four/five-seat cabin and covered tail boom, which was built by Agusta for anti-submarine duties with the Italian Navy and for other customers. Westland-built Sioux used by the British services have been replaced by Gazelles. **Data** (47G-3B-1): Rotor diameter 37ft $1\frac{1}{2}$in (11.32m). Fuselage length 31ft 7in (9.63m). Gross weight 2,950lb (1,338kg). Max speed 105mph (169km/h). Range 315 miles (507km). Photo: Bell 47G, Venezuela.

Bell Model 214 (Isfahan) USA

During 1970, Bell flew the prototype of an improved version of the UH-1H, known as the Model 214 Huey Plus. Powered by a 1,900shp Lycoming T53-L-702 turboshaft, it had an enlarged rotor, strengthened airframe and increased gross weight of 11,000lb (4,995kg). From this prototype was developed the Model 214A with a T55-L-7C engine and after demonstrations in Iran, the Iranian government placed an order for 287 examples of the Model 214A, powered in the production model by the 2,930shp Lycoming LTC4B-8D engine, derated to 2,050shp. Known in Iran as the Isfahan, the first production Model 214A flew on March 13, 1974 and deliveries began in April 1975. The Imperial Iranian Army has subsequently ordered 39 Model 214Cs, which are similar but are equipped for search and rescue duties. Original plans to manufacture 400 additional Model 214As at a new plant in Isfahan have been abandoned following events in that country. **Data** (Model 214A): Rotor diameter 50ft 0in (15.24m). Gross weight with external load 15,000lb (6,803kg). Cruising speed 161mph (259km/h). Range 283 miles (455km). Photo: Model 214A Isfahan, Iran.

Bell UH-1 Iroquois (and Agusta-Bell 204B/205)

USA/Italy

Deliveries of the HU-1A (Model 204) Iroquois, with T53-L-1A engine, began on June 30, 1959, for utility transport and casualty evacuation, with six seats or two stretchers. First flown in 1960, the HU-1B (now UH-1B) had a larger cabin for eight passengers or three stretchers, and 960shp T53-L-5 engine. Large numbers were built for the US Army, and for the Australian, Austrian, Italian, Netherlands, Norwegian, Saudi Arabian, Spanish, Swedish and Turkish Services, and by Fuji in Japan. The UH-1C was similar with 1,100shp T53-L-11 engine and wide-chord rotor. The UH-1D (Model 205) has a larger cabin, for 12–14 troops or six stretchers, and a T53-L-11 driving a larger-diameter rotor. In addition to large US Army orders, this model serves in numerous foreign air arms and was built by Dornier for the German Services. For the US Army and New Zealand, the UH-1H superseded the D, with 1,400shp T53-L-13 engine, and 118 of this model were produced in Taiwan for the Chinese Nationalist Army. A similar version used by the Canadian Armed Forces is known as the CH-118, and the USAF bought 30 HH-1Hs for local base rescue duties. A version of the UH-1B won a US Marines design contest for an assault support helicopter in 1962 and is in service as the UH-1E; in 1963 the USAF adopted the UH-1F, with 1,100shp T58-GE-3 engine, for support duties. The HH-1K is a Navy air-sea rescue version of the UH-1E; the TH-1L and UH-1L are Navy training and utility versions. In Italy, Agusta has built equivalent models in large numbers as AB-204 and AB-205, and for the Italian and Spanish Air Arms a special version was developed for anti-submarine duties. Special features of this variant, known as the AB-204AS, include an automatic approach-to-hover system and all-weather instrumentation, sonar equipment, optional AN/APN-195 search radar and provision to carry two Mk44 homing torpedoes. The power plant is a 1,290shp General Electric T58-GE-3 turboshaft, and the gross weight is 9,500lb (4,310kg). **Data** (UH-1H): Rotor diameter 48ft 0in (14.63m). Fuselage length 41ft 10¾in (12.77m). Gross weight 9,500lb (4,309kg). Max speed 127mph (204km/h). Range 318 miles (511km) at 127mph (204km/h). Photo: UH-1H.

Bell UH-1N and Model 212 (and Agusta-Bell AB-212ASW)

USA/Italy

The Bell Model 212 was developed from the basic Model 205 Huey during 1968 to take advantage of the Pratt & Whitney (Canada) PT6T coupled turboshaft engine, offering improved performance and twin-engined safety. Initial orders were placed simultaneously by the US government and the Canadian government. The US version was designated UH-1N and a total of 300 has been built for service with the USAF, USN and Marine Corps, including some UH-1N command transports. The Canadian variant was designated CUH-1N when ordered but now serves with the Canadian Armed Forces as the CH-135. Deliveries of the UH-1N, with 1,800shp Pratt & Whitney T400-CP-400 engine, began in 1970, followed by the first CUH-1N in May 1971. During 1973, 14 Bell 212s were ordered for use by the Peruvian Air Force; the Argentine Air Force has ordered eight, and several other air forces have acquired Model 212s for general duties. The Bell 212 is also built in Italy by Agusta, and this company has developed an extensively-modified version for anti-submarine search and attack as the AB-212ASW. Carrying search radar, sonar and homing torpedoes, the AB-212ASW has been ordered by the Italian Navy, Peru and Turkey, and the general-purpose AB-212 has been ordered by the Austrian Army. **Data** (AB-212ASW): Rotor diameter 48ft 0in (14.63m). Fuselage length 46ft 0in (14.02m). Gross weight 11,196lb (5,079kg). Max speed 122mph (196km/h). Range 414 miles (667km). Photo (*below left*): AB-212ASW, Spain.

Boeing E-4

USA

The well-known Boeing 747 "jumbo-jet" entered USAF service in 1974 to serve as the National Emergency Airborne Command Post and HQ Strategic Air Command airborne command post, able to control the entire US deterrent force of manned bombers and missiles in time of war or crisis. The first three aircraft were delivered to E-4A interim standard, with electronic systems transferred from EC-135 command posts, and will be updated eventually to E-4B standard, with new avionics having greater capabilities. Three new-build E-4Bs are also being procured by the USAF, and the first of these, less the complete avionics, flew on June 8, 1978. The E-4s are each powered by four 52,500lb (23,815kg) st General Electric F103-GE-100 turbofans, which replaced the Pratt & Whitney F105-PW-100s fitted temporarily to the first two. **Data:** Span 195ft 8in (59.64m). Length 231ft 4in (70.51m). Gross weight (E-4A) 778,000lb (352,895kg). Unrefuelled endurance 12 hours Photo (*see page 2*): E-4B.

Boeing T-43A and Model 737

USA

Choice of the Boeing 737 as a new navigation trainer to replace the Convair T-29 was announced by the USAF in May 1971. This type, powered by two Pratt & Whitney JT8D turbofans, had been produced previously only in commercial versions. The USAF order for T-43As was for 19; the first flew on April 10, 1974 and deliveries to Mather AFB were completed in mid-1974. Each has positions in the cabin for 12 students, four advanced students and three instructors. Among air forces operating 737s as standard or VIP transports are those of Brazil and Venezuela. **Data** (T-43A): Span 93ft 0in (28.35m). Length 100ft 0in (30.48m). Gross weight 115,500lb (52,390kg). Max speed 586mph (943km/h). Range over 2,000 miles (3,200km). Photo: Model 737, Venezuela.

Boeing Vertol CH-46 Sea Knight   USA/Japan

The Sea Knight is a derivative of the Boeing Vertol 107-II tandem-rotor helicopter, which itself originated as a Piasecki design. Three Model 107s underwent US Army evaluation and the type was then adopted by the US Marine Corps as the CH-46A Sea Knight with 1,250shp General Electric T58-GE-8B engines; the first example flew on October 16, 1962. After 160 CH-46A, production switched to the CH-46D, with 1,400shp T58-GE-10 engines; 266 "Ds" were built, and a change was then made to the CH-46F with added avionics and instrument panel changes, about 174 being built by the time production ended in 1970. During 1975, the Marine Corps began a programme to convert 276 Sea Knights to CH-46E standard, with 1,870shp T58-GE-16 engines and other improvements. For use in supplying stores to combatant vessels at sea, the US Navy bought 14 UH-46As and 10 UH-46Ds, similar to the Marine Corps models. Variants of the Model 107 were supplied by Boeing to Canada for use by the RCAF as CH-113 Labradors and by the Army as CH-113A Voyageurs; and to Sweden (with Bristol Siddeley Gnome engines) for use by the Air Force and Navy as HKP-7s. **Data** (CH-46D): Rotor diameter 51ft 0in (15.55m) each. Fuselage length 44ft 10in (13.66m). Gross weight 23,000lb (10,442kg). Max speed 166mph (267km/h) at sea level. Range 230 miles (370km). Photo: UH-46D, US Navy.

Boeing Vertol CH-47 Chinook   USA

The Vertol Model 114 tandem-rotor helicopter was selected in March 1959 as the winner of a US Army design competition for a "battlefield mobility" helicopter, capable of carrying a two-ton load internally or eight tons on an external sling. Five prototypes were ordered with the designation YHC-1B, and the first of these flew on September 21, 1961, by which time the Vertol company had become a Division of Boeing. Delivery to the Army began in December 1962. The basic designation had been changed to H-47 in July 1962, and the first production version became the CH-47A, with 2,200shp T55-L-5 or, later, 2,650shp T55-L-7 engines. In early October 1966, the CH-47B made its first flight, with 2,850shp T55-L-7C engines, and production of this version began in 1967. On October 14, 1967, Boeing Vertol flew the first CH-47C, with 3,750shp T55-L-11 engines, and the first production type reached Vietnam in 1968. A total of 699 was delivered to the US Army; in addition, the RAAF bought 12, Iran 76, Italy 10, Spain 7 and Canada 8 (as CH-147s). The examples for Italy and Iran are built in Italy by Agusta/Meridionali. During 1977, Boeing-Vertol was converting one each of the CH-46A, B and C models to YCH-47D prototypes, with 3,700shp T55-L-712 engines, composite rotor blades and improved instrumentation; the Army plans eventually to convert 361 of its Chinooks to this standard. In 1978, it was announced that 30 of the CH-147 model were to be bought for the RAF as Chinook HC.Mk1s; other customers include Greece, Libya, South Korea and Argentina. **Data** (CH-47C): Rotor diameter (each) 60ft 0in (18.29m). Length 51ft 0in (15.54m). Gross weight 46,000lb (20,865kg). Max speed 190mph (306km/h) at sea level. Mission radius 115 miles (185km) at 160mph (257km/h) with 13,450lb (6,080kg) payload. Photo: CH-47C, US Army.

Britten-Norman BN-2A Islander and Defender   Great Britain

Among the first military customers for the basic Islander was the Abu Dhabi Defence Force, which has four for communications duties. Numerous others are now in use with various overseas Services, including the Ghana Air Force (8) and Jamaica Defence Force (2). Intended for more specific military roles, including search and rescue, border patrol and reconnaissance, the Defender appeared in 1971. It has nose-mounted Bendix or RCA radar, and gun or rocket pods on four pylons under the wings. The Maritime Defender differs in having a larger search radar. First orders for the Defender came from the Sultan of Oman's Air Force, for eight, and from the Malagasy Air Force; among more recent customers are the Belgian Army (12), Mauritanian Islamic Air Force (9), Guyana Defence Force (8), Indian Navy (5), Philippine Navy (at least 10) and several others with one or two examples each. The basic BN-2A is powered by 260hp Lycoming O-540-E4C5 engines and was first flown on June 13, 1965. The Defender has 300hp IO-540s. **Data** (Defender): Span 49ft 0in (14.94m) or 53ft 0in (16.15m). Length 35ft 8in (10.86m). Gross weight 6,600lb (2,993kg). Cruising speed 165mph (265km/h) at 10,000ft (3,050m). Range up to 1,723 miles (2,772km) with optional tanks in wingtips. Photo: Defender, Botswana.

CAARP/Mudry CAP 10 and CAP 20   France

Developed from the well-known Piel Emeraude, the side-by-side two-seat CAP 10 is intended for training, touring or aerobatic use. Construction is of wood, except for fabric covering on the rear fuselage and some plastics components, such as the engine cowlings. Standard power plant is a 180hp Lycoming IO-360-B2F. Thirty of the first 50 CAP 10s built were delivered to the French Air Force, for service with the Equipe de Voltige

Aérienne at Salon-de-Provence, and at the basic flying training school at Clermont-Ferrand-Aulnat. The Equipe de Voltige also acquired six CAP 20s, which are single-seat derivatives of the CAP 10 with a 200hp Lycoming AIO-360-B1B engine. **Data** (CAP 10): Span 26ft 5¼in (8.06m). Length 23ft 11½in (7.30m). Gross weight 1,829lb (830kg). Max speed 168mph (270km/h). Range 745 miles (1,200km). Photo: CAP 10.

Canadair CL-215   Canada

The CL-215 amphibian was evolved as a specialised water-bomber, following several years' close study by Canadair of the requirements for this type of operation. The prototype flew for the first time on October 23, 1967; first customers were the Province of Quebec and the Securité Civile of France, each of which acquired fifteen. Being designed for simplicity of operation and maintenance, and capable of operating from short airstrips, small lakes and bays, the CL-215 is equally suited to a variety of other duties. Thus, the Spanish Air Force has ten which are intended

primarily for search and rescue, carrying up to 18 passengers or nine stretchers, but are available for other tasks, including fire-fighting. The Hellenic Air Force flies eight CL-215s for general transport and fire-fighting duties; the Royal Thai Navy has two for search and rescue. **Data:** Two 2,100hp Pratt & Whitney R-2800-83AM2AH engines. Span 93ft 10in (28.60m). Length 65ft 0½in (19.82m). Gross weight 43,500lb (19,731kg). Max cruising speed 181mph (291km/h). Range 1,405 miles (2,260km). Photo: CL-215, Thailand.

CASA 207 Azor

Spain

The Azor flew for the first time on September 28, 1955 and was produced subsequently for the Spanish Air Force in two versions, under the designation T.7. The first series of ten aircraft are CASA C.207-As (T.7As), equipped to carry a crew of four and 30–40 passengers in an air-conditioned cabin. The second series of ten, known as CASA C.207-Cs (T.7Bs) are freighters with a large cargo-door. Powered by 2,040hp Bristol Hercules 730 engines, all the C.207s remain in second-line service with the Spanish Air Force although the Aviocar is replacing this type for routine transport operations. **Data:** Span 91ft 2½in (27.80m). Length 68ft 5in (20.85m). Gross weight 36,375lb (16,500kg). Max speed 283mph (455km/h). Range 1,620 miles (2,610km).

CASA C.101 Aviojet

Spain

The Spanish Ministerio del Aire signed a contract with CASA in September 1975 for the construction of four prototypes (plus two static test specimens) of a new advanced jet trainer for use by the Ejercito del Aire. The C.101 was designed along conventional lines, with a straight wing and a single 3,500lb (1,590kg) st Garrett-AiResearch TFE 731-2 engine. Construction is on modular lines, with space for additional equipment that may be required to meet future training needs. The design also provides for the addition of weapons on six wing pylons and a fuselage centreline hardpoint, up to a total external load of 4,410lb (2,000kg), and the 3,700lb (1,680kg) st TFE 731-3 engine may be adopted in due course. The first prototype of the C.101 flew at Getafe on June 27, 1977, the second on September 30, and the other two in the first half of 1978. Deliveries of 60 production models to the Ejercito del Aire are scheduled to begin in 1980. **Data:** Span 34ft 9½in (10.60m). Length 40ft 2¼in (12.25m). Gross weight (trainer) 10,360lb (4,700kg). Max speed Mach 0.69 at 25,000ft (7,620m).

CASA C.212 Aviocar

Spain

Design of the C.212 was undertaken to provide a locally-produced replacement for the CASA C.352L (Ju 52/3m) and Douglas C-47 transport aircraft serving with the Spanish Air Force. The Spanish Air Ministry ordered two prototypes in September 1968 and these flew, respectively, on March 26 and October 23, 1971, powered by 755hp AiResearch TPE 331 turboprops. Orders totalled 136 for six countries by early 1978, including more than 50 for the Spanish Air Force, 25 for the Portuguese Air Force, five for Ecuador, four for the Royal Jordanian Air Force and 25 for the armed forces of Indonesia, where an Aviocar assembly line has been opened by Nurtanio. The Spanish Air Force orders include the C.212A (T.12B) utility transport, C.212B (TR.12A) photo-survey version, C.212AV (T.12C) VIP transport and C.212E navigation trainer. The 138th production Aviocar, under construction in early 1978 as the C.212-10, has an increased gross weight of 16,500lb (7,485kg) and 865hp engines. **Data** (C.212C): Span 62ft 4in (19.00m). Length 49ft 10½in (15.20m). Gross weight 14,330lb (6,500kg). Max speed 223mph (359km/h). Range 300-1,100 miles (480-1,750km). Photo: C.212A (T.12B), Spain.

Cessna O-1 Bird Dog

USA

One of the first light liaison and reconnaissance aircraft developed for the US Army Field Forces after the end of World War II, the O-1 (formerly L-19) Bird Dog won a design competition in April 1950. By March 1964, a total of 3,431 had been delivered to the Army under the designations O-1A and O-1E and to the Marine Corps as O-1B (60 built). The Marines also received 25 O-1Cs, a similar but more powerful type with square-cut fin. TO-1A, TO-1D and TO-1E versions were used by the Army as trainers. The USAF used the modified O-1F and O-1G for forward air control duties in Vietnam. The O-1 was also supplied to France (90), Canada, Cambodia, Austria, Brazil, Chile, Indonesia, Italy, Kenya, South Korea, Laos, Lebanon, Norway, Pakistan, the Philippines, Spain, Thailand, Turkey and South Vietnam, and was built in Japan by Fuji; it remains in service in several of these countries. **Data** (O-1E): One 213hp Continental O-470-11. Span 36ft 0in (10.9m). Length 25ft 10in (7.89m). Gross weight 2.430lb (1,103kg). Max speed 115mph (184m/h). Range 530 miles (848km). Photo: O1, Pakistan.

Cessna O-2　　　　　　　　　　　　　　USA

The USAF adopted this version of the "push and pull" Cessna 337 Super Skymaster late in 1966, to replace the Cessna O-1 in FAC (forward air controller) missions, for which purpose a number of modifications were introduced including four underwing pylons for gun pods, rockets, flares, etc. Powered by two 210hp Continental IO-360-C/D engines, the O-2 has dual controls for the pilot and observer, and can carry one passenger. The USAF acquired 346, and 12 were purchased by the Iranian Imperial AF. In addition, the USAF acquired more than 100 O-2Bs, equipped for psychological warfare duties with high-power air-to-

ground broadcast systems; these are no longer in service. The Ecuadorean Air Force and Venezuelan Navy are among military users of the basic Skymaster. In France, Reims Aviation produces the similar F-337 in several military versions, some with STOL modifications. **Data:** Span 38ft 2in (11.63m). Length 29ft 9in (9.07m). Gross weight 5,400lb (2,450kg). Max speed 199 mph (320km/h). Photo: Reims FTB 337.

Cessna T-41 Mescalero　　　　　　　USA

In 1964 the USAF ordered 170 standard Cessna 172 light aircraft as basic trainers, under the designation T-41A; a further 34 followed in 1967, and 96 remained in service in 1977. Eight T-41As were delivered to Ecuador, 20 to Greece, 5 to Honduras and 20 to Peru. The US Army bought 255 similar T-41Bs, with a 210hp Continental IO-360-D engine. Also similar are the T-41C, of which Cessna delivered 52 to the USAF Academy, and the T-41D, 226 of which were built for MAP supply to various nations including Bolivia, Colombia, Dominican Republic, Ecuador, Indonesia, Laos, the Philippines, Thailand and Turkey. Other mili-

tary users of the Cessna 172 include the Malagasy Air Force, the Royal Saudi Air Force and the Irish Army Air Corps, which has eight Reims-built FR.172Hs. Other countries use various Cessna lightplanes including the Model 180, with tailwheel undercarriage and 230hp Continental O-470-R engine, and the Model 182 with O-470-R and nose-wheel undercarriage. **Data** (T-41A): One 145hp Continental O-300-C engine. Span 35ft 10in (10.92m). Length 26ft 11in (8.20m). Gross weight 2,300lb (1,043kg). Max speed 138mph (222km/h). Range 720 miles (1,160km). Photo: T-41A, Peru.

Cessna U-3, Model 310, 402 & 411　　　　USA

The U-3A (originally known as the L-27A) is the commercial Cessna 310A (first flown on January 3, 1953) as modified for a USAF design competition for a light twin-engined administrative liaison and cargo aircraft. It won this competition, and an initial contract for 80 was subsequently doubled. The U-3A seats five in a roomy cabin, and can be identified by its unswept fin. It was followed by 36 "all-weather" U-3Bs, based on the commercial 310E with swept fin. Nine other air forces operate standard Cessna 310s. The French Air Force acquired 12 somewhat similar but larger six/eight-seat Cessna 411s, with 340hp GTSIO-520 turbo-supercharged engines, and 12 Cessna 310s which serve in the communications role at the CEV bases at Bretigny and Istres. Twelve somewhat larger Cessna 402s were bought by the Royal Malaysian Air Force. **Data** (U-3A): Two 240hp Continental O-470-M piston-engines. Span 36ft (10.97m). Length 27ft 1in (8.25m). Gross weight 4,600lb (2,086kg). Max speed 232mph (373km/h). Range 850 miles (1,368km). Photo: Model 411, France.

Cessna U-17　　　　USA

The Cessna 185 Skywagon has been adopted for military duties by several nations and has also been built in quantity under USAF contract for delivery to foreign nations, with the designation U-17. Since 1963 a total of 169 U-17As and 136 U-17Bs, plus some U-17Cs with O-470-L engines, have been delivered. Among the nations which received U-17s under this programme were Bolivia, Costa Rica, South Vietnam and Laos. Skywagons, powered by the 300hp Continental IO-520-D engine, have also been purchased direct from Cessna by the South African Air Force and Peru. The larger Model 207 Turbo-Skywagon has been purchased by the Indonesian Air Force. **Data:** Span 35ft 10in (10.92m). Length 25ft 9in (7.85m). Gross weight 3,300lb (1,500kg). Max speed 178mph (286km/h). Range 1,075 miles (1,730km). Photo: Model 185, Jamaica.

Convair C-131 (and Canadair CC-109)   USA

The USAF procured substantial numbers of the basically-civil Convair Model 240/340/440 series in two groups—as T-29 special purpose trainers and as C-131 transports. None of the T-29s remain in service but MAC's 89th MAW, Special Missions, in Washington still operates four VC-131Hs in the short-range VIP transport role; these are converted C-131Ds with 3,750shp Allison T56-A-9 turboprops. During 1977, the US Coast Guard acquired 22 C-131As ex-USAF, from long-term storage for conversion to HC-131A search-and-rescue aircraft. Seventeen of these have entered the USCG inventory, with the original R-2800 piston engines. A few Convair-liners still operate with other air forces, including that of Italy; while the Canadian Armed Forces has in service seven CC-109 Cosmopolitans, these being Canadair-built versions of the CV-440 with Allison T56 engines. **Data** (VC-131H): Span 105ft 4in (32.10m). Length 79ft 2in (24.13m). Gross weight 54,600lb (24,788kg). Cruising speed 342mph (550km/h). Range 1,605 miles (2,582km). Photo: Convair 440 (T.14), Spain.

Convair F-102 Delta Dagger   USA

Convair initiated design of the Delta Dagger in 1950, basically by scaling up in size its earlier XF-92A, the world's first jet-powered delta. Two prototype YF-102s flew, respectively, on October 24, 1953, and January 11, 1954. When initial trials revealed deficiencies in performance, a YF-102A was built with the first-ever area-ruled ('waisted') fuselage. It soon proved itself capable of supersonic speed, and 875 similar F-102As were built for service with Air Defense Command, each powered by a 17,200lb (7,808kg) st Pratt & Whitney J57-P-23 or -25 afterburning turbojet and armed with up to four Falcon missiles. They were supplemented by 63 TF-102A combat trainers, with wider front fuselage containing two side-by-side seats. After many years of USAF service, about 60 F-102As and TF-102As were passed on to the Turkish and Hellenic Air Forces; but the only Delta Daggers operational in 1978 were being flown by a single Turkish squadron. Many others have been converted into PQM-102 pilotless target drones for the USAF. **Data** (F-102A): Span 38ft 1½in (11.62m). Length 68ft 4½in (20.81m). Gross weight approx 32,000lb (14,515kg). Max speed Mach 1.25 (825mph; 1,328km/h). Max range approx 1,100 miles (1,770km). Photo: F-102A, Turkey.

Dassault MD-312/315 Flamant   France

The MD-315 Flamant entered service originally as a light transport, powered by two 580hp SNECMA-Renault 12S-02-201 engines and with accommodation for a crew of two and ten passengers or freight. A total of 137 were built. Another passenger-carrying version is the MD-312 six-seat communications aircraft, of which 142 were built. Flamants remain active with the French Air Force, serving alongside other types in three Escadrilles de Liaison Aériennes. Three Flamants are also in service with the Tunisian Air Force.

The Flamant can be adapted for freighting or ambulance duties and is a development of the original MD-303 prototype, which first flew on February 10, 1947. **Data** (MD-315): Span 67ft 10in (20.68m). Length 41ft (12.50m). Gross weight 12,760lb (5,800kg). Max speed 236mph (380km/h). Range 755 miles (1,215km). Photo: MD-312, France.

Dassault MD-452 Mystère IVA   France
and Super Mystère B-2

Altogether, 421 Mystère IVAs were built, all but the first 50 with a 7,716lb (3,500kg) st Hispano-Suiza Verdon 350 turbojet. None remains in first-line service, but a few still fly in Israel and India; others equip the 8e *Escadre de Transformation* of the French Air Force, at Cazaux, where they will continue to be used for weapon training until replaced by Alpha Jets. The supersonic Super Mystère B-2, evolved from the Mystère IV series, retired from French service in 1977. Israel, which purchased 24, still had one squadron operational in a fighter-bomber role at the time of the Holy Day

War in 1973. By that time, the original Atar 101G turbojet fitted to these aircraft had been replaced by a 9,300lb (4,218kg) st Pratt & Whitney J52-P-8A, with lengthened jet pipe, as installed in early Israeli Skyhawks. Twelve of these J52-engined Super Mystères were sold to Honduras in 1976/77. **Data** (Mystère IVA): Span 36ft 5$\frac{1}{2}$in (11.12m). Length 42ft 1$\frac{1}{2}$in (12.85m). Gross weight 18,700lb (8,482kg). Max speed 695mph (1,120km/h) at sea level. Endurance 1hr 10min (clean). Photo: Mystère IVA, France.

Dassault-Breguet Falcon 10 MER   France

The Falcon 10 was developed by Dassault-Breguet in the late 'sixties as a "baby brother" for the successful Mystère/Falcon 20 business jet (page 155). Basically a scaled-down version of that design, it has smaller overall dimensions and less powerful engines; but a more advanced wing bestows on the Falcon 10 a somewhat higher cruising speed. The cabin normally seats four, with a crew of two. The first Falcon 10 flew on December 1, 1970, with General Electric CJ610 engines, followed by a second prototype on October 15, 1971, with 3,230lb (1,466kg) st Garrett-AiResearch TFE 731-2 engines which have been adopted as the production standard. Two Falcon 10s were acquired by the French Aéronavale, to be used as systems trainers for the Super Etendard programme and for fleet support and instrument training duties in general; these are known as Falcon 10 MER (*Marine Entrainement Radar*). **Data:** Span 42ft 11in (13.08m). Length 45ft 5in (13.85m). Gross weight 18,740lb (8,500kg). Max speed 568mph (915km/h).

Dassault-Breguet Falcon 20   France

Several air forces use this small, high-speed aircraft for VIP transport duties, including the RAAF, which has three operated by No 34 Squadron at Fairbairn, the Canadian Armed Forces with seven (some converted for use as ECM trainers), and the Belgian, French and Norwegian Air Forces.

Powered in this version by two General Electric CF700 turbofans, each of 4,200 or 4,250lb (1,905 or 1,928kg) st, the Falcon 20 normally carries a crew of two and eight passengers, but is able to take up to 14 seats in its main cabin in less luxurious layouts. The French Air Force also has two Falcon ST fitted with the same radar and navigation systems as those carried by a Mirage III fighter, and uses them to train combat pilots in the use of this equipment; the Libyan Air Force has one, similarly equipped. **Data:** Span 53ft 6in (16.30m). Length 56ft 3in (17.15m). Gross weight 28,660lb (13,000kg). Max speed 534mph (860km/h). Range 2,220 miles (3,570km) at 466mph (750km/h).

De Havilland DHC-1 Chipmunk

Canada/Great Britain

First original design by de Havilland Canada, the Chipmunk was built in quantity on both sides of the Atlantic, DHC producing a total of 218 and 1,014 being built by de Havilland in the UK. Most of those operated by the RAF have been replaced by Bulldogs but some remain in use in Air Experience Flights, for the benefit of the ATC, and have undergone a programme to give them a further 10-year life. Chipmunks were supplied to about a dozen overseas air forces and are still used in the training role by a few of them, including those of Burma, Sri Lanka and Thailand, and the Irish Air Corps. **Data** (T.Mk 10): One 145hp Gipsy Major 8 piston-engine. Span 34ft 4in (10.46m). Length 25ft 5in (7.48m). Gross weight 2,014lb (915kg). Max speed 138mph (222km/h). Range 280 miles (450km). Photo: T.Mk 20, Ireland.

De Havilland DHC-2 Mk 1 Beaver and U-6

Canada

The Beaver first flew on August 16, 1947, and was the second original design of the Canadian de Havilland company. A high proportion of the total of 1,657 built were supplied to 20 military air forces, including 968 delivered to the USAF and US Army under the designation U-6A (formerly L-20A); some are now TU-6As for training use. Of 42 acquired by the British Army Air Corps as Beaver AL.Mk 1, only a few remain in use in 1978. Beavers can operate on wheels, floats or skis or as amphibians, and with the US Forces have operated in the Arctic. **Data:** One 450hp P. & W. R-985-AN-1 or -3 piston-engine. Span 48ft (14.64m). Length 30ft 4in (9.24m). Gross weight 5,100lb (2,313kg). Max speed 140mph (225km/h). Range 778 miles (1,252km).

De Havilland DHC-3 Otter and U-1　　Canada

First flown on December 12, 1951, the 11-seat Otter is "big brother" to the Beaver. A total of 460 were built for military and commercial use and about 11 air forces have flown the type. The 69 Canadian Armed Forces Otters were supplied primarily for Arctic search and rescue, paratroop dropping and photographic duties. The US Army purchased a trial batch of six YU-1s in 1955 and followed this order with another for 84 U-1As which were used as supply aircraft in forward areas, and now serve in the utility and communications role, and as TU-1A trainers. U-1Bs were US Navy purchases for use in the Antarctic. All Otters can operate on wheels, floats or skis. **Data:** One 600hp R-1340 piston-engine. Span 58ft (17.69m). Length 41ft 10in (12.80m). Gross weight 8,000lb (3,629kg). Max speed 160mph (257km/h). Range 945 miles (1,520km).

De Havilland DHC-6 Twin Otter and UV-18　Canada

The original 19-passenger DHC-6 made its first flight on May 20, 1965. Both the Series 100 and Series 200 have 579eshp Pratt & Whitney PT6A-20 turboprops, while the Series 300 has 652eshp PT6A-27 engines, increased gross weight and higher performance. Over 600 Twin Otters have been delivered to date, mostly for service with airlines and as business aircraft. Military orders have come from the Argentine Air Force (5) and Army (3); Canadian Armed Forces (9, designated CC-138); Chilean Air Force (11); Ecuadorean Air Force (3); Jamaica Defence Force (1); Peruvian Air Force (12, including 8 floatplanes); Royal Norwegian Air Force (5); Uganda Police Air Wing (1); Paraguayan Air Force (1) and Panamanian Air Force (1). Early in 1976, the US Army acquired two as UV-18As for service in Alaska, and the USAF bought two UV-18Bs in 1977 to be used at the Air Academy. **Data:** Span 65ft 0in (19.81m). Length 51ft 9in (15.77m). Gross weight 12,500lb (5,670kg). Max speed 210mph (338km/h). Range 794 miles (1,277km). Photo: Twin Otter, Argentine Navy.

De Havilland (Hawker Siddeley) D.H.104 Dove, Devon and Sea Devon, and Sea Heron C.Mk1

Great Britain

The Dove was adopted for service with the RAF in 1948, as the Devon C.Mk1. A change of designation to C.Mk2 indicated replacement of the original 380hp Gipsy Queen 70-4 or -71 engines with Gipsy Queen 175s; introduction of an enlarged Heron-type canopy was indicated by the designation C.Mk2/2. The Devon's primary role was that of staff transport, most of the 30 or so examples acquired having been allocated for the personal use of officers commanding Groups and Commands. A few remain in service with No 207 Communications Squadron. Thirteen similar aircraft were acquired by the Royal Navy for communications duties, as Sea Devon C.Mk20s. Eight continue in use, with No 781 Squadron, together with four Sea Heron C.Mk1s, with four Gipsy Queen engines and seats for 14–17 passengers. About a dozen other air forces have used Doves in the communications and training role. **Data:** Span 57ft (17.40m). Length 39ft 3in (11.96m). Gross weight 8,950lb (4,060kg). Max speed 230mph (370km/h). Range 880 miles (1,415km). Photo: Sea Heron.

De Havilland Vampire

Great Britain

Having flown for the first time on September 20, 1943, the Vampire is one of the oldest jet fighters still in service. The Dominican Republic has a fighter-bomber squadron of F.Mk1s and FB.Mk50s, acquired from Sweden. Rhodesia has a squadron of FB.Mk9s. Switzerland uses some FB.Mk6s as trainers. Also in service is the two-seat training variant of the Vampire, first flown in private-venture prototype form on November 15, 1950. The prototype was followed by two examples for evaluation by the Royal Navy, and then by production deliveries for the RAF, under the designation T.Mk11. A total of 804 Vampire Trainers was eventually built, including 73 Sea Vampire T.Mk22s for the Fleet Air Arm; Australian licence production accounted for another 109 as Mks33, 34 and 35. Trainers were exported to about 20 countries and are still used by several, including Burma, Rhodesia, Chile, Venezuela and Switzerland. **Data** (T.Mk11): Span 38ft 0in (11.58m). Length 34ft 6½in (10.51m). Gross weight 11,150lb (5,060kg). Max speed 549mph (885km/h). Range 853 miles (1,370km). Photo: FB.Mk6, Switzerland.

158

Dornier Do 27 Germany

Until aircraft manufacture was permitted again in Germany, many German designers worked abroad. Thus, the prototype of this design, designated Do 25 and powered by a 150hp ENMA Tigre G-IVB engine, was built in Spain to meet a Spanish Air Force requirement. It flew on June 25, 1954, and was followed by the prototype Do 27 with 275hp Lycoming GO-480 engine on June 27, 1955. Production of the latter was transferred to Germany, where the first of 428 Do 27As ordered for the German Air Force and Army flew on October 17, 1956. Others were acquired by about ten air forces and are still used by the Israeli, Maltese, Nigerian, Swedish, Swiss and Turkish Services; 50 were built in Spain as CASA 127s for the Spanish Air Force. The basic Do 27A is a five-seater, convertible for freighting and casualty evacuation. The Do 27H has a 340hp GSO-480 engine. **Data** (Do 27A): Span 39ft 4½in (12.0m). Length 31ft 6in (9.6m). Gross weight 4,070lb (1,850kg). Max speed 141mph (227km/h). Range 685 miles (1,100km). Photo: CASA 127 (L.9), Spain.

Dornier Do 28D Skyservant Germany

The 14/15-seat Skyservant is a successor to the STOL Do 28, of which 120 were built. A few Do 28s serve in military guise for communications duties. The Do 28D represented a completely new design, with much increased capacity, and the prototype flew on February 23, 1966. After seven Do 28Ds had been built, production switched to the Do 28D-1/2 with a small increase in wing span and higher gross weight. The largest single order for the Do 28D-2 was from the German Armed Forces, comprising 20 for the Navy and 101 for the Luftwaffe. Two were bought by the Turkish Army for its Flying Training School and other military users include the Zambian, Israeli, Malawi, Ethiopian, Nigerian and Kenyan Air Forces. The Skyservant is powered by two 380hp Lycoming IGSO-540 engines. **Data:** Span 51ft 0¼in (15.55m). Length 37ft 5¼in (11.41m). Gross weight 8,470lb (3,842kg). Max cruising speed 170mph (273km/h). Range 1,255 miles (2,020km). Photo: Do 28D-2, Luftwaffe.

Douglas A-3 Skywarrior　　　　　　　USA

The Skywarrior was the largest aircraft that had been produced for carrier operations when the prototype first flew on October 28, 1952, designated XA3D-1. All Skywarriors were built with A3D designations, changed to A-3 in 1962. The first production three-seat A-3A flew on September 16, 1953, and deliveries to the Navy began in March 1956. The A-3B, which began to reach the fleet in 1957, had more powerful engines and provision for flight refuelling; 164 were built. The EA-3B for electronic countermeasures had a crew compartment in the bomb-bay, seating four, and

first flew on December 10, 1958; 24 were built. The final operational deployment of the Skywarrior, continuing in 1978, was as the KA-3B flight refuelling tanker and the EKA-3B tanker aircraft/countermeasures or strike (TACOS) version, 30 examples of which were converted from A-3Bs. **Data** (A-3B): Two 10,500lb (4,763kg) st Pratt & Whitney J57-P-10 turbojets. Span 72ft 6in (22.07m). Length 76ft 4in (23.27m). Gross weight 73,000lb (33,112kg) Max speed 610mph (982km/h) at 10,000ft (3,050m). Range over 2,900 miles (4,667km). Photo: EKA-3B.

Douglas C-47 and C-117 Skytrain　　USA
and Dakota

C-47 variants remain in service with many air forces throughout the world, sometimes under the British name Dakota. The C-47 Skytrain was the basic production model for the USAF, supplemented by the externally-similar C-117A, B and C staff transports. The C-117D was an improved model for the US Navy with new wings and tail and 1,535hp Wright R-1820 engines. Heavily-armed gunship versions of the type, designated AC-47D "Spooky", operated in Vietnam with great effectiveness; some AC-47s were later transferred

to Cambodia. The few C-47s used in Canada now carry the designation CC-129. **Data** (C-47): Two 1,200hp Pratt & Whitney R-1830-90C piston engines. Span 95ft (28.95m). Length 64ft 5½in (19.64m). Gross weight 26,000lb (11,793kg). Max speed 229mph (369km/h). Range 1,500 miles (2,414km) Photo: C-47, Dominican Republic.

Douglas C-54 Skymaster   USA

In production as a new commercial transport when America entered the war in 1941, the Douglas DC-4 was immediately taken over as a military transport, and more than 1,000 were built for the USAF and US Navy. Numerous sub-variants were produced and in small numbers the Skymaster continues to serve as a personnel or freight transport with about a dozen air forces. In the Spanish Air Force, the type is known as the T-4. Standard payload is 50 troops or 32,000lb (14,515kg) of cargo. **Data:** Four 1,450hp Pratt & Whitney R-2000 piston-engines. Span 117ft 6in (35.8m). Length 93ft 11in (28.63m). Gross weight 73,000lb (33,112kg). Max speed 274mph (441km/h). Range (normal) 1,500 miles (2,410km). Photo: DC-4, SAAF.

Douglas C-118 Liftmaster and   USA
DC-6/DC-7 variants

The USAF acquired a total of 101 DC-6Cs for service with MATS, under the designation C-118A, following development under military contracts of the prototype DC-6. Designated XC-112A, this prototype first flew on February 15, 1946, and was a development of the C-54. A further 65 similar aircraft were purchased by the US Navy and contributed to MATS operations—61 as R6D-1s and four as R6D-1Zs with executive interiors. These were subsequently redesignated C-118B and VC-118B respectively, and were assigned to Reserve units (to replace C-54s), with which a few were still being flown in 1978. Commercial DC-6/DC-7 variants passed into military service elsewhere, such as six DC-6A/BFs used for long-range logistic support by the Portuguese Air Force, and five in service with the Paraguayan Air Force. **Data** (C-118): Span 117ft 6in (35.81m). Length 105ft 7in (32.18m). Gross weight 102,000lb (46,266kg). Max speed 360mph (579km/h). Range 3,860 miles (6,212km). Photo: C118B, US Navy.

EKW C-3605   Switzerland

This is the final variant in a family of general-purpose monoplanes originated by the Swiss factory of Eidgenössiches Konstruktionswerkstätte (EKW) in 1939, when the C-3601 was flown for the first time. The Swiss Air Force took delivery, between 1942 and 1945, of 150 C-3603s and ten C-3604s as reconnaissance bombers. After they had been replaced by newer types, 35 C-3603s remained in service as target tugs and two as trainers, powered by the Hispano HS 12Y-51 engine. On August 19, 1968, EKW flew the C-3605, a converted C-3603 with a 1,150shp Avco Lycoming T5307A turboprop engine. The Swiss Air Force ordered conversion of 23 of the surviving C-3603s to this standard for continued use as target tugs and these began to enter service in 1972. **Data:** Span 45ft 1in (13.74m). Length 39ft 5$\frac{3}{4}$in (12.03m). Gross weight 8,185lb (3,710kg). Max speed 268mph (432km/h). Range 610 miles (970km).

Fairchild C-119 Flying Boxcar   USA

A total of 1,051 Flying Boxcars was built for the USAF and for countries associated with the Mutual Aid Programme. Production versions for the USAF comprised the C-119B and C, with R-4360 engines, and the C-119F and G, which switched to R-3350s. The US Navy had 39 C-119Bs as R4Q-1 and 58 C-119Fs as R4Q-2, later designated C-119F. Eight C-119Gs were converted into unarmed C-119Ks and supplied through MAP to the Ethiopian Air Force, which obtained at least ten more C-119s in second-hand deals with other air forces. By 1978, the principal remaining users of the Flying Boxcar were the Chinese Nationalist Air Force, with about 40, the Italian Air Force with some 20 C-119G/Js and the Indian Air Force with about 32 C-119Gs. During 1963-64, 26 of the Indian Air Force machines were modified to Steward-Davis Jet Packet standard, by having a Westinghouse J34-WE-36 auxiliary turbojet mounted above the fuselage. More powerful Orpheus turbojets have since replaced the J34s. **Data** (C-119K): Two 3,700hp Wright R-3350-99 TC18EA2 piston engines, plus two 2,850lb (1,293kg) st General Electric J85-GE-17 turbojets. Span 109ft 3in (33.30m). Length 86ft 6in (26.36m). Gross weight 77,000lb (34,925kg). Max speed 243mph (391km/h) at 10,000ft (3,050m). Range 990 miles (1,595km) with max payload. Photo: C-119K, Ethiopia.

Fairchild C-123 Provider

USA

This tactical assault transport was derived from a cargo glider designed in 1949 by Chase Aircraft. Five pre-production C-123Bs were built for Chase at Willow Run by the Kaiser-Frazer Corporation in 1953, after which the production contract was transferred to Fairchild. As the C-123B Provider, Fairchild flew the first of 300 on September 1, 1954. First flown on July 30, 1962, the YC-123H added CJ610 podded turbojets under each wing and was tested in South Vietnam in the counter-insurgency role. A modification programme was put in hand for the conversion of 183 aircraft to similar standard, with J85 engines in the pods; the first of these, designated C-123K, flew on May 27, 1966. Many of the USAF Providers used in Vietnam were transferred to the VNAF, but were withdrawn in the closing stages of the war. Other users of the type included the Cambodian Air Force, but these aircraft also were flown out to Thailand, which had about 30 in service in 1978. The Chinese National-ist Air Force has about 10 and four US Air Force Reserve squadrons flew C-123s in 1978. **Data:** Two 2,300hp Pratt & Whitney R-2800-99W piston-engines and two 2,850lb (1,293kg) st General Electric J85-GE-17 turbojets. Span 110ft 0in (33.53m). Length 76ft 3in (23.92m). Gross weight 60,000lb (27,215kg). Max speed 228mph (367km/h) at 10,000ft (3,050m). Normal range 1,035 miles (1,666km) with 15,000lb (6,800kg) payload. Photo: C-123B, Venezuela.

Fairchild FH-1100

USA

This five-seat utility helicopter had its origin in the Hiller OH-5A, designed for evaluation in the US Army's competition for a light observation heli-copter (LOH). The prototype OH-5A flew on Janu-ary 26, 1963, and after the Hughes OH-6A had been chosen for production, Fairchild (which had taken over Hiller) continued development and manufacture of the OH-5A as a private venture for both commercial and military use. The developed version was redesignated FH-1100 and the first production model was completed on June 3, 1966. The Philippine Air Force placed the first military contract, for eight. Others subsequently went into service with the Argentine Army, and in Costa Rica, Nigeria, Panama, El Salvador and Thailand. Power plant is a 317shp Allison 250-C18 turboshaft. **Data:** Rotor diameter 35ft 4¾in (10.79m). Fuselage length 29ft 9½in (9.08m). Gross weight 2,750lb (1,247kg). Max cruising speed 127mph (204km/h). Range 348 miles (560km). Photo: FH-1100, Argentine.

FMA I.A.35 Huanquero   Argentina

The I.A.35 Huanquero (first flown September 21, 1953) was built in four versions for the Argentine Air Force. The first production machine flew on March 29, 1957; of the total of 47 delivered about 40 remained in service in 1978. The I.A.35 Type IA is an advanced instrument flying and navigation trainer, carrying two pilots, radio operator, instructor and four pupils. Type III is an ambulance version with accommodation for a crew of three, four patients and attendant. Type IV is a photographic version. Each of these three models is powered by two 620hp I.A.19R El Indio engines.

Fourth version, being replaced by the I.A.58 Pucara, is the Type IB for weapon training, powered by 750hp I.A.19R engines and armed with two 0.50in machine-guns, plus underwing racks for 440lb of bombs or rockets. **Data** (Type IA): Span 64ft 3in (19.60m). Length 45ft 10in (13.98m). Gross weight 12,540lb (5,700kg). Max speed 225mph (362km/h). Range 975 miles (1,570km).

FMA I.A.50 G.II   Argentina

In its original Mk I form, this design utilised many components of the Huanquero, including the twin-fin tail unit. The I.A.50 G.II introduced many changes, including a single swept fin and rudder, de-icing equipment, a shorter rear fuselage and more powerful (930hp) Turboméca Bastan VI-A turboprops. The first of two prototypes flew on April 23, 1963, followed by one pre-production model and two series of 18 and 15 production aircraft. The first batch comprised 14 troop transports, a VIP transport and two survey aircraft for the Argentine Air Force and one Navy staff transport. One example was fitted with skis and another

furnished as a Presidential transport. **Data:** Span 64ft 3¼in (19.59m). Length 50ft 2½in (15.30m). Gross weight 16,200lb (7,350kg). Max speed 310mph (500km/h). Max range 1,600 miles (2,575km).

Fokker-VFW F.28   Netherlands

First military order for an F.28 of the basic Mk 1000 series, announced in 1970, came from the Argentine Air Force, for use as a Presidential aircraft. Another was acquired by the Dutch Royal Flight; one was delivered for the President of Colombia, another for VIP use by the Government of Nigeria and similar aircraft to the Congo Republic, Peru and Togo. The Malaysian government bought two and the Argentine Air Force acquired five Mk 1000C freighters for operation by LADE. Another Mk 1000C and a Mk 1000 went to Ivory Coast. The F.28 prototype made its first flight on May 9,

1967 and deliveries for commercial use began on February 24, 1969. All aircraft sold by 1978 for military or government VIP use were to Mk 1000/1000C standard, with 9,850lb (4,468kg) st Rolls-Royce RB. 183-2 Spey Mk 555-15 engines. Current commercial aircraft are the Mk 3000 and Mk 4000, with improved engines and greater wing span. **Data** (Mk 1000): Span 77ft 4¼in (23.58m). Length 89ft 10¾in (27.40m). Gross weight 65,000lb (29,485kg). Max cruising speed 528mph (849km/h) at 21,000ft (6,400m). Range 956 miles (1,538km). Photo. Mk1000, Ivory Coast.

Fuji LM-1/LM-2 Nikko and   Japan
KM-2 (T-3)

The LM-1 Nikko is a liaison aircraft, developed from the Beech T-34 Mentor by Fuji, who built the latter under licence in Japan. It retains the standard 225hp Continental O-470-13A engine of the trainer, and differs only in the centre-fuselage structure which seats four persons in pairs, with side doors and a removable hatch for loading bulky freight. The first Nikko flew on June 6, 1955, and 27 were delivered subsequently to the Japan Ground Self-Defence Force. Some were converted to LM-2 standard, with more powerful engine and optional fifth seat. Generally similar in appearance

are KM-2 two/four-seat primary trainers of the Maritime Self-Defence Force; but these have a 340hp Lycoming IGSO-480-A1C6 engine. The KM-2B trainer is similar, but with only two seats in tandem like the original Mentor; 54 of these are in process of being acquired by the JASDF under the designation T-3, to replace Mentors. **Data** (KM-2): Span 32ft 10in (10.0m). Length 26ft 0¾in (7.94m). Gross weight 3,860lb (1,750kg). Max speed 230mph (370km/h). Range 570 miles (915km). Photo: KM-2B.

Fuji T1   Japan

Designed to replace the T-6 piston-engined trainers of the JASDF, the prototype of this tandem two-seat intermediate jet trainer was ordered in 1956 and flew on January 19, 1958. The first 40 production machines each had a 4,000lb (1,814kg) st Bristol Siddeley Orpheus 805 turbojet and bear the company designation T1F2 (JASDF designation T1A). They were followed by 20 T1F1s (T1B) with 2,645lb (1,200kg) st Ishikawajima-Harima J3-

IHI-3, the prototype of which flew on May 17, 1960. Both versions have provision for one 0.50in machine-gun and 1,500lb (680kg) of underwing bombs, rockets or missiles instead of drop tanks. **Data** (T1A): Span 34ft 5in (10.50m). Length 39ft 9in (12.12m). Gross weight 11,000lb (5,000kg). Max speed 575mph (925km/h). Range 1,210 miles (1,950km). Photo: T1A.

Grumman C-2A Greyhound   USA

Grumman developed the C-2A under US Navy contract as a carrier on-board delivery (COD) aircraft, taking the E-2A Hawkeye (see p. 50) as the basis for the design. The wing, main landing gear, flight deck and tail unit are basically the same as the equivalent components of the E-2A, the fuselage being the obvious new feature. This was designed to seat up to 39 passengers in a high-density layout, and can also accommodate a wide variety of stores and supplies used on an aircraft carrier, including spare jet engines, small vehicles and standard US freight pallets. Loading

doors and a ramp are incorporated in the rear fuselage. The initial US Navy order was for three C-2A airframes, including one for static testing. The first prototype flew on November 18, 1964, and the Navy began accepting production C-2As in 1966. Manufacture of the production batch of 17 ended in 1968. **Data:** Two 4,050shp Allison T56-A-8A or 8B turboprops. Span 80ft 7in (24.56m). Length 56ft 8in (17.27m). Gross weight 54,830lb (24,870kg). Max speed 352mph (567km/h). Range 1,650 miles (2,660km) at 297mph (478km/h) at 27,300ft (8,320m).

Grumman HU-16 Albatross   USA

The XJR2F-1 Albatross prototype, built for the US Navy as a utility transport amphibian, first flew on October 24, 1947. The USAF ordered a total of 305, as SA-16As, for search and rescue. Most of these were converted to SA-16B with increased span and higher weights. Designations were changed to HU-16A and HU-16B respectively in 1962. The US Navy purchased aircraft similar to the SA-16A as UF-1s, and put in hand a similar conversion programme, to produce UF-2s; these became HU-16C and HU-16D respectively, while the Coast Guard version became HU-16E. Nations still using the type in 1978 include Argentina, Brazil, Chile, Indonesia, Japan, Mexico, Nationalist China, Pakis-

tan, the Philippines, Spain, Thailand and Venezuela. A special model for anti-submarine duties was produced in 1961, with a large nose radome, retractable MAD in the rear fuselage, an ECM radome on the wing, an underwing search-light and provision for carrying depth charges. Sixteen were supplied to Norway and seven to Spain; during 1969, the Norwegian aircraft were transferred to Greece and Spain. Peru also has four. The Albatross has two 1,425hp Wright R-1820-76A engines. **Data:** Span 96ft 8in (29.46m). Length 62ft 10in (19.18m). Gross weight 37,500lb (17,010kg). Max speed 236mph (379km/h) at sea level. Photo: Anti-submarine HU-16B.

Grumman TC-4C Academe and VC-11A   USA

A single example of the Grumman Gulfstream executive transport was purchased for use by the US Coast Guard in 1963 with the designation VC-4A. Together with a single Gulfstream II jet, designated VC-11A, it serves as a VIP transport. Plans to buy a training variant for use by the USN as TC-4B were shelved; but in December 1966 the Navy ordered nine TC-4Cs as flying classrooms for training bombardier/navigators for service in the A-6 Intruder. For this purpose a large radome was incorporated in the nose and the cabin was modified to house a complete A-6 avionics system.

Powered by two 2,185ehp Rolls-Royce Dart 529-8X turboprops, the TC-4C made its first flight on June 14, 1967 and these aircraft were being progressively updated to incorporate TRAM sensors in 1978/79. **Data:** Span 78ft 6in (23.92m). Length 67ft 11in (20.70m). Gross weight 36,000lb (16,330kg). Max cruising speed 348 mph (560km/h). Photo: VC-4A.

Grumman TF-9J Cougar

USA

The Cougar was evolved as a sweptwing derivative of the straight-wing Panther, the first jet fighter built for the US Navy by Grumman. Cougar single-seat fighters were designated originally F9F-6 to -8 (later F-9), but none remain in service. The TF-9J tandem two-seat operational training version (first flown April 4, 1956) was used for combat missions in Vietnam, and still equips a number of training units in the US. It has an 8,500lb (3,855kg) st Pratt & Whitney J48-P-8A turbojet and provision for two 20mm cannon and 2,000lb (907kg) of underwing stores. A total of 399 TF-9Js was built. **Data:** Span 34ft 6in (10.51m). Length 48ft 6in (14.78m). Gross weight 20,600lb (9,344kg). Max speed 705mph (1,135km/h). Range 1,000 miles (1,610km).

HAL HAOP-27 Krishak Mk 2

India

This two/three-seat air observation post aircraft was developed by Hindustan from its two-seat Pushpak light aircraft and utilises the same basic fabric-covered metal wing. The first of two proto-types flew in November 1959, with a 190hp Continental engine. Production Krishaks, of which 68 were supplied to the Indian Army, have 225hp Continental O-470-J engines. Dual controls are standard and the cabin can be adapted to carry a stretcher for air ambulance duties. **Data:** Span 37ft 6in (11.43m). Length 27ft 7in (8.41m). Gross weight 2,800lb (1,270kg). Max speed 130mph (209km/h). Max range 500 miles (805km).

HAL HJT-16 Kiran   India

This side-by-side two-seat jet basic trainer was designed to replace the Indian Air Force's Vampires. Detailed design work began in 1961, under the leadership of Dr. V. M. Ghatage, but the need to give priority to the HF-24 fighter delayed the first flight of the prototype Kiran until September 4, 1964. A second prototype followed and deliveries of the initial series of 24 pre-production aircraft began in March 1968. The total Indian Air Force/Navy requirement is for 190, of which 125 had been delivered by January 1978; from the 119th aircraft, deliveries have been of the Kiran Mk IA with two underwing hardpoints for weapons or drop-tanks. Standard power plant of the Kiran Mk I/IA is the 2,500lb (1,135kg) st Rolls-Royce Viper 11 turbojet, but Hindustan has under development the Kiran II with a derated Orpheus 701 engine, built-in gun armament, updated avionics and four hardpoints on the wings. Flight testing of the first of two Kiran II prototypes began on July 30, 1976. **Data** (Kiran Mk I): Span 35ft 1¼in (10.70m). Length 34ft 9in (10.60m). Gross weight 9,039lb (4,100kg). Max speed 432 mph (695km/h). Endurance 1 hr 45 min on internal fuel. Photo: Kiran Mk1.

HAL HPT-32   India

Design of a new fully-aerobatic basic trainer for use by the Indian Air Force as a replacement for the HT-2 was launched by Hindustan Aeronautics in 1975 and a conventional low-wing piston-engined monoplane was evolved. The first of two prototypes of the HPT-32 flew on January 6, 1977, at Bangalore and upon conclusion of flight trials an initial production batch was expected to be ordered by the IAF. These, like the prototypes, will have fixed tricycle landing gear but the HPT-32 has been designed to have a retractable under-carriage in later versions. With side-by-side seat-ing for pupil and instructor, the HPT-32 has pro-vision for a third seat in the rear of the cockpit and is designed to be used for a wide range of *ab initio* training, including instrument, navigation, night flying and formation flying, and also for armed patrol, observation, weapon training, glider towing and target towing. It is powered by a 260hp Lycom-ing AEIO-540-D4B5 flat-six engine. **Data:** Span 31ft 2in (9.50m) Length 25ft 4in (7.72m). Gross weight 3,490lb (1,583kg). Max speed 145mph (233km/h). Range 745 miles (1,199km).

HAL HT-2   India

India's first domestically-designed aeroplane, the HT-2 was a product of the Hindustan Aeronautics factory at Bangalore. The first HT-2, a conventional tandem-seat basic trainer, flew on August 13, 1951, with a de Havilland Gipsy Major 10 engine. The second prototype, flown on February 19, 1952, had a 155hp Blackburn Cirrus Major III engine and production HT-2s for the Indian Air Force and Navy are to this standard. **Data:** Span 35ft 2in (10.72m). Length 24ft 8½in (7.53m). Gross weight 2,240lb (1,016kg). Max speed 130mph (209km/h). Range 350 miles (563km).

Helio U-10   USA

Service interest in the Helio Courier STOL aircraft was first shown in 1952 when the US Army acquired a single aircraft for evaluation under the original designation YL-24. Six years later, the USAF bought three of the more powerful five-seat Super Couriers, with 295hp Lycoming GO-480-G1D6 engine, under the designation L-28A (now U-10A), to evaluate operational techniques of STOL aircraft. Full-span leading-edge slats, large flaps, one-piece horizontal tail surfaces and a slow-turning oversize propeller enable this version to take off in 114 yards (104m) and land in 70 yards (64m) with a full load, and to remain controllable at speeds down to 30mph (48km/h). Large numbers entered USAF service for counter-insurgency duties in Vietnam, South America and elsewhere, including U-10Bs with paradrop door and extra fuel giving an endurance of 10 hours. The U-10D has a gross weight of 3,600lb (1,633kg) and provision for an aerial camera and air-to-ground broadcast system. **Data:** Span 39ft (11.89m). Length 31ft (9.45m). Gross weight 3,400lb (1,542kg). Max speed 167mph (269km/h). Range up to 1,380 miles (2,220km). Photo: U-10D.

Hispano HA-200 Saeta and HA-220 Super Saeta

Spain

The HA-200 serves with the Spanish Air Force as the E-14 two-seat advanced flying and armament trainer. The first prototype flew on August 12, 1955, followed by five pre-production models and 30 HA-200As (first flight October 11, 1962) with 880lb (400kg) st Turboméca Marboré IIA turbojets and armament of two 7.7mm machine-guns and underwing rockets. Also in service, but allocated to a counter-insurgency squadron, are HA-200Ds (C-10Bs), with modernised systems; of 55 built, 40 have the heavier armament specified for the HA-200E, which was to be powered by 1,058lb (480kg) st Marboré VI turbojets, but did not enter production. From it was developed the single-seat HA-220 ground-attack aircraft (C-10C), of which 25 were built for the Spanish Air Force and continue to equip a light strike squadron. **Data** (HA-220): Span 34ft 2in (10.42m). Length 29ft 5in (8.97m). Gross weight 8,157lb (3,700kg). Max speed 413 mph (665km/h). Range 1,055 miles (1,700km). Photo: HA-220.

Hughes AH-64

USA

In November 1976, the US Army announced that two YAH-64 prototypes had won a competitive fly-off against the Bell YAH-63, and that the Hughes design would be developed as the Army's new Advanced Attack Helicopter (AAH) to replace the HueyCobra in the 1980s. As the next stage, the prototypes are being fitted with advanced electronics, electro-optical equipment and weapon fire control systems, for continued evaluation; and three pre-production AH-64s are to join the test programme. No production decision is to be taken until at least 1980. Meanwhile Martin Marietta and Northrop are engaged in a follow-on competition to provide the aircraft's target acquisition and designation system (TADS) and pilot's night vision system (PNVS). Layout of the AH-64 is conventional for a helicopter gunship, with co-pilot/gunner and pilot in tandem, and nose-mounted PNVS. Armament comprises a 30mm Hughes XM-230 chain gun in an underfuselage turret, and up to 16 Hellfire anti-tank missiles, 76 rockets or a mix of the two on four attachments under the stub-wings. Equipment includes a stabilised sight, forward-looking infra-red sighting, a laser rangefinder and target designator, and laser tracker. The power plant comprises two 1,536shp General Electric T700-GE-700 turboshaft engines, as in the Sikorsky Black Hawk. The Army is expected to acquire the first 18 of a total 536 AAHs in FY 1981. **Data:** Rotor diameter 48ft 0in (14.63m). Length 49ft 5in (15.06m). Gross weight 17,400lb (7,892kg). Max speed 191mph (307km/h). Range 359 miles (578km) on internal fuel.

Hughes OH-6A Cayuse and Model 500M-D Defender

USA

The OH-6A was chosen by the US Army for production in May 1965. Deliveries began in 1966 against contracts which eventually totalled 1,434. The OH-6A is powered by a 252.5shp Allison T63-A-5A turboshaft, driving a four-blade main rotor, and carries a crew of two, plus two passengers or four soldiers sitting on the floor, or equivalent freight. The similar Hughes 500M has been delivered to several foreign armed forces including the Spanish Navy (anti-submarine use) and is built by Kawasaki in Japan (as OH-6J for JGSDF) and BredaNardi in Italy (for Italian Army). Latest military variant is the Model 500M-D Defender,

with 420shp Allison 250-C20B turboshaft, five-blade main rotor, a small T-tail, self-sealing tanks, armour and provision for a variety of weapons, including 14 rockets and a Minigun, a 30mm chain gun, ASW weapons or four TOW air-to-surface missiles. The Defender has been ordered by Colombia (10) and Mauritania (4), Israel (30) and South Korea (100, of which 66 will be locally built). **Data** (500M-D): Rotor diameter 26ft 5in (8.05m). Length 23ft 0in (7.01m). Gross weight 3,000lb (1,360kg). Max speed 160mph (258km/h). Range 335 miles (540km). Photo: Kawasaki-Hughes OH-6J.

Hughes TH-55A Osage

USA

Hughes entered the light helicopter field in 1955, when it began design and development of the two-seat Model 269. The prototype flew in October 1956. The design was then simplified for production and the US Army purchased five of the resulting Model 269A for evaluation, under the designation YHO-2HU; commercial sales began in 1961. The version now in production, as Model 300C, has three seats and a 190hp Lycoming HIO-360 engine. In mid-1964, the US Army ordered 20 Model 269A-1s, under the designation TH-55A, and

follow-up orders brought the total of TH-55As to 792, to meet the Army's needs for a standard light helicopter primary trainer. Small numbers were bought for military use by other countries, including Algeria, Brazil, Colombia, Guyana, India and Nicaragua. Kawasaki built 38 TH-55Js for the JGSDF in Japan. **Data** (TH-55A): Rotor diameter 25ft 3½in (7.71m). Length 21ft 11¾in (6.80m). Gross weight 1,670lb (757kg). Max speed 86mph (138km/h). Range 204 miles (328km).

Hunting Pembroke   Great Britain

First to order military versions of the Prince feeder-liner was the Royal Navy; but the last of its Sea Prince T.Mk 1s, equipping the Air Observer School at Culdrose, was scheduled for retirement during 1978. The RAF acquired 44 Pembroke C.Mk 1 staff transports, each powered by two 540/560hp Alvis Leonides 127 piston-engines and furnished to carry a crew of two and eight passengers. To prolong their life into the 1980s, a modernisation programme was begun during 1969, under which 14 of the Pembrokes were re-sparred. They equip No 60 Squadron at Wildenrath, Germany, which operates six aircraft at a time on communications duties. About eight Pembroke C.52s (Tp83s) continue to serve with the Swedish Air Force. **Data:** Span 64ft 6in (19.66m). Length 46ft 0in (14.02m). Gross weight 13,500lb (6,125kg). Max speed 224mph (360km/h). Range 1,150 miles (1,850km). Photo: C.Mk1.

Israel Aircraft Industries IAI-201 Arava   Israel

Israel Aircraft Industries began development of this twin-turboprop STOL light transport in 1966 and first flew the IAI-101 civil prototype on November 27, 1969, followed by a second on May 8, 1971. Because of the prospect of immediate orders, effort was switched to the military IAI-201, of which a prototype was flown on March 7, 1972. This was powered by two 750shp Pratt & Whitney PT6A-34 engines and had accommodation for 24 fully-equipped troops, 17 paratroops and a despatcher, twelve stretchers and two seated casualties or medical attendants, or $2\frac{1}{2}$ tons of freight. The first production Arava 201 flew on February 4, 1973. Deliveries to the Mexican Air Force began later in 1973 and 60 had been sold by early 1978, to the Israeli Air Force (14) and armed services in Central and South America. Arava 101 and 201 prototypes were used by the Israeli Air Force during the Holy Day War in October 1973. **Data:** Span 68ft 9in (20.96m). Length 42ft 9in (13.03m). Gross weight 15,000lb (6,803kg). Max speed 203mph (326km/h). Max range 812 miles (1,306km).

Ilyushin II-12 and II-14 (NATO code-names: Coach and Crate)

USSR

The II-12 (NATO *Coach*) first flew in 1944 as a general-purpose military transport to succeed the Li-2, the Russian-built Dakota. It could carry only 27 passengers because of its high structure weight, but was put into service by the Soviet Air Force, with 1,775hp Shvetsov ASh-82FNV two-row radials.

The II-14 (NATO *Crate*) appeared in 1953, with reduced structure weight and 1,900hp ASh-82T engines. In the II-14P, gross weight was reduced to 36,380lb (16,500kg), leading to improved take-off and climb performance while carrying 18–26 passengers. In the II-14M, which appeared in 1956, the fuselage was stretched by 3.3ft (1.0m) and the

gross weight restored to 38,000lb (17,235kg) with 32 passengers.

Air forces of the Warsaw Pact nations, and their allies, continue to fly the II-14 in some numbers, including versions specially equipped for ECM duties. **Data** (II-14M): Span 103ft 11in (31.67m). Length 73ft 3½in (22.34m). Gross weight 38,000lb (17,235kg). Max speed 258mph (415km/h). Range 937 miles (1,508km). Photo: II-14.

Ilyushin II-18 (NATO code-name: Coot)

USSR

Familiar for many years as one of Russia's standard airliners and one which was exported widely to countries in the Soviet sphere of influence, the II-18 appeared quite late in military service, although a prototype was seen in Soviet Air Force markings as early as 1958. The II-18 had first flown in July 1957 and entered airline service less than two years later, powered by 4,000shp Ivchenko AI-20K turboprops. In commercial operation it carries up to 122 passengers and can probably carry about the same number of troops when used in the military role. Some are used as VIP transports in Russia, and it is thought that China, as well as the air forces of Afghanistan, Bulgaria, Czechoslovakia, East Germany, Guinea, Poland,

Romania, Syria and Yugoslavia, has the type in small-scale military transport service. A number of II-18s has been converted for electronic surveillance duties, with a large underfuselage pod, a smaller one on each side of the forward fuselage, and numerous smaller antennae (NATO *Coot-A*, as illustrated). **Data:** Span 122ft 8½in (37.40m). Length 117ft 9in (35.90m). Gross weight 141,100lb (64,000kg). Cruising speed 388mph (625km/h). Range 2,300 miles (3,700km). Photo: *Coot-A* elint version.

Kaman SH-2 Seasprite

USA

The Seasprite was developed and produced originally as a single-engined utility helicopter, powered by a 1,250shp T58-GE-8B turboshaft. The prototype flew for the first time on July 2, 1959. Subsequently, the US Navy took delivery of 88 UH-2As, equipped for all-weather operation, and 102 UH-2Bs, with instruments for VFR operation only. Conversion of the entire inventory to twin-engined configuration was undertaken under the basic designation of UH-2C, deliveries beginning in August 1967. In 1971, two Seasprites were modified for evaluation in an anti-ship missile defence (ASMD) role under the US Navy's LAMPS (Light Airborne Multi-Purpose System) programme. As a result of these tests, 20 Seasprites were converted to SH-2D LAMPS configura-

tion, with Canadian Marconi LN 66 high-power surface search radar in a chin housing, towed magnetic anomaly detector on the starboard side of the fuselage, sonobuoys, smoke markers, flares, homing torpedoes and other equipment. The first SH-2D flew on March 16, 1971, and this version has been followed by conversion of 87 more Seasprites to improved SH-2F standard, with new rotor, LN 66HP radar, a repositioned tailwheel midway along the rear fuselage, 1,350shp T58-GE-8F engines and other changes. The SH-2Ds have been uprated to "F" standard. **Data** (SH-2F): Rotor diameter 44ft 0in (13.41m). Length, nose and blades folded, 38ft 4in (11.68m). Gross weight 12,800lb (5,805kg). Max speed 165mph (265km/h). Range 422 miles (679km). Photo: SH-2F.

Kamov Ka-25 (NATO code-name: Hormone) USSR

The Ka-25 (NATO code name *Hormone-A*) was first seen in prototype form in the Soviet Aviation Day display over Moscow on July 9, 1961. It then carried two dummy air-to-surface missiles, on outriggers on each side of its cabin. No such installation has been seen on production Ka-25s, which serve on board ships of the Soviet Navy, including the aircraft carrier *Kiev* and the helicopter cruisers *Moskva* and *Leningrad*; but there is a weapons bay below the cabin floor of most aircraft, able to house ASW torpedoes and nuclear depth charges. Equipment includes an undernose search radar, optional equipment pod at the base of the central tail-fin and cylindrical housing above the tail-boom, and, usually, inflatable pontoons on each wheel of the undercarriage. A version with special electronics to acquire targets for ship-launched missiles has the NATO reporting name of *Hormone-B*, and can be identified by its more spherical nose radome. The Ka-25 has a commercial counterpart in the Ka-25K which was exhibited at the 1967 Paris Aero Show, and is itself used also for transport and general-purpose duties. **Data** (based on Ka-25K): Rotor diameter 51ft 8in (15.74m). Length 32ft 0in (9.75m). Gross weight 16,100lb (7,300kg). Max speed 137mph (220km/h). Max range 405 miles (650km). Photo: *Hormone-A*.

Kamov Ka-26 (NATO code-name: Hoodlum) USSR

First flown in 1965, the Ka-26 is a standard civilian general-purpose helicopter in the Soviet Union and other East European countries. Its military use is less widespread; by 1978 it had been identified only with the Air Forces of the Soviet Union, Sri Lanka (Ceylon) and Hungary. By podding the two 325hp Vedeneev M-14V-26 radial engines, and mounting them on short stub-wings, Kamov was able to make the whole rear fuselage detachable aft of the two-seat flight deck. Standard fuselage pods accommodate six passengers or equivalent freight. Minus pod, the aircraft can be operated as a flying crane; or the space under the rotor can be occupied by a platform for a ton of cargo. **Data:** Rotor diameter 42ft 8in (13.00m). Length 25ft 5in (7.75m). Gross weight 7,165lb (3,250kg). Max speed 105mph (170km/h). Normal range 248 miles (400km). Photo: KA-26, Hungary.

Kawasaki KV-107   Japan

During 1962, Kawasaki flew the first example of the Boeing Vertol 107 tandem-rotor helicopter built in Japan under licence, and since 1965 the company has held world-wide sales rights in the KV-107 from Boeing. In addition to the series of KV-107/II variants offered by Kawasaki, the company has developed the improved KV-107/IIA, with 1,400shp General Electric CT58-140-1 engines (which can be of Japanese origin, built by Ishikawajima). Production is continuing to meet the requirements of the Japanese armed forces, which have bought nine KV-107/II-3 or IIA-3 mine-countermeasures variants (JMSDF), 54 KV-107/II-4 or IIA-4 transports (JGSDF) and 24 KV-107/II-5 or

IIA-5 search and rescue versions (JASDF). The Swedish Navy also bought eight KV-107/II-5s which were fitted in Sweden with Gnome engines to standardise with the HKP-7s previously acquired from the USA. **Data** (KV-107/IIA): Rotor diameter 50ft 0in (15.24m) each. Fuselage length 44ft 7in (13.59m). Gross weight 21,400lb (9,706kg). Max speed 158mph (254km/h). Range 682 miles (1,097km). Photo: KV-107/II-4.

Lockheed C-140 JetStar   USA

Five JetStars, designated C-140A, are used by USAF's Air Force Communications Service which is responsible for checking world-wide military navigation aids. Six others, designated VC-140B, are 11/16-seat transports operated by the Special Air Missions Wing of Military Airlift Command. Three JetStars were acquired by the Federal German Air Force for VIP transport duties; others are operated by the air forces of Indonesia (1), Libya (1), Mexico (1) and Saudi Arabia (2). The

prototype JetStar flew on September 4, 1957, powered by two Bristol Siddeley Orpheus turbojets. Production models have four 3,000lb (1,360kg) st Pratt & Whitney JT12A-6A or 3,300lb (1,497kg) st JT12A-8 engines, mounted in pairs on each side of the rear fuselage. **Data:** Span 54ft 5in (16.60m). Length 60ft 5in (18.42m). Gross weight 42,000lb (19,051kg). Max speed 566mph (911km/h). Range 2,235 miles (3,595km). Photo: VC-140B.

Lockheed EC-121 Super Constellation   USA

The only military versions of the Super Constellation airliner still flying with the US armed services are EC-121 Warning Star airborne early warning and control (AEW & C) aircraft, distinguished by large radomes above and below the fuselage. EC-121Ts of the 915th AEW & C Group, US Air Force Reserve, perform Aerospace Defense Command's airborne radar surveillance mission, with seven of the aircraft flying from Florida and three patrolling off Iceland. These models are each powered by four 3,250hp Wright R-3350-91 piston

engines and are distinguished by wingtip tanks. Similar EC-121S Warning Stars of the 193rd Tactical Early Warning Group, Air National Guard, are based at Harrisburg, Pennsylvania. The L-1049Gs taken over from Air-India by the Indian Air Force, for the maritime search role, are being retired as the Indian Navy's Il-38s enter service. **Data** (EC-121T): Span 126ft 2in (38.45m). Length 116ft 2in (35.40m). Gross weight 143,600lb (65,135kg). Max speed 321mph (516km/h). Range 4,600 miles (7,400km). Photo: EC-121M.

Lockheed T-33A and RT-33A   USA

The final single-seat fighter version of America's first operational jet-fighter, the Shooting Star, was the F-80C, with a 5,400lb (2,450kg) st Allison J33-A-35 turbojet and armament of six 0.50in machine-guns and two 1,000lb bombs or ten rockets. The T-33A advanced trainer is similar, except for having two seats in tandem, and is still used by nearly 30 air forces throughout the world, in some cases in AT-33 armed trainer/attack form. A total of 5,691 T-33As, and similar T-33Bs for the US Navy, were built by Lockheed, and USAF still uses at least 300 for combat support duties, and for proficiency and

radar target evaluation training. A further 210 were produced under licence by Kawasaki in Japan. Canadair built 656 as CL-30 Silver Stars with the 5,100lb (2,313kg) st Rolls-Royce Nene 10. Also in service in Pakistan, Thailand and Yugoslavia is the RT-33A photographic-reconnaissance aircraft with camera-carrying nose. **Data** (T-33A): Span 38ft 10½in (11.85m). Length 37ft 9in (11.51m). Gross weight 14,440lb (6,550kg). Max speed 600mph (965km/h). Range 1,345 miles (2,165km). Photo: T-33A (E.15), Spain.

Lockheed U-2 and TR-1   USA

Designation of this Lockheed design in the USAF's Utility category was a deliberate attempt to mislead, since the specific role of the aircraft when first produced in 1954 was strategic reconnaissance over Soviet and other territory. A number of U-2s operated in this role until 1960, when one was destroyed over Russia and its pilot captured. Subsequently, a number were modified to WU-2A and WU-2C configuration for high-altitude weather flights. Some were supplied to the Chinese Nationalist Air Force for reconnaissance over mainland China, but were withdrawn after several had been shot down. Production of the type is believed to have totalled 53 in several versions, including five two-seat U-2Ds. The first U-2As had 11,200lb (5,080kg) st J57-P-37A turbojets. The U-2B had the 17,000lb (7,710kg) st

J75-P-13 engine and several continue in service for special high-altitude reconnaissance and weather flights. All have similar dimensions, except for the U-2R, which is 63ft (19.20m) long, with a span of 103ft (31.40m). A new variant, of which 25 were ordered in the FY79 budget, is the TR-1 high-altitude stand-off surveillance aircraft. This will have a J75-P-13 engine and a high-resolution side-looking radar, enabling it to see deep into a foreign country without crossing its borders. Dimensions will be similar to those of the U-2R. **Data** (U-2B): Span 80ft (24.38m). Length 49ft 7in (15.11m). Gross weight over 21,000lb (9,525kg). Max speed 528mph (850km/h) above 36,000ft (11,000m). Service ceiling 80,000ft (24,400m). Range approx 4,000 miles (6,435km). Photo: U-2R.

Max Holste M.H.1521 Broussard   France

The M.H.1521 Broussard is a six-seat utility transport suitable for service in regions where airfields are few and maintenance facilities scanty. It is powered by a 450hp Pratt & Whitney R-985 engine and has large slotted flaps which enable it to take off in under 220 yards (200m). With two seats removed, there is room for two stretchers; all passenger seats are removable for cargo-carrying operations. The prototype flew for the first time on November 17, 1952, and was followed by a second

prototype and 27 pre-production aircraft. Initial orders for 180 production Broussards for the French Army and Air Force were stepped up to a total of 335 in 1957 and a few were still serving in 1978. Small numbers were passed on to many former French colonies, to help each form the nucleus of an air force. **Data:** Span 45ft 1in (13.75m) Length 28ft 4½in (8.65m). Gross weight 5,953lb (2,700kg). Max speed 161mph (260km/h). Range 745 miles (1,200km).

MBB 223 Flamingo   Spain

First flown on March 1, 1967, this all-metal light aircraft was developed in Germany by the former SIAT company, now part of MBB, after winning a 1962 design competition organised by the German Ministry of Economics. Only 50 were built in Germany, including a batch of 15 MBB 223A1 two-seat utility/trainers for the Turkish Air Force. Production was then transferred to CASA in Spain, where a further series of 50 was built, including 32 for the Syrian Air Force. Most of the CASA aircraft are 223K1s, which are fully aerobatic when flown as single-seaters. The jigs and tools were next transferred to Pilatus in Switzerland, which in 1977 was building a further 16 of these trainers for the Syrian Air Force. Power plant is a 200hp Lycoming AIO-360. **Data** (223K1): Span 27ft 2in (8.28m). Length 24ft 4½in (7.43m). Gross weight 1,810lb (821kg). Max speed 155mph (249km/h).

MBB BO 105   Germany

This twin-turbine utility helicopter has been adopted for large-scale service with the German Army in two special versions. The first, designated BO 105VBH, is a five-seat liaison and observation helicopter of which 227 have been ordered to replace Alouette IIs from 1979. The BO 105PAH 1 is an anti-tank version, carrying six Hot missiles on outriggers and fitted with a stabilised sight above the cabin Following trials with two prototypes, 210 production PAH 1s are being manufactured for the German Army. The standard utility version is in military service in the Netherlands, Nigeria and the Philippines, powered by two 420shp Allison 250-C20B turboshafts. **Data:** Rotor diameter 32ft 3½in (9.84m). Fuselage length 28ft 1in (8.56m). Gross weight 5,070lb (2,300kg). Max speed 167mph (270km/h). Range 408 miles (656km). Photo: BO 105PAH 1.

MBB HFB 320 Hansa   Germany

The unique sweptforward wings of the Hansa were adopted to permit the wing centre-section structure to pass through the fuselage without impairing the space available in the main cabin, and to give passengers an exceptional downward view. Standard versions carry seven or twelve passengers. The prototype flew for the first time on April 21, 1964, and deliveries began in September 1967. Current Hansas have 3,100lb

(1,406kg) st General Electric CJ610-9 turbojets in rear-mounted pods. Eight were delivered to the *Luftwaffe* for VIP transport and military flight test duties. Others have been equipped for ECM missions, and for flight checks and avionics calibration. **Data:** Span 47ft 6in (14.49m). Length 54ft 6in (16.61m). Gross weight 20,280lb (9,200kg). Max speed 513mph (825km/h). Range 1,472 miles (2,370km) at 420mph (675km/h). Photo. ECM.

McDonnell Douglas C-9 Nightingale/Skytrain II   USA

The USAF selected the C-9A Nightingale version of the commercial DC-9 Series 30 during 1967 to meet a requirement for a new aeromedical transport. The initial order was for eight; thirteen more were ordered subsequently. The C-9A can carry up to 40 patients on stretchers or more than 40 in standard seats and contains a special-care compartment. Powered by 14,500lb (6,575kg) st Pratt & Whitney JT8D-9 turbofans, the first C-9A was delivered to Scott AFB on August 10, 1968. Three VC-9Cs ordered in 1974 are for use as VIP

transports. Also based on the DC-9 Series 30, the US Navy's C-9B Skytrain II is a fleet logistic support transport of which 11 were ordered. The Italian and Kuwait Air Forces each fly two DC-9 Srs 30s as VIP transports. **Data** (C-9A): Span 93ft 5in (28.47m). Length 119ft 3½in (36.37m). Gross weight 108,000lb (48,988kg). Max cruising speed 565mph (909km/h) at 25,000ft (7,620m). Range more than 2,000 miles (3,220km). Photo: DC-9 Srs 30, Italy.

McDonnell Douglas KC-10A   USA

In December 1977, the USAF chose this development of the DC-10 wide-bodied airliner as its new Advanced Tanker/Cargo Aircraft (ATCA). The need for such an aircraft had been underlined during the 1973 war in the Middle East, when many countries refused landing rights to USAF transports ferrying urgent cargoes to Israel. Ability to carry 36,650 US gallons (135,510 litres) of fuel for its own use, and for transfer to other aircraft at an unprecedented high rate, will enable the KC-10A to provide support for many types of US and Allied combat aircraft on a global basis. Based on the DC-10 Series 30CF, the first KC-10A is expected to fly in the Spring of 1980, powered by three General Electric CF6-50C1 tur-

bofans, each rated at 52,500lb (23,815kg) st. Major changes compared with the basic airliner will include the addition of bladder fuel cells in the lower cargo compartments, a refuelling boom, hose and drogue, with operator's station, and military avionics. The main cargo hold will continue to be available for freight. Initial USAF requirement is for about 20 KC-10As. **Data:** Span 165ft 4$\frac{1}{2}$in (50.41m). Length 181ft 7in (55.35m). Gross weight 590,000lb (267,619kg). Max cruising speed 564mph (908km/h). Able to deliver 200,000lb (90,720kg) of fuel to aircraft 2,200 miles (3,540km) from its base, and return.

Mikoyan/Gurevich MiG-15   USSR
(NATO code-names: Fagot and Midget)

The MiG-15 first flew on December 30, 1947, and was produced in very large numbers, in Czechoslovakia and Poland as well as in Russia. The basic version (S-102 in Czechoslovakia, LiM-1 in Poland) had an RD-45 turbojet, which was a copy of the Rolls-Royce Nene with a rating of around 5,450lb (2,470kg) st. This engine was replaced by a developed 5,950lb (2,700kg) st Klimov VK-1 turbojet in the MiG-15*bis* (S-103 in Czechoslovakia, LiM-2 in Poland). Armament comprised one 37mm N-37 and two 23mm NR-23 cannon.
The basic single-seat fighter (NATO *Fagot*) was supplied in large numbers to countries in the

Soviet sphere of influence and a few examples survive. The tandem two-seat MiG-15UTI operational trainer (NATO code-name Midget) was also built in quantity, with an RD-45 turbojet (this version being known as the CS-102 in Czechoslovakia). The MiG-15UTI is a standard advanced trainer in more than 30 countries, including the Soviet Union. **Data** (MiG-15UTI): Span 33ft 1in (10.08m). Length 32ft 11$\frac{1}{4}$in (10.04m). Gross weight 11,905lb (5,400kg). Max speed 630mph (1,015km/h). Range 885 miles (1,424km) at 32,800ft (10,000m) with underwing tanks. Photo: MiG-15UTI, USSR.

MIL (WSK-PZL-Swidnik) Mi-2 (NATO code-name: Hoplite)   Poland

By utilising two small and lightweight turboshaft engines, mounted above the cabin, Mil produced a helicopter that can carry $2\frac{1}{2}$ times the payload of the piston-engined Mi-1 without any significant change in overall dimensions. Known in Russia as the V-2, the Mi-2 was announced in the Autumn of 1961 and has since been in large-scale production, exclusively at the WSK-Swidnik in Poland, for both military and civil use. Many hundreds have been delivered. The basic version carries a pilot and up to eight passengers and is powered by 400 or 450

shp Isotov GTD-350P turboshaft engines. The ambulance version carries four stretchers and an attendant: cargo can be carried internally or slung underneath from a hook. Air forces that operate the Mi-2 include those of Czechoslovakia, Hungary, Poland, Romania and the Soviet Union. **Data:** Rotor diameter 47ft 6¾in (14.50m). Length 39ft 2in (11.94m). Normal gross weight 7,826lb (3,550kg). Max speed 130mph (210km/h). Max range 360 miles (580km) at 118mph (190km/h). Version with anti-tank missiles.

MIL Mi-4 (NATO code-name: Hound)   USSR

Soviet counterpart of the American Sikorsky S-55, the Mi-4 has been in service with the Soviet Air Force since 1953. Powered by a 1,700hp Shvetsov ASh-82V piston engine, the basic transport version carries a crew of two and 14 troops, or 3,525lb (1,600kg) of freight or vehicles, which are loaded via clamshell rear doors beneath the tailboom. The fairing under the front fuselage can house a navigator or observer, and carries a machine-gun. This can be supplemented with air-to-surface rockets for army support duties. Although largely superseded by turbine-powered types in the Soviet Services, Mi-4s continue to operate with about 25 foreign air forces. Most are transports, but anti-

submarine variants can also be seen, with undernose search radar, an MAD towed "bird" stowed against the rear of the fuselage pod, and racks for flares, markers or sonobuoys on each side of the cabin. First identified in 1977 was a communications jamming Mi-4, with multiple antennae projecting from the front and rear of the cabin on each side. **Data:** Rotor diameter 68ft 11in (21.00m). Length 55ft 1in (16.80m). Gross weight 17,200lb (7,800kg). Max speed 130mph (210km/h). Range 250 miles (400km) with 8 passengers. Photo: *Hound-B*, Soviet Navy.

MIL Mi-6 (NATO code-name: Hook)　　　USSR

At least 850 Mi-6s appear to have been built since the prototype was first revealed in 1957. They remain the largest helicopters yet produced in such numbers, and are used for transport and assault duties by the air forces of Bulgaria, Egypt, Iraq, Syria and North Vietnam, as well as the Soviet Union. Despite its size, the Mi-6 has a conventional layout, except for the small fixed wings which offload its main rotor in cruising flight. Two 5,500shp Soloviev D-25V (TV-2BM) turboshaft engines drive the five-blade main and four-blade tail rotors. Payload can include a crew of 5 and 65 passengers, or 41 stretcher patients, or 26,450lb (12,000kg) of freight or vehicles, loaded via rear clamshell doors. Some aircraft have a nose gun. When the Mi-6 is used in a flying crane role, the wings are normally removed. **Data:** Rotor diameter 114ft 10in (35.00m). Length 108ft 10½in (33.18m). Gross weight 93,700lb (42,500kg). Max speed 186mph (300km/h). Range 652 miles (1,050km) with 9,480lb (4,300kg) payload.

MIL Mi-8 (NATO code-name: Hip)　　　USSR

Similar in overall size to the Mi-4, and able to use Mi-4 rotor blades and secondary gearboxes in an emergency, the Mi-8 made its first appearance in 1961 poweded by a single 2,700shp Soloviev turboshaft engine. A version with two 1,500shp Isotov TV2-117A turboshafts flew for the first time on September 17, 1962, and became the prototype for more than 5,000 production Mi-8s that have since entered service, mainly with the Soviet Air Force and at least 25 other air forces throughout the world. The standard assault transport carries a crew of two or three and up to 32 passengers or 8,820lb (4,000kg) of internal freight. Three tons can be carried externally, and all versions can be fitted with two twin-racks for bombs or pods each containing sixteen 57mm rockets. Twelve stretcher patients and a medical attendant can be carried on return flights from combat areas. **Data:** Rotor diameter 69ft 10¼in (21.29m). Length 60ft 0¾in (18.31m). Gross weight 26,455lb (12,000kg). Max speed 161mph (260km/h). Range 264 miles (425km) with 28 passengers. Photo: *HipC*, USSR.

MIL Mi-10 (NATO code-name: Harke)　　　USSR

This very large flying crane was put back into production in 1976, to meet a Soviet military requirement, and more than 60 are thought to be in service. The Mi-10 was first displayed at Tushino on Aviation Day 1961. Subsequent study of photographs showed it to be almost identical with the Mi-6 above the line of the cabin windows, but the depth of the cabin is reduced considerably and the tailboom deepened to give a continuous flat undersurface. The stalky four-leg undercarriage enables loads as big as prefabricated buildings or a motor coach to be carried on an open cargo platform between the legs, plus 28 passengers or freight in the cabin. With two 5,500shp Soloviev D-25V turboshafts, max payload is 33,070lb (15,000kg). **Data:** Rotor diameter 114ft 10in (35.00m). Fuselage length 107ft 9¾in (32.86m). Gross weight 96,340lb (43,700kg) Max speed 124mph (200km/h). Range 155 miles (250km) with 26,455lb (12,000kg) payload.

MIL Mi-14 (NATO code-name: Haze)　　　USSR

A float-equipped version of the Mi-8 was reported to be under development in the Soviet Union in early 1974, with the designation V-14 (Mi-14). This is now believed to be the shore-based anti-submarine helicopter (known to NATO as *Haze*) which, with the Ka-25, has largely replaced Mi-4s in the Soviet Navy's force of around 500 helicopters. Although the power plant is similar to that of the Mi-8, the addition of a boat-hull, with a sponson on each side, should give the aircraft a degree of amphibious capability. Other features that can be identified in the few pictures released to date include a large undernose radome, a towed magnetic anomaly detection (MAD) "bird" stowed against the rear of the fuselage pod, and fully-retractable undercarriage. Dimensions, weights and performance should be generally similar to those of the Mi-8.

MIL Mi-24 (NATO code-name: Hind) USSR

Regiments of Mi-24s are based at Parchim and Stendal, northwest and west of Berlin, near the border with West Germany, giving a completely new dimension to the mobility and hitting power of the Warsaw Pact ground forces confronting NATO in Europe. The initial multi-role version, known to NATO as *Hind-A*, has been followed by the complementary *Hind-C* and *D*. The first of these is an armed assault transport, carrying a crew of four on a large flight deck and a squad of eight heavily-armed combat troops in its armoured cabin. Four pylons under its stub-wings enable it to carry up to 128 rockets or other weapons to keep down the heads of any opposition in the drop zone. In addition, the assault craft are intended to be escorted by *Hind-D* gunships, with weapon operator and pilot in tandem cockpits in a completely redesigned front fuselage. Additional wingtip pylons carry "fire and forget" anti-tank missiles, and there is a four-barrel Gatling-type gun under the nose. A special sensor pack is believed to house infra-red and low-light-level TV for operations by night or in bad weather. An indication of performance may have been given by records set by Soviet women pilots in an aircraft designated A-10, with two 1,500shp Isotov turboshafts, which is likely to be an Mi-24; the records include a speed of 212.105mph (341.35km/h) over a 15/25km course. More than 650 *Hinds* had been delivered by 1978. **Data** (estimated): Rotor diameter 55ft 9in (17.00m). Length 55ft 9in (17.00m). Gross weight 22,000lb (10,000kg). Photo: *Hind-A*.

Mitsubishi MU-2 Japan

The first prototype of this 6/14-seat STOL utility transport flew on September 14, 1963, powered by two 562shp Turboméca Astazou turboprop engines. The early production versions had 605shp AiResearch TPE 331-25A turboprops and a 3ft 3½in (1.0m) greater wing span than the prototypes. Initial military versions were the MU-2C, of which four were delivered to the Japanese Ground Self-Defence Force, with reconnaissance cameras and provision for two nose machine-guns, bombs, rockets, etc.; and the MU-2E search and rescue model, of which 16 were produced for the Japanese Air Self-Defence Force, with nose radome, extra fuel, bulged observation windows and sliding door for lifeboat dropping. Military designations are LR-1 and MU-2S respectively. They have been followed by four more LR-1s and seven MU-2A search and rescue aircraft, all with 724ehp TPE 331-6-251M engines, corresponding to commercial MU-2K. **Data** (MU-2K): Span 39ft 2in (11.95m). Length 33ft 3in (10.13m). Gross weight 9,920lb (4,500kg). Max cruising speed 365mph (590km/h). Range 1,680 miles (2,700km). Photo: MU-2S.

Mitsubishi T-2   Japan

Development of this tandem two-seat supersonic trainer for the Japanese Air Self-Defence Force began in September 1967, when Mitsubishi was named as prime contractor. The first of two XT-2 prototypes flew for the first time on July 20, 1971. Production orders were then placed for 59 T-2s, made up of 28 T-2 advanced trainers, 29 T-2A combat trainers and two prototypes for the F-1 close-support fighter version (see page 87). Thirty-five were delivered by the Spring of 1977, with completion of the order scheduled for August

1979. The T-2 was Japan's first home-designed supersonic aircraft, powered by two licence-built Rolls-Royce/Turboméca Adour turbofans, each rated at 7,070lb (3,207kg) st with afterburning. The combat trainer version has a 20mm cannon in the front fuselage and seven attachments for external stores. **Data:** Span 25ft 11in (7.90m). Length 58ft 4¾in (17.80m). Gross weight 20,833lb (9,450kg). Max speed 1,060mph (1,700km/h) at 36,000ft (11,000m). Ferry range 1,610 miles (2,600km).

NAMC YS-11   Japan

First flown in prototype form on August 30, 1962, the basic YS-11-100 is a 52/60-passenger short-range transport powered by two 3,060ehp Rolls-Royce Dart Mk 542-10K turboprop engines. It entered commercial service in the Spring of 1965. Military versions include the YS-11-103/105 32/48-seat VIP transport (4 for JASDF), YS-11-112 cargo transport (1 for JMSDF), YS-11A-218 transport (1

for JASDF), YS-11A-206 anti-submarine trainer (4 for JMSDF), YS-11A-305 passenger/cargo transport (1 for JASDF), and YS-11A-402 cargo transport (7 for JASDF). **Data** (YS-11-200 series): Span 104ft 11¾in (32.00m). Length 86ft 3¼in (26.30m). Gross weight 54,010lb (24,500kg). Max cruising speed 291mph (469km/h). Max range 2,000 miles (3,215km).

Neiva C-42 and L-42 Regente   Brazil

The Regente is of all-metal construction. It flew for the first time on September 7, 1961 and was ordered for the Brazilian Air Force in two versions. These comprised 80 C-42 four-seat utility models and 40 air observation post L-42s, with stepped-down rear fuselage for improved all-round visibility. The prototype Regente had a 145hp Continental O-300 engine, but the production models are powered by a 210hp Continental IO-360-D. **Data:** Span 29ft 11½in (9.13m). Length 23ft 8in (7.21m). Gross weight 2,293lb (1,040kg). Max speed 153mph (246km/h). Range 590 miles (950km). Photo: C-42.

Neiva N621 Universal (T-25)   Brazil

This two/three-seat basic trainer was designed to meet a Brazilian Air Force requirement for a replacement for its Fokker S-11/S-12 Instructors and T-6 Texans. The prototype flew for the first time on April 29, 1966, and was followed on April 7, 1971, by the first of 160 production Universals delivered in 1971–75 to the Air Forces of Brazil (170) and Chile (10). The power plant is a 300hp Lycoming IO-540-K1D5 piston-engine and construction is all-metal. The pilot and instructor sit side-by-side, with space for a third person to the rear. The Brazilian Air Force designation is T-25. Under development in 1978 is a prototype of the N622 Universal II (T-25A), with a 400hp Lycoming IO-720 engine and six underwing attachments for light bombs and rocket pods. **Data:** Span 36ft 1in (11.00m). Length 28ft 2½in (8.60m). Gross weight 3,748lb (1,700kg). Max speed 195mph (315km/h). Max range 975 miles (1,570km).

Nord 3202 and 3212 France

One hundred of these two-seat primary trainers were acquired to replace the Stampe SV-4 biplanes that had been used for basic, aerobatic, and blind-flying instruction at French Army training schools. The original version was the Nord 3200 (first flown September 10, 1954) with a 260hp Salmson 8.AS.04 engine. Then came the Nord 3201 (first flown June 22, 1954) which was similar except for its 170hp SNECMA-Régnier engine. A further engine change led to the production-type

Nord 3202 (first flown April 17, 1957), with a 240hp Potez 4D.32 engine in the first 50 machines and a 260hp Potez 4D.34 in the last 50. When fitted with a radio-compass for instrument flying training, the designation is changed to Nord 3212. **Data** (4D.32 engine): Span 31ft 2in (9.50m). Length 26ft 8in (8.12m). Gross weight 2,690lb (1,220kg). Max speed 161mph (260km/h). Range 620 miles (1,000km). Photo: Nord 3202.

North American (and Cavalier) USA
F-51D Mustang

About 50 North American F-51D Mustang fighters of World War II vintage remain in first-line service, primarily in South America and Indonesia. Each is powered by a 1,695hp Packard V-1650-7 (Rolls-Royce Merlin) piston-engine and is armed with six 0.50in wing-mounted machine-guns, plus two 1,000lb bombs and 5in rockets on eight underwing attachments. The aircraft serving in Bolivia were acquired from Cavalier Aircraft Corporation, which received a USAF contract in 1967 to build (from existing components) a small batch of Mustangs for counter-insurgency duties with certain air forces which received MAP assistance. The basic

Cavalier F-51D is a tandem two-seat fighter assembled from component parts, some manufactured as new. The height of the fin is increased, and armament and avionics are updated to 1968 standards. The US Army bought two Cavalier F-51Ds as chase 'planes and for weapons trials. The Cavalier TF-51D trainer, also delivered in small numbers, has four guns, dual controls and a larger canopy. **Data** (Cavalier F-51D): Span 37ft 0½in (11.29m). Length 32ft 2½in (9.81m). Gross weight 12,500lb (5,670kg). Max speed 457mph (735km/h). Max range 1,980 miles (3,185km) at 290mph (466km/h) Photo: F-51D, Dominican Rep.

North American T-6 Texan

USA

Remembered in Britain as the Harvard, this veteran two-seat basic trainer remained in production in the United States and, later, Canada, from 1938 until 1954 and more than 10,000 were built. In 1949–50, a total of 2,068 early models were modernised as T-6G Texans, and considerable numbers of these are still in service with more than 25 air forces throughout the world. The Texan has a 550hp Pratt & Whitney R-1340-AN-1 engine and can carry underwing rockets and light bombs for weapon training and close support duties. **Data:** Span 42ft (12.80m). Length 29ft 6in (8.99m). Gross weight 5,617lb (2,548kg). Max speed 212mph (341km/h). Range 870 miles (1,400km). Photo: T-6, Dominican Republic.

Northrop T-38A Talon

USA

Structurally, the T-38A two-seat supersonic basic trainer is almost identical with the F-5A/B tactical fighter (see page 94). It lacks the fighter's wing leading-edge flaps and is powered by two 3,850lb (1,746kg) st General Electric J85-GE-5A afterburning turbojets. The first prototype ordered by the USAF flew on April 10, 1959, powered by YJ85-GE-1 engines without afterburners. The second aircraft was similar and was followed by four YT-38 trials aircraft with 3,600lb (1,633kg) st YJ85-GE-5 afterburning engines. The first production T-38As became operational in March 1961 and a total of 1,187 were eventually built. Forty-six were purchased by the *Luftwaffe* for training German pilots in the USA; the Nationalist Chinese Air Force received 30; the US Navy has five; and the Portuguese Air Force has six. **Data:** Span 25ft 3in (7.70m). Length 46ft 4½in (14.12m). Gross weight 11,820lb (5,360kg). Max speed Mach 1.3 (860mph; 1,385km/h). Range 1,140 miles (1,835km).

Pazmany/CAF PL-1B Chienshou Taiwan

In 1968 the Chinese Nationalist Air Force was looking for a small primary trainer which could be built in Taiwan as the first stage in creating an aircraft industry. The type selected was the PL-1, of which construction plans are marketed by the designer, Ladislao Pazmany of San Diego, California. The slightly modified prototype, designated PL-1A and powered by a 125hp Lycoming O-290-D engine, was built in 100 days at the Aeronautical Research Laboratory, Taichung, and flew for the first time on October 26, 1968. It was followed by two more PL-1A prototypes, and then by the first of 50 production PL-1Bs (10 for the Chinese Army) with wider cockpit, larger rudder and more powerful (150hp) Lycoming O-320-E2A engine. The PL-1B is a side-by-side two-seater, of all-metal construction. **Data:** Span 28ft (8.53m). Length 19ft 8in (5.99m). Gross weight 1,440lb (653kg). Max speed 150mph (241km/h). Max range 405 miles (650km). Photo: PL-1B Chienshou.

Piaggio P.149D Italy

The P.149 started out as a four-seat touring development of the P.148 two/three-seat primary trainer, with a tricycle undercarriage and more powerful engine. It was flown in prototype form (with 260hp Lycoming GO-435) on June 19, 1953, but did not enter large-scale production until West Germany chose it as the standard basic trainer/liaison aircraft for the *Luftwaffe*. The first of 72 Piaggio-built P.149Ds (with 270hp GO-480) was delivered to Germany in May 1957, and was followed six months later by the first of 190 which were licence-built by Focke-Wulf. About 40 of these continue in service, and P.149Ds are used also by the air forces of Nigeria and Uganda. Up to five persons can be carried in the liaison role. **Data:** Span 36ft 6in (11.12m). Length 28ft 9½in (8.78m). Gross weight 3,704lb (1,680kg). Max speed 192mph (310km/h). Range 680 miles (1,095km).

Piaggio P.166M (and Albatross) Italy

Piaggio developed the P.166 light transport from its P.136 twin-engined amphibian, with a normal fuselage instead of a flying-boat hull, but with similar basic outline. More than 100 were built, including 51 P.166Ms for training, ambulance and communications duties with the Italian Air Force. Powered by two 340hp Lycoming GSO-480-B1C6 engines, driving pusher propellers, the P.166M can carry up to ten people or items of freight as large as an Orpheus turbojet. Final production version was the P.166S, of which the South African Air Force

purchased 20 (in two batches) for coastal patrol, with the local name Albatross. No military orders had been reported for the latest P.166-DL2 with 380hp Lycoming IGSO-540 engines, or the turbo-prop P.166-DL3, by 1978. **Data** (P.166M): Span 46ft 9in (14.25m). Length 38ft 1in (11.60m). Gross weight 8,115lb (3,680kg). Max speed 222mph (357km/h). Range 1,200 miles (1,930km). Photo: P.166S Albatross, SAAF.

Piaggio PD-808 Italy

The El Segundo Division of Douglas Aircraft Company was responsible for the basic design of this 6/10-seat twin-jet utility transport; detail design and manufacture were entrusted to Piaggio. The Italian Government paid for two prototypes, and the first of these flew on August 29, 1964. Of the 13 PD-808s which went into service subsequently with the Italian Air Force, four are six-seat VIP transports, six are PD-808TA com-

munications aircraft and three are ECM aircraft with a crew of five. Power is provided by two 3,360lb (1,524kg) st Rolls-Royce Bristol Viper 526 turbojets, mounted on the sides of the rear fuselage. **Data:** Span 43ft 3½in (13.20m). Length 42ft 2in (12.85m). Gross weight 18,000lb (8,165kg). Max speed 529mph (852km/h). Range 1,322 miles (2,128km).

Pilatus P.2   Switzerland

This tandem two-seat basic trainer, like all aircraft designed for the Swiss armed forces, is capable of operating from high-altitude alpine airfields and has a sturdy structure. It is powered by a 465hp Argus As 410A-2 engine and carries comprehensive night flying instrumentation, oxygen and radio equipment. The prototype flew for the first time on April 27, 1945, and was followed by 53 production models for the Swiss Air Force. The first 27, designated P-2/05s, were intended only for flying training. The remainder, designated P-2/06s, each have a 7.9mm machine-gun in the fuselage and underwing racks for practice bombs and rockets for weapon training, plus provision for cameras in the rear cockpit for observer training. **Data:** Span 36ft 1in (11.00m). Length 29ft 9in (9.07m). Gross weight 4,335lb (1,966kg). Max speed 211mph (340km/h). Range 535 miles (860km).

Pilatus P.3   Switzerland

The tandem two-seat Pilatus P-3 is used by the Swiss Air Force as a basic trainer, before the pupil graduates on to the Vampire jet advanced trainer. The first of two prototypes flew on September 3, 1953, and a total of 72 were acquired by the Swiss Air Force to replace its T-6 Texans, a few also serving in the liaison role. Power plant is a 260hp Lycoming GO-435-C2A piston-engine, and one 7.9mm machine-gun and racks for two rockets or four small bombs can be fitted for weapon training. **Data:** Span 34ft 1½in (10.40m). Length 28ft 8in (8.75m). Gross weight 3,300lb (1,500kg). Max speed 193mph (310km/h). Range 465 miles (750km).

Pilatus PC-6 Porter and PC-6/A/B/C Turbo-Porter (and Fairchild AU-23A Peacemaker)

Switzerland/USA

This family of aircraft stemmed from the basic Swiss Pilatus PC-6 Porter 8/10-seat STOL utility transport, with a Lycoming piston-engine. Turbo-Porters, similar except for having a Turboméca Astazou (PC-6/A series), Pratt & Whitney PT6A (PC-6/B series) or AiResearch TPE 331 (PC-6/C series) turboprop, were manufactured also by Fairchild in the USA. From them was evolved the AU-23A Peacemaker, of which 15 were acquired by the USAF for evaluation, 14 later being assigned to the Royal Thai Air Force. Powered by a 650shp TPE 331-1-101F, the AU-23A carries a side-firing 20mm cannon and has five racks under its

fuselage and wings for gun or rocket pods, bombs, broadcasting equipment, or camera and flare packs. Five more AU-23As were bought by the Thai Police, and another batch of 20 was delivered to the Thai Air Force in 1975/76. Military customers for Porters and Turbo-Porters include the Australian Army, Austria, Angola, Bolivia, Colombia, Ecuador, Israel, Peru and Sudan. **Data:** (PC-6/B2): Span 49ft 8in (15.13m). Length 36ft 1in (11.00m). Gross weight 4,850lb (2,200kg). Max cruising speed 161mph (259km/h). Max range 1,006 miles (1,620km). Photo: PC-6, Switzerland.

Pilatus PC-7 Turbo-Trainer

Switzerland

In the mid-sixties, Pilatus decided to update the P.3 intermediate trainer by developing a turboprop version. An early P.3 was retrofitted with a 550shp Pratt & Whitney PT6A-20, and flew for the first time in its new form on April 12, 1966. Known originally as the P.3B, it was subsequently redesignated PC-7 Turbo-Trainer. The project was revived in the Spring of 1975, by which time the design had undergone considerable refinement. The original framed canopy was replaced by a one-piece type. Provision for underwing tanks superseded the

former wingtip tanks. The engine is now a 550shp PT6A-25A. The result is a thoroughly modern, fully-aerobatic tandem two-seater, for which orders had been placed by the air forces of Burma, Mexico and Bolivia by 1978, when production was at the rate of 2–3 aircraft per month. Deliveries began in July 1978. **Data:** Span 34ft 1½in (10.40m). Length 32ft 0in (9.75m). Gross weight 5,952lb (2,700kg). Max cruising speed 252mph (405m/h). Max range 807 miles (1,300km).

Piper L-4, L-18, L-21 and U-7A USA

At least two air forces (those of Indonesia and Paraguay) still have in service some original L-4 Piper Cubs, with 65hp Continental O-170-3 engine. Far more numerous, and flown by about 10 air forces, are L-18s and U-7s, based on the post-war Super Cub. The 105 standard Super Cub 95s (90hp Continental C90) purchased as L-18Bs were all supplied to Turkey. They were followed by 838 similar L-18Cs for the US Army and America's allies, including France, Israel and Norway, where a few may still be seen. Last version of the Piper Cub to serve with the US forces, the U-7A (formerly L-21A) went into production in 1951 with a 125hp Lycoming O-290-11 engine. Thirty went to the US Army and 120 to the USAF, from which they passed to other operators. They were followed by 582 U-7Bs (originally L-21Bs), with 135hp O-290-D2 engine, of which about 70 were fitted with tandem wheels on each leg for operation from rough ground. All of these Cub variants are tandem two-seaters, for observation and liaison duties. **Data** (U-7A): Span 35ft 3in (10.73m). Length 22ft 7in (6.88m). Gross weight 1,580lb (717kg). Max speed 123mph (198km/h). Range 770 miles (1,240km). Photo: L-21 Portugal.

Piper PA-28-140 Cherokee 140 USA

First country to adopt this two/four-seat sporting and training aircraft for military use was Tanzania, which took delivery of five in the first half of 1972. They are being used as *ab initio* trainers for the Tanzanian People's Defence Force Air Wing. The Cherokee 140 is powered by a 150hp Lycoming O-320 engine. Two of the "stretched" six/seven-seat Cherokee Six version of the same basic design are operated by the Chilean Army and one by the Tanzanian Air Wing. Five Cherokee Arrows, with retractable undercarriage, have been loaned to the Finnish Air Force by private owners. **Data** (Cherokee 140): Span 36ft 2in (11.02m). Length 23ft 3½in (7.10m). Gross weight 2,150lb (975kg). Max speed 142mph (229km/h). Max range 839 miles (1,350km). Photo: Chincul Cherokee Arrow Trainer, developed in the Argentine from the standard Cherokee Arrow.

Piper PA-31 Turbo Navajo USA

The prototype of the basic Navajo six/nine-seat light transport was flown on September 30, 1964, as the first of a new Piper family of larger aircraft for business and commuter airline service. It was followed by the turbocharged Turbo Navajo and then, in 1970, by the PA-31P Pressurised Navajo. The French Navy has 12 Navajos and the Argentine Navy has four. The Chilean Army has one Turbo Navajo. The Spanish Air Force has one Pressurised Navajo; the Nigerian Air Force has two Pressurised Navajo and one Navajo Chieftain, the

Syrian Air Force has two for air survey duties, and the Kenya Air Force has two Chieftains. **Data** (Turbo Navajo): Powered by two 310hp Lycoming TIO-540-A engines. Span 40ft 8in (12.40m). Length 32ft 7½in (9.94m). Gross weight 6,500lb (2,948kg). Max speed 261mph (420km/h). Max range 1,730 miles (2,780km). Photo: Navajo French Navy.

Piper U-11A Aztec USA

The PA-23-250 Aztec was introduced by Piper in 1959 as a five-seat development of their Apache four-seat light twin, with more powerful engines and swept fin. The US Navy ordered 20 of this original version, with 250hp Lycoming O-540-A1A engines, "off the shelf" for utility transport duties and some of these remain in service under the designation U-11A (originally UO-1). The later six seat Turbo Aztec E, with 250hp TIO-540-C1A engines and longer nose, serves with the Spanish Air Force, which acquired six in 1972 (as E.19). The French Air Force also bought two Aztecs. The

Malagasy Air Force has one, Nigeria one, the Peruvian Navy one, Senegal one and Uganda two. **Data** (Turbo Aztec E): Span 37ft 2½in (11.34m). Length 31ft 2¾in (9.52m). Gross weight 5,200lb (2,360kg). Max speed 253mph (407km/h). Range 1,310 miles (2,108km). Photo: Aztec (E.19), Spain.

PZL-104 Wilga/Gelatik 32   Poland/Indonesia

The original Wilga 1 prototype flew for the first time on April 24, 1962, powered by a 180hp Narkiewicz WN-6B engine. The fuselage and tail unit were then redesigned completely, giving the aircraft its present unique spindly outline. The resulting Wilga 2 flew on August 1, 1963, with a 195hp WN-6RB engine. Other prototypes followed, equipped for both four-seat liaison and agricultural duties, including one with a Continental O-470 engine. Thirty-nine of this version were built under licence in Indonesia, with the name Gelatik

(Rice-bird) and are serving with the Indonesian Air Force. Early aircraft have a 225hp O-470-13A; Gelatik 32s have a 230hp O-470-L. The Polish Air Force has received standard Polish-built Wilgas, and a few are in service with the Egyptian Air Force, with 260hp Al-14R radial engines, to replace its Yak-12s. **Data** (Gelatik): Span 36ft 5in (11.10m). Length 26ft 6¾in (8.10m). Gross weight 2,711lb (1,230kg). Max speed 127mph (205km/h). Range 435 miles (700km). Photo: Wilga 35, Poland.

PZL-Mielec TS-11 Iskra   Poland

The TS-11 Iskra (Spark) flew for the first time on February 5, 1960. It came second to the Czech L-29 Delfin in the competition to find a new jet trainer for the Warsaw Pact nations; but Poland decided to continue development and production of the Iskra to meet its own requirements and the first formal delivery to the Air Force was made in March 1963. Quantity deliveries began in the following year and several hundred had been built by 1978. Design is conventional, with two seats in tandem and a 2,205lb (1,000kg) st nationally-designed SO-3 turbojet (1,760lb; 800kg st HO-10 in

early aircraft). A version known as the Iskra 100 has a 23mm gun in its nose and four underwing racks for bombs or rockets. Current production versions are the improved Iskra 200 flying trainer and 200SB armament trainer, which is available also in single-seat form for light attack duties. First export customer was the Indian Air Force, which acquired 90 for use as armament trainers. **Data:** Span 33ft 0in (10.07m). Length 36ft 5in (11.17m). Gross weight 8,465lb (3,840kg). Max speed 447mph (720km/h). Range 907 miles (1,460km). Photo: Iskra 100, India.

RFB Fantrainer   Germany

First military prototypes to emerge from Rhein-Flugzeugbau's years of experiments with ducted fan propulsion systems are two Fantrainers, the first of which flew in late October 1977. Of extremely neat layout, the Fantrainer has the now customary sloping tandem cabin, giving the instructor a clear view forward over the head of his pupil. The first prototype, designated AWI-2, is powered by two 150hp Audi NSU/RFB Wankel EA 871-L rotating-piston engines, mounted one above the other in the centre-fuselage and driving a Dowty Rotol seven-blade variable-pitch ducted fan built into the cruciform rear fuselage. The second prototype, designated ATI-2, has a Lycoming turboshaft engine. Production models are projected with turboshafts of up to 800shp, for training, counterinsurgency, helicopter escort, anti-helicopter and liaison duties. The prototypes were funded by the Federal German Defence Ministry, which was evaluating the Fantrainer in 1978 as a potential replacement for the Luftwaffe's Piaggio P.149Ds. **Data** (AWI-2): Span 31ft 6in (9.60m). Length 29ft 4in (8.94m). Gross weight 3,483lb (1,580kg). Max speed 220mph (354km/h). Range 1,150 miles (1,850km).. Photo: ATI-2.

Rockwell International T-2 Buckeye   USA

No prototype of the Buckeye was built and the first of the original series of 217 T-2A production models for the US Navy flew on January 31, 1958. This version, no longer in service, was a tandem two-seater with a 3,400lb (1,540kg) st Westinghouse J34-WE-48 turbojet, and was suitable for the complete syllabus of naval training. On August 30, 1962 North American flew the first of two YT-2B prototypes (converted from T-2As), built to evaluate the potential of the airframe when fitted with two 3,000lb (1,360kg) st Pratt & Whitney J60-P-6 turbojets. A total of 97 T-2Bs was built for the Navy in 1964–69; the first flew on May 21, 1965. During 1968, a prototype T-2C was produced by installing 2,950lb (1,339kg) st General Electric J85-GE-4 engines in a T-2B, and the Navy took delivery of 231 in 1968–75. Twenty-four T-2Ds for Venezuela differ from the T-2C only in electronics and deletion of carrier landing capability; but the second batch of 12 were supplied with attack kits providing six underwing hardpoints for 3,500lb (1,588kg) of external stores. Forty T-2Es for Greece have similar attack capability. **Data** (T-2C): Span 38ft 1½in (11.62m). Length 38ft 3½in (11.67m). Gross weight 13,179lb (5,977kg). Max speed 522mph (840km/h). Range 1,047 miles (1,685km). Photo: T-2D Venezuela.

Rockwell International T-39 Sabreliner

USA

The Sabreliner prototype flew for the first time on September 16, 1958, with two General Electric J85 turbojets; but production models for military use have 3,000lb (1,360kg) st Pratt & Whitney J60 (JT12) engines. The T-39A (143 delivered) is a pilot proficiency trainer and administrative support aircraft in service with the USAF. The six T-39B aircrew trainers have Doppler radar and NASARR all-weather search and ranging radar. The US Navy's 42 T-39Ds have a Magnavox radar system for maritime radar training. Seven CT-39E rapid response airlift jets acquired by the USN are similar to the commercial Sabreliner 40, while 12 CT-39Gs have the longer fuselage of the Sabreliner 60. A further variant is the T-39F, equipped to train "Wild Weasel" ECM operators. **Data** (T-39A/D): Span 44ft 5in (13.54m). Length 43ft 9in (13.34m). Gross weight 17,760lb (8,055kg). Max cruising speed 502mph (808km/h). Range 1,950 miles (3,138km). Photo: CT-39G, US Navy.

Saab-91 Safir

Sweden

The Saab-91A two/three-seat basic trainer, first flown in prototype form on November 20, 1945, had a 145hp D.H. Gipsy Major 10. The Saab-91B changed to a 190hp Lycoming O-435-A engine and remains a standard basic trainer of the Swedish Air Force (75 delivered as SK50B) and Norwegian (25) and Ethiopian (16) air forces. The Saab-91C differs from the B only in having four seats and was sold to the Swedish Air Force (14 SK50Cs) and Ethiopia (14). Final version was the Saab-91D, which differs from the C in having a 180hp Lycoming O-360-A1A engine, propeller spinner, more powerful generator and rudder trim. Orders for the D were received from the air forces of Finland (35), Tunisia (15, no longer in use) and Austria (24). **Data** (Saab-91D): Span 34ft 9in (10.60m). Length 26ft 4in (8.03m). Gross weight 2,660lb (1,205kg). Max speed 165mph (265km/h). Range 660 miles (1,060km). Photo: Saab-91D Austria.

Saab Supporter

Sweden

This aircraft had its origin in the MFI-9/Bölkow Junior series, designed by Bjorn Andreasson and used as lightweight attack aircraft by the Biafran forces in the Nigerian civil war. When Saab took over the MFI company, they supported development of the two/three-seat Saab-MFI 15 for military training and general-purpose duties. This aircraft was superseded in production by the Supporter (originally Saab-MFI 17), which differs primarily in having provision for six underwing attachments for up to 660lb (300kg) of rocket pods, wire-guided anti-tank missiles, droppable containers or other stores. Power plant is a 200hp Lycoming IO-360-A1B piston-engine. The Suppor-ter entered production in the Autumn of 1972; orders have included 45 for the Pakistan Air Force and Army, and 32 for the Royal Danish Air Force and Army. **Data:** Span 29ft 0$\frac{1}{2}$in (8.85m). Length 22ft 11$\frac{1}{2}$in (7.00m). Gross weight 2,645lb (1,200kg). Max speed 146mph (236km/h). Endurance 5hr 10min. Photo: Supporter, Denmark.

Shenyang F-9
(NATO code-name: Fantan)

China

Although the Chinese State Aircraft Factory at Shenyang produced a small number of MiG-21s, under the designation F-8, the Chinese Air Force preferred the Shenyang F-6 variants of the MiG-19. The latter was, therefore, selected as the basis for the F-9 (NATO *Fantan-A*), of which the accompanying three-view drawing is believed to depict the main features. Scaled-up a little from the MiG-19, the F-9 has lateral air intakes to permit the installation of a comparatively large radar scanner in a pointed nose radome. The prototype is believed to have flown in the early seventies, and F-9s were said to be operational with both strike squadrons of the Chinese Air Force and the Naval Air Force by 1977. The following data, like the three-view, should be regarded as provisional. **Data:** Span 33ft 5in (10.20m). Length 50ft 0in (15.25m). Gross weight 22,050lb (10,000kg). Max speed nearly Mach 2.0. Combat radius 500 miles (800km).

200

Shorts Skyvan Series 3M

Great Britain

The prototype of this military version of the Shorts Skyvan Srs. 3 STOL utility transport flew for the first time in early 1970. It is powered by two 715shp Garrett-AiResearch TPE 331-201 turboprops and can carry 22 equipped troops, 16 paratroops and a despatcher, 12 stretcher cases and two medical attendants or 5,200lb (2,358kg) of freight. Entry to the cabin is via a rear loading ramp. Special equipment includes a Bendix weather radar on the nose, anchor cables for parachute static lines, inward-facing paratroop seats, stretcher mounts and roller conveyors in the cabin floor. Initial deliveries comprised two aircraft for the Austrian Air Force and the first of 16 for the Sultan of Oman's Air Force. Others are used by the Argentine Naval Prefectura (5), Royal Thai Police (3), the Nepalese Army (2), the Ghana Air Force (6), the Yemen Arab Republic Air Force (2), and the Air Arms of Ecuador, Mauritania and Indonesia. The Singapore Air Defence Command acquired six in 1973. **Data:** Span 64ft 11in (19.79m). Length 41ft 4in (12.60m). Gross weight 14,500lb (6,577kg). Max cruising speed 203mph (327km/h). Max range 670 miles (1,075km).

SIAI-Marchetti S.208M

Italy

The prototype of the S.208 five-seat light aircraft flew for the first time on May 22, 1967. It embodies many components of SIAI-Marchetti's popular S.205 series, but introduced one more seat and a more powerful (260hp) Lycoming O-540-E4A5 engine. In addition to civilian production, the company built 44 of a version designated S.208M for the Italian Air Force. This differs from the standard model by having a jettisonable cabin door, and is intended for liaison and training duties. **Data:** Span 35ft 7½in (10.86m). Length 26ft 3in (8.00m). Gross weight 3,307lb (1,500kg). Max speed 199mph (320km/h). Max range 1,250 miles (2,000km).

SIAI-Marchetti SF.260, Warrior and Sea Warrior

Italy

The prototype of this two/three-seat aircraft, designed by Ing. Stelio Frati, was built by Aviamilano as the F.250 and flew on July 15, 1964. Production was undertaken by SIAI-Marchetti, who exchanged the original 250hp engine for a 260hp Lycoming O-540-E4A5 and redesignated the aircraft SF.260. In addition to manufacturing civil-registered SF.260s, many for use as airline trainers, SIAI-Marchetti received orders for military SF.260Ms for the Air Forces of Italy (20), Morocco (2), Belgium (36), Zaïre (12), Singapore (16), Zambia (8), Thailand (12) and the Philippines (32). This version (first flown on October 10, 1970) has a larger rudder and specialised equipment for military training. A strengthened and armed version, with wing pylons for up to 661lb (300kg) of bombs or rockets, is known as the SF.260W Warrior and first flew in May 1972; 16 were ordered by the Philippine Air Force, 12 by Tunisia, 10 by the Irish Air Corps, and 3 by the Comores Islands. Production of a large batch for Libya was underway in 1978. The SF.260SW Sea Warrior has photorecce and radar equipment in wingtip tanks, for surveillance, search/rescue and supply missions, **Data** (SF.260W): Span 27ft 4¾in (8.35m). Length 23ft 3½in (7.10m). Gross weight 2,866lb (1,300kg). Max speed 196mph (315km/h). Operational radius 57–345 miles (92–556km). Photo: SF.260W.

SIAI-Marchetti SM.1019E

Italy

This two-seat light military STOL aircraft is a turboprop development of the Cessna L-19/O-1 Bird Dog which can be produced either as a new airframe or by extensive modification of existing aircraft. The entire airframe is updated to meet current operational requirements, and is fitted with new, angular vertical tail surfaces and a lengthened nose for the 400shp Allison 250-B17 turboprop. Up to 500lb of rockets, gun pods, missiles, bombs or camera packs can be carried on two underwing racks. The first of two prototype SM.1019s flew on May 24, 1969, and production of 100 aircraft for the Italian Army Aviation component began in 1974. **Data:** Span 36ft (10.97m). Length 27ft 11½in (8.52m). Gross weight 3,196lb (1,450kg). Max cruising speed 184mph (296km/h). Range 840 miles (1,352km). Photo: SM.1019E with AS.12 missiles.

Sikorsky S-55 and H-19 Chickasaw USA

The H-19 is the military counterpart of the civil Sikorsky S-55, with accommodation for a crew of two and up to ten troops or six stretchers. The parent company built 1,281, of which most went to the US armed forces. Versions included the USAF's UH-19B, Army UH-19D, Marine CH-19E and Naval UH-19F, all with 800hp Wright R-1300-3 engine, and the Army's UH-19C with 600hp Pratt & Whitney R-1340. Others were manufactured in Japan by Mitsubishi. More than 20 air forces used versions of the S-55 and H-19 for utility transport,

search and rescue, casualty evacuation and other duties. Few remain in service, although some operators have extended the life and capability of their aircraft by converting them to Helitec S-55T standard, with a 650shp Garrett-AiResearch TSE 331 turboshaft replacing the original piston engine. **Data** (S-55T): Rotor diameter 53ft (16.15m). Length 42ft 3in (12.88m). Gross weight 7,200lb (3,265kg). Max speed 114mph (183km/h). Range 370 miles (595km). Photo: H-19D, Brazil.

Sikorsky S-58 USA
(H-34 Seabat, Choctaw, Seahorse)

On June 30, 1952, Sikorsky received a US Navy contract for a prototype anti-submarine helicopter to be designated XHSS-1. This aircraft flew on March 8, 1954, and was followed by 1,821 production helicopters of the S-58 series. Most were delivered to the US services, for a wide variety of duties, under the names Seabat (Navy), Seahorse (Marines) and Choctaw (Army), but many were exported. For the French Army and Navy, Sud-Aviation built 166 S-58s, plus five for Belgium. Westland in the UK built a turbine-powered

version known as the Wessex (which see). Few of the military S-58s remain in service. However, the Argentine Air Force has had some of its remaining aircraft converted to S-58T standard, with an 1,875shp Pratt & Whitney (Canada) PT6T-6 Twin-Pac twin-turbine power plant. **Data** (S-58T): Rotor diameter 56ft 0in (17.07m). Length 47ft 3in (14.40m). Gross weight 13,000lb (5,896kg). Max speed 138mph (222km/h). Range 278 miles (447km). Photo: S-58, Costa Rica.

Sikorsky S-61B (H-3 Sea King) USA

The Sikorsky S-61 was developed to provide the US Navy with an anti-submarine "hunter-killer". It was designed around two General Electric T58 turboshaft engines, with a watertight hull to permit operation on and off water. The prototype, designated XHSS-2, flew on March 11, 1959. Deliveries of production HSS-2s to operational ASW units began in September 1961; altogether 255 were built, with 1,250shp T58-GE-8B engines. Their designation was changed to SH-3A Sea King in July 1962; conversions included 12 HH-3A armed search and rescue helicopters, 105 SH-3G utility helicopters, and SH-3H multipurpose helicopters for ASW and defence against missiles. Forty-one CH-124s (similar to SH-3As) were delivered to the Canadian Armed Forces; 73 similar HSS-2s and 2As had been delivered to the JMSDF by Mitsubishi by early 1977, when 10 more HSS-2As remained to be built. With uprated engines (1,400shp T58-GE-10s), the SH-3D appeared in 1965; 98 were built by Sikorsky, including 22 for the Spanish Navy and four for the Brazilian Navy. Eleven specially-equipped VH-3Ds are operated by the Executive Flight Detachment based in Washington for VIP duties. SH-3Ds continue in production by Agusta for the Italian Navy and Iran; in Britain, Westland produce a family of SH-3D variants as the Sea King and Commando. Other Sikorsky-built variants include four S-61D-4s (similar to SH-3D) for the Argentine Navy; nine S-61A transports (similar to SH-3A) for long-range air/sea rescue duties with the Royal Danish Air Force; and 38 S-61A-4 Nuri 31-seat transports for the Royal Malaysian Air Force. **Data** (SH-3D): Rotor diameter 62ft 0in (18.90m). Length 54ft 9in (16.69m). Gross weight 18,626lb (8,449kg). Max speed 166mph (267km/h). Range 625 miles (1,005km). Armament 840lb (381kg) of homing torpedoes, depth charges, etc. Photo: SH-3H.

Sikorsky S-61R USA
(H-3 Jolly Green Giant/Pelican)

On February 8, 1963, the USAF ordered 22 CH-3C general-purpose helicopters, based on the S-61 but with new stabilising sponsons for amphibious operation, a hydraulically-operated rear loading ramp and built-in auxiliary power unit. An S-61R civil prototype flew on June 17, 1963, followed a few weeks later by the first CH-3C, with 1,300shp T58-GE-1 engines. By the time deliveries began in December 1963, another 19 had been ordered to fill a further USAF requirement for a long-range rotary-wing support system. In February 1966 production was switched to the CH-3E with 1,500shp T58-GE-5s; 42 were built to this standard, and the 41 CH-3Cs were modified to CH-3Es. Subsequently, 50 CH-3Es were converted into HH-3E Jolly Green Giants for the USAF Aerospace Rescue and Recovery Service, with defensive armament, armour plating, jettisonable fuel tanks and rescue hoist. Forty unarmed HH-3F Pelicans were built for extended search and rescue operations with the US Coast Guard. Basic accommodation of all models is for a crew of two or three, 30 troops, 15 stretcher patients or 5,000lb (2,270kg) of cargo. Agusta have built 12 HH-3Fs for SAR duties with the Italian Air Force, and others for foreign operators. **Data** (CH-3E): Rotor diameter 62ft 0in (18.90m). Length 57ft 3in (17.45m). Gross weight 22,050lb (10,000kg). Max speed 162mph (261km/h). Range 465 miles (748km). Photo: Agusta-built HH-3F.

Sikorsky S-64 Skycrane (CH-54 Tarhe) USA

The highly-functional Skycrane consists of a "backbone" structure carrying a cab for three crew at the front, two 4,500shp Pratt & Whitney T73-P-1 turboshaft engines and the main rotor above the centre of gravity, and a tail rotor. The underside of the backbone is flattened, enabling bulky cargoes to be clamped tightly beneath it, between the stalky main undercarriage legs. The payload can be carried in interchangeable Universal Military Pods, each accommodating 45 combat-equipped troops, 24 stretcher patients, a surgical unit or field command or communications post. The first of three S-64A prototypes flew on May 9, 1962. In June 1963, the US Army ordered six, as CH-54A Tarhes, to evaluate the heavy-lift concept as an aid to battlefield mobility. After trials in Vietnam, the Army ordered about 60 CH-54As, followed by ten CH-54Bs with 4,800shp T73-P-700 engines, high-lift rotor blades and gross weight of 47,000lb (21,319kg). Typical loads carried in Vietnam included 20,000lb (9,072kg) armoured vehicles and up to 87 troops; more than 380 damaged aircraft were retrieved. **Data** (CH-54A): Rotor diameter 72ft 0in (21.95m). Length 70ft 3in (21.41m). Gross weight 42,000lb (19,050kg). Max speed 126mph (203km/h). Range 230 miles (370km).

Sikorsky S-65A (H-53 Sea Stallion)　　　　USA

On October 14, 1964, Sikorsky flew the prototype of the CH-53A Sea Stallion heavy assault transport for the US Marines, with accommodation for a crew of three, 37 combat-equipped troops, 24 stretcher patients or internal or external freight. Deliveries of production models, with two 2,850shp General Electric T64-GE-6 turboshaft engines, began in mid-1966. These aircraft were operational in Vietnam from January 1967, primarily to carry cargo, vehicles and equipment such as 105mm howitzers, loaded into the amphibious fuselage via rear doors. The first improved CH-53D, with 3,925shp T64-GE-413s, was delivered in March 1969, and the Marines received a total of 265 As and Ds. Simultaneously, the USAF Aerospace Rescue and Recovery Service acquired eight HH-53Bs, with 3,080shp T64-GE-3s, armament, flight refuelling probe and jettisonable ex-

ternal tanks; followed by 64 HH-53Cs with 3,925shp T64-GE-7s. The German armed forces acquired 112 CH-53Gs, assembled under licence; Israel had eight CH-53s, the Iranian Navy six; and the Austrian Air Force has two S-65Oes for rescue work in the Alps. RH-53Ds supplied to the US Navy (30) and Iran (6) have 4,380shp T64-GE-415 engines, special towing equipment to sweep mechanical, acoustic and magnetic mines, and max gross weight of 50,000lb (22,680kg). **Data** (CH-53D): Rotor diameter 72ft 2¾in (22.02m). Length 67ft 2in (20.47m). Gross weight 42,000lb (19,050kg). Max speed 196mph (315km/n). Range 257 miles (413km). Photo: CH-53, Israel.

Sikorsky CH-53E　　　　USA

To meet a US Navy/Marine Corps requirement for a new heavy-duty multi-purpose helicopter, Sikorsky proposed this version of the H-53 with a third engine, larger-diameter rotor with seven titanium blades, and uprated transmission. The first of two YCH-53E development aircraft flew on March 1, 1974; the second has flown at a gross weight of 70,000lb (31,751kg), unmatched by any other helicopter outside the Soviet Union. Two pre-production CH-53Es have demonstrated their capability of performing the Navy's vertical on-board delivery mission for ships at sea, and 49 are to be acquired, with about two-thirds going to the Marine Corps. In addition to removing battle-damaged aircraft from

carrier decks, the CH-53Es will be capable of airlifting 93 per cent of a Marine division's combat items, and of retrieving 98 per cent of Marine tactical aircraft without disassembly. **Data:** Power plant, three 4,380shp General Electric T64-GE-415 turboshaft engines. Rotor diameter 79ft 0in (24.08m). Length 73ft 9in (22.48m). Gross weight 69,750lb (31,638kg). Max speed 196mph (315km/h). Range 306 miles (492km).

Sikorsky S-70 (H-60 Black Hawk)　　　　USA

Three YUH-60A prototypes were built initially, to compete with three Boeing Vertol YUH-61As, in the programme to provide the US Army with a new utility tactical transport aviation system (UTTAS). The first YUH-60A flew on October 17, 1974, and Sikorsky's design was declared the winner of a seven-month fly-off evaluation on December 23, 1976. The intention is to procure 1,107 production UH-60A Black Hawks by 1985, to replace UH-1s in selected assault helicopter, air cavalry and aeromedical evacuation units. Powered by two 1,543shp General Electric T700-GE-700 turboshaft engines, the UH-60A will carry a crew of three and a fully-equipped infantry squad of 11 troops, four stretcher patients, internal cargo or 8,000lb (3,630kg) of slung cargo. Two side-firing machine-guns can be fitted for protection during drops. A first contract for 15 aircraft was placed in FY 1977,

with total funding for 368 aircraft by FY 1980. In addition, the US Navy ordered five prototype SH-60Bs in September 1977, to initiate development of the 204 aircraft that will eventually replace SH-2F Seasprites, as the Navy's LAMPS III shipboard ASW and ASV helicopters. They will be similar to the UH-60A except for automatic blade-folding, added surface search radar, MAD, sonobuoys, two homing torpedoes and other specialised equipment. **Data** (UH-60A): Rotor diameter 53ft 8in (16.36m). Length 50ft 0¾in (15.26m). Gross weight 20,250lb (9,185kg). Max speed 184mph (296km/h). Range 373 miles (600km). Photo: YUH-60A.

Socata Rallye

France

The Rallye began life as a three/four-seat light-plane designed by the old Morane-Saulnier company to meet a requirement of the French official Service de la Formation Aéronautique (SFA). The prototype flew for the first time on June 10, 1959, with a 90hp Continental engine. Since then, many different versions have been produced, with engines of up to 235hp. The current manufacturer is Socata, a subsidiary of Aérospatiale, which delivered the 3,000th Rallye in May 1977. Current versions include the two-seat Rallye 100S

(S for Sport), first flown on March 30, 1973, and the first aircraft in the series cleared for spinning. Ten were delivered to the French Navy Training School at Lanvéoc-Poulmic in April 1974. The French Navy also has five 2/4-seat Rallye 100STs. The 180hp MS.893A Rallye Commodore has been supplied to the Dominican Military Aviation Corps and ordered by the French Air Force. **Data** (100S): Span 31ft 11in (9.74m). Length 23ft 1¼in (7.05m). Gross weight 1,653lb (750kg). Max speed 121mph (195km/h). Range 465 miles (750km). Photo: 235G.

Soko G2-A Galeb

Yugoslavia

First flown in prototype form in May 1961, the G2-A Galeb tandem two-seat basic trainer is conventional in design and, like many of its counterparts in other countries, is powered by a Rolls-Royce Viper turbojet. The second prototype embodied improvements and was representative of the production version, of which many are in service with the Yugoslav Air Force. The engine in the production G2-A is a Viper 11 Mk22-6 of 2,500lb (1,134kg) st. For weapon training or light

attack duties, it is fitted with two 0.50in machine-guns and underwing racks for bombs and rockets. Two G2-A Galebs have been supplied to Zambia. Current export model is the G-2A-E, with updated equipment; first customer was reported to be Libya. **Data** (G2-A): Span 38ft 1½in (11.62m). Length 33ft 11in (10.34m). Gross weight 8,440–9,480lb (3,828–4,300kg). Max speed 505mph (812km/h). Range 770 miles (1,240km).

Swearingen Merlin IIIA   USA

This eight/eleven-seat pressurised transport has
the same wings, undercarriage and basic engines
as the longer-fuselage Metro II. The original Merlin
III was certificated in July 1970; additional cabin
windows, system and flight deck improvements
and cabin refinements came with the current
Merlin IIIA, which is powered by two 840shp Garrett-AiResearch TPE 331-3U-303G turboprops.
Success as a commercial business transport led to
a Belgian Air Force order for six, which were
delivered in 1976. Four are operated by the Argentine Army. **Data:** Span 46ft 3in (14.10m). Length
42ft 2in (12.85m). Gross weight 12,500lb (5,670kg).
Max cruising speed 325mph (523km/h). Range at
max cruising speed 1,968 miles (3,167km). Photo:
Merlin IIIA, Belgium.

Swearingen Metro/Merlin IVA   USA

The original Metro and current Metro II are
equipped normally as 19/20-passenger pressurised commuter airliners, but have an easily
convertible passenger/cargo interior. Kits are
available for adaptation to business transport, air
ambulance (ten stretcher patients) or air survey
photographic configurations. The twin engines are
940shp Garrett-AiResearch TPE 331-3UW-303G
turboprops. A more luxurious 12/15-passenger
executive model is available as the Merlin IVA.
Customers for this include the South African Air
Force, which has six for VIP transportation and
one equipped as an air ambulance. The Argentine
Air Force has two fitted out for "critical care"
ambulance duties, with normal accommodation
for two stretchers and five seated casualties or
attendants, and with provision for four more
stretchers in the rear of the cabin. **Data** (Merlin
IVA): Span 46ft 3in (14.10m). Length 59ft 4¾in
(18.10m). Gross weight 12,500lb (5,670kg). Max
cruising speed 310mph (499km/h). Range at max
cruising speed 1,575 miles (2,534km).

Tupolev Tu-124　　　　　　　USSR
(NATO code-name: Cookpot)

This scaled-down version of the Soviet Union's first jet airliner, the Tu-104, flew in June 1960 as the first Soviet transport aircraft fitted with turbofan engines. In addition to its use by a number of airlines, notably Aeroflot, the Tu-124 is in service with the Soviet, East German, Indian and Iraqi Air Forces. The standard airline version is powered by two 11,905lb (5,400kg) st Soloviev D-20P turbofans and accommodates 56 passengers. **Data:** Span 83ft 9½in (25.55m). Length 100ft 4in (30.58m). Gross weight 83,775lb (38,000kg). Max speed 603mph (970km/h). Max range 1,305 miles (2,100km). Photo: TU-124, India.

Tupolev Tu-134A　　　　　　USSR
(NATO code-name: Crusty)

This 64/80-seat transport is basically a rear-engined development of the Tu-124, powered by two 14,990lb (6,800kg) st Soloviev D-30 turbofans. In the same class as the BAC One-Eleven and McDonnell Douglas DC-9, it is standard short/medium-range equipment of Aeroflot and other East European airlines. In addition, it is operated in small numbers by the air forces of the Soviet Union, Bulgaria, East Germany, Hungary and Poland. Examples can be seen with both western-style nose radome and a glazed nose with shallow undernose radome. **Data:** Span 95ft 2in (29.01m). Length 121ft 6½in (37.05m). Gross weight 103,600lb (47,000kg). Max cruising speed 550mph (885km/h). Range with max payload 1,243 miles (2,000km). Photo: TU-134A, Poland.

UTVA-60 and UTVA-66   Yugoslavia

The Yugoslav Air Force has a number of these sturdy four-seat utility aircraft built by the Fabrika Aviona UTVA at Pancevo. The UTVA-60, powered by a 270hp Lycoming GO-480-B1A6 engine, was manufactured in utility and ambulance versions. In addition, there was a floatplane version, designated UTVA-60H, with 296hp Lycoming GO-480-G1H6 engine. The UTVA-60H is known to be in military service, as is the developed UTVA-66, which exists in the same versions and has a 270hp GSO-480-B1J6 engine, fixed leading-edge slots, larger tail surfaces, increased fuel capacity, provision for underwing armament such as gun packs, and other changes. **Data** (UTVA-66): Span 37ft 5in (11.40m). Length 27ft 6in (8.38m). Gross weight 4,000lb (1,814kg). Max speed 155mph (250km/h). Max range 466 miles (750km). Photo: UTVA-66.

UTVA-75   Yugoslavia

Design of this side-by-side two-seat training, glider-towing and utility lightplane was begun in 1974 by the UTVA and Prva Petoletka companies, in association with the major Yugoslav aeronautical research establishments. The first of two prototypes flew on May 20, 1976, proving so successful that the first five of the initial batch of 30 production UTVA-75s had been completed by March 1977. Layout of the all-metal aircraft is conventional. The engine is a 180hp Lycoming IO-360-B1F, and there are two underwing attachments for light armament, including two pairs of rocket launch-tubes. **Data:** Span 31ft 11in (9.73m). Length 23ft 4in (7.11m). Gross weight 2,116lb (960kg). Max speed 136mph (220km/h). Range with external tanks 1,242 miles (2,000km). Photo: UTVA-75 with rocket tubes.

Valmet Viinka   Finland

This side-by-side two-seat trainer was developed as the Leko-70, a name representing an abbreviation of "Lentokone", the Finnish word for "aeroplane". The prototype flew for the first time on July 1, 1975. On January 28, 1977, the Finnish Air Force ordered 30 production models to replace its Saab-91D Safirs, with deliveries to begin in April 1979. Construction is all-metal; power plant is a 200hp Lycoming AEIO-360-A1B6, equipped for aerobatic flying. **Data:** Span 32ft 3¾in (9.85m). Length 24ft 7¼in (7.50m). Gross weight 2,645lb (1,200kg). Max speed 149mph (240km/h). Range 630 miles (1,015km).

VFW-Fokker VFW 614   Germany

The unique overwing engine pods of this twin-turbofan short-haul transport appeared to offer a number of attractions. The undercarriage legs could be kept shorter than with underwing pods, and there were none of the T-tail/deep-stall complications encountered with some rear-engine designs. However, the VFW 614 failed to find a commercial market in competition with airliners such as the Fokker F.28, and the production line was closed in early 1978 after sales of only sixteen had been announced. Three of these are operated by the *Luftwaffe*. Powered by two 7,280lb (3,302kg) st Rolls-Royce M45H Mk 501 turbofans, the VFW 614 is equipped normally to carry either 40 or 44 passengers in four-abreast seating. **Data:** Span 70ft 6½in (21.50m). Length 67ft 7in (20.60m). Gross weight 44,000lb (19,950kg). Max speed 443mph (713km/h). Range with 40 passengers 748 miles (1,204km).

Vickers-Slingsby T.61E Venture T.Mk 2
Great Britain

This side-by-side two-seat motor-glider had its origin in the German Scheibe SF-25B Falke (Falcon), of which Vickers-Slingsby manufactured 35 under licence in 1971-74. Impressed by the possibilities of the type for low-cost training and air experience flying, the UK Ministry of Defence evaluated a prototype (XW983) as the Venture T.Mk 1. It then ordered 15 of the improved T.61E version, powered by a Rollason-modified 1600cc Volkswagen car engine and with many components of glassfibre, including the plywood-encased wing main spar. Named Venture T.Mk 2, these are for use by the Air Training Corps. **Data:** Span 50ft 2½in (15.30m). Length 24ft 9¼in (7.55m). Gross weight 1,350lb (612kg). Max speed 100mph (160km/h).

Westland Commando
Great Britain

Based on the Sea King, the Commando is intended to operate primarily on tactical troop transport, logistic support, cargo transport and casualty evacuation duties. It can be used also for ground support and search and rescue. The Mk 1 version, which accommodates up to 21 troops and has a retractable undercarriage, is externally similar to the Sea King, except for the absence of the latter's search radar in a hump above the fuselage. Five were ordered by Saudi Arabia, on behalf of Egypt. The first of these flew on September 12, 1973. The more specialised Commando Mk 2 has two 1,660shp Rolls-Royce Gnome H.1400-1 turboshaft engines, a fixed undercarriage, provision for a wide range of guns, missiles and other weapons, and accommodation for a crew of two, up to 28 troops, internal or external freight or stretchers; it flew for the first time on January 16, 1975. Saudi Arabia's contract included 19 of this version, two of them furnished as VIP Mk 2Bs. Three Mk 2As and a VIP Mk 2C were ordered by the Qatar Emiri Air Force, and four more by an undisclosed customer. Fifteen Commandos were ordered by the MoD in 1978 to replace Wessex HU Mk 5s in the commando support role. **Data** (Mk 2): Rotor diameter 62ft 0in (18.90m). Length 55ft 10in (17.02m). Gross weight 21,000lb (9,525kg). Max speed 137mph (220km/h). Range 276 miles (445km) with max payload. Photo: Commando VIP.Mk 2B, Egypt.

Westland Sea King　　　　　　　Great Britain

This is the Sikorsky SH-3D Sea King (see page 204), built under licence initially for the Royal Navy, whose HAS.Mk 1 differs in having 1,500shp Rolls-Royce Gnome H.1400 engines, an automatic flight control system of the kind installed in the Wessex HAS.Mk 3, long-range sonar with Doppler processing, AW391 search radar in a dorsal hump fairing, Doppler navigation system, a crew of four, provision for a machine-gun, and armament of four Mk 44 homing torpedoes or Mk 11 depth charges. The first of 56 HAS.Mk 1s for the Royal Navy flew on May 7, 1969; the first of 21 uprated HAS.Mk 2s, with 1,660shp Gnome H.1400-1 engines, followed on June 18, 1976, and Mk 1s are being modified to this standard. These aircraft equipped five operational squadrons, two flights and a training squadron in 1978. Fifteen Sea King

HAR.Mk 3s began to re-equip two RAF search and rescue (SAR) squadrons in 1978. Export orders have included 22 Sea King Mk 41s for SAR duties with the Federal German Navy, 17 ASW Mk 42s for the Indian Navy, 10 SAR Mk 43s for the Norwegian Air Force, 6 ASW Mk 45s for the Pakistan Navy, 6 ASW Mk 47s for the Egyptian Navy, 5 SAR Mk 48s for the Belgian Air Force, and 10 Mk 50s for the Royal Australian Navy, with Gnome H.1400-1 engines and improved sonar. **Data** (Mk 2): Rotor diameter 62ft 0in (18.90m). Length 55ft 9¾in (17.01m). Gross weight 21,000lb (9,525kg). Max speed 137mph (220km/h). Range 764 miles (1,230km). Photo: Sea King HAR.Mk 3.

Westland Wasp/Scout　　　　　Great Britain

The anti-submarine Wasp and Scout light liaison helicopter are variants of the same design, which had its origin in the private-venture Saunders-Roe P.531. Evaluation of three early models led to a Royal Navy contract for development and production of the Wasp HAS.Mk 1, with a 710shp (derated) Rolls-Royce Nimbus 503 turboshaft engine, folding tailboom, four individual undercarriage legs with castoring wheels, armament of two Mk 44 homing torpedoes or other external stores, and accommodation for a crew of two, with provision for three passengers or for a stretcher across the rear of the cabin. The first Wasp flew on October 28, 1962, and aircraft of this type still equipped 35 Royal Navy flights in 1978,

operating from five classes of frigates and destroyers. Export customers included South Africa (17), New Zealand (3), Netherlands (12) and Brazil (9). The first pre-production Scout for the British Army Air Corps flew on August 4, 1960; the production Scout AH.Mk 1 has a 685shp Nimbus 101 or 102 engine, skid undercarriage, fixed tail and gross weight of 5,300lb (2,404kg). Export customers were the Royal Australian Navy (2) and Uganda Police Air Wing (1). **Data** (Wasp HAS.Mk 1): Rotor diameter 32ft 3in (9.83m). Length 30ft 4in (9.24m). Gross weight 5,500lb (2,495kg). Max speed 120mph (193km/h). Range 270 miles (435km). Photo: Scout AH.Mk 1.

Westland Wessex

Great Britain

The prototype for the Wessex was a Sikorsky HSS-1 (S-58) imported by Westland, re-engined with a Gazelle turboshaft and first flown in this form on May 17, 1957. The Royal Navy ordered a production version, designated Wessex HAS.Mk 1, for anti-submarine duties in the hunter-killer role; the first operational squadron was commissioned in July 1961. The HAS.Mk 1 had a 1,450shp Gazelle 161 engine, dipping sonar and strike weapons, and carried a crew of four. An assault transport version, carrying 16 troops, entered service in 1962. The HAS.Mk 1 was superseded by the HAS.Mk 3, with 1,600shp Gazelle 165 and large dorsal radome, which still equipped seven flights on County Class destroyers and a training squadron in 1978. Also still in service for Commando assault, training and fleet requirements are three squadrons of Wessex HU.Mk 5s, with a 1,550shp Rolls-Royce Gnome 112/113 twin-turbine power plant, accommodation for a crew of 1–3, 16 troops, seven stretchers or 4,000lb (1,814kg) of freight, and provision for carrying machine-guns, rockets, torpedoes and air-to-surface missiles. The RAF has three squadrons of similar, twin-engined Wessex HC.Mk 2s; and two airframes were converted to HCC.Mk 4 standard for The Queen's Flight. Export models were delivered to the Royal Australian Navy (27 HAS.31B with 1,540shp Gazelle 162) and Iraq (9 Mk 52, similar to Mk 2). **Data** (HU.Mk 5): Rotor diameter 56ft 0in (17.07m). Length 48ft 4½in (14.74m). Gross weight 13,500lb (6,120kg). Max speed 132mph (212km/h). Range 478 miles (770km). Photo: Wessex HU.Mk 5.

Westland Whirlwind

Great Britain

The Whirlwind began, in its Series 1 form, as a licence-built Sikorsky S-55 (see page 203) but later underwent considerable development. In the Series 2, the usual Wright or Pratt & Whitney piston-engine was replaced by a 750hp Alvis Leonides Major, giving considerably improved performance. The Series 3, first flown on February 28, 1959, switched to a 1,050hp Rolls-Royce Gnome H.1000 turboshaft. A total of more than 400 Series 1 and 2 Whirlwinds were built for civil and military use, including many for the RAF, Royal Navy and seven other air forces. A few remain in RAF service for search and rescue duties, as HAR Mk 10, these being conversions of earlier piston-engined Marks. The Qatar Emiri Air Force has two Series 3 Whirlwinds; the Brazilian Navy has five and the Nigerian Air Force one. **Data** (Srs.3): Rotor diameter 53ft (16.15m). Length 44ft 2in (13.46m). Gross weight 8,000lb (3,630kg). Max speed 106mph (170km/h). Range 300 miles (482km). Photo: Whirlwind HAR.Mk 10.

Westland/Aérospatiale Lynx   Great Britain/France

Basic versions of the Lynx are an all-weather general-purpose helicopter for the British Army (Lynx AH.Mk 1), and frigate-borne anti-submarine hunter-killer versions for the Royal Navy (HAS.Mk 2) and French Navy, to replace types such as the Wasp. Orders totalled 285 by the Autumn of 1978, of which 160 were for the British forces, 26 for the French Navy, and the others for Argentina, Brazil, Denmark, Egypt, the Netherlands, Norway and Qatar. The last 30 of 50 Lynx for Egypt are to be supplied in knocked-down form for local assembly, prior to manufacture of a further 230 or more in that country. Standard power plant comprises two 900shp Rolls-Royce BS.360-07-26 Gem turboshaft engines. Accommodation is for a basic crew of two, or pilot and up to ten troops, three stretchers and an attendant, or 2,000lb (907kg) of internal freight. There is provision for a 20mm cannon or two Miniguns in the cabin, but other armament and equipment vary according to role. Dual controls are optional, as are electronics such as Decca Doppler and navigation computer with roller map display. The ASW version can carry two homing torpedoes or Mk 11 depth charges, a wide range of missiles and search radar. **Data** (HAS.Mk 2): Rotor diameter 42ft 0in (12.80m). Length 39ft 1¼in (11.92m). Gross weight 10,500lb (4,763kg). Max speed 167mph (269km/h). Range 390 miles (628km). Photo: Naval Lynx, Argentina.

Yakovlev Yak-18 and Yak-18T   USSR
(NATO code-name: Max)

In a variety of forms, the sturdy all-metal Yak-18 has been the standard primary trainer of the Soviet Air Force and civil flying schools since 1946, and is also in service in a dozen other countries. Numerous versions have appeared since the early tandem two-seat Yak-18 (*Max*) with 160hp M-11FR engine and tail-wheel landing gear. These include the Yak-18U with nose-wheel and longer fuselage; Yak-18A with 300hp AI-14RF engine; Yak-18P single-seat version of the -18A with forward-retracting or inwards-retracting landing gear; Yak-18PM single-seat aerobatic version; Yak-18PS tail-wheel version of the PM; and the four-seat Yak-18T, with wider centre fuselage and enclosed cabin, which entered service in the early 1970s. **Data** (Yak-18T): Powered by 360hp Vedeneev M-14P engine. Span 36ft 7¼in (11.16m). Length 27ft 4¾in (8.35m). Gross weight 3,637lb (1,650kg). Max speed 183mph (295km/h). Range 560 miles (900km). Photo: Yak-18T.

Yakovlev Yak-40
(NATO code-name: Codling)

USSR

Confirmation that this unique little tri-jet transport is in military, as well as commercial, service came in the Summer of 1971, when two Yak-40s were seen in Yugoslav Air Force markings. By 1973, three had been delivered to this Air Force, and other military use of the type is likely. The Yak-40 first flew on October 21, 1966, and more than 800 had been built by Summer 1976, mostly for Aeroflot, which operates them on several thousand short-haul routes inside the Soviet Union. The three

3,300lb (1,500kg) st Ivchenko AI-25 turbofans enable the Yak-40 to take off in 2,625ft (800m) with a full load of 27–32 passengers. It can operate from grass or dirt strips, will take off and climb on any two engines and maintain cruising height on one. **Data:** Span 82ft 0¼in (25.0m). Length 66ft 9½in (20.36m). Gross weight 35,275lb (16,000kg). Max speed 373mph (600km/h). Max range 1,240 miles (2,000km). Photo: Yak-40, Yugoslavia.

Photo Credits

Index